D1567227

Social
Pain

Social Pain

Neuropsychological and Health Implications of Loss and Exclusion

Edited by
Geoff MacDonald and
Lauri A. Jensen-Campbell

American Psychological Association • Washington, DC

Published by
American Psychological Association
750 First Street, NE
Washington, DC 20002
www.apa.org

To order
APA Order Department
P.O. Box 92984
Washington, DC 20090-2984
Tel: (800) 374-2721; Direct: (202) 336-5510
Fax: (202) 336-5502; TDD/TTY: (202) 336-6123
Online: www.apa.org/pubs/books/
E-mail: order@apa.org

In the U.K., Europe, Africa, and the Middle East, copies may be ordered from
American Psychological Association
3 Henrietta Street
Covent Garden, London
WC2E 8LU England

Typeset in Goudy by Circle Graphics, Inc., Columbia, MD

Printer: Maple-Vail Book Manufacturing, York, PA
Cover Designer: Mercury Publishing Services, Rockville, MD

The opinions and statements published are the responsibility of the authors, and such opinions and statements do not necessarily represent the policies of the American Psychological Association.

Library of Congress Cataloging-in-Publication Data

Social pain : neuropsychological and health implications of loss and exclusion / edited by Geoff MacDonald and Lauri A. Jensen-Campbell. — 1st ed.
    p. ; cm.
  Includes bibliographical references and index.
  ISBN-13: 978-1-4338-0874-6
  ISBN-10: 1-4338-0874-9
  1. Pain 2. Loss (Psychology) 3. Neuropsychology. I. MacDonald, Geoff, 1972- II. Jensen-Campbell, Lauri A. III. American Psychological Association.
  [DNLM: 1. Social Alienation—psychology. 2. Pain—psychology. 3. Social Behavior. WM 600 S6775 2011]

  QP401.S63 2011
  616'.0472—dc22
                                    2010010034

British Library Cataloguing-in-Publication Data

A CIP record is available from the British Library.

Printed in the United States of America
First Edition

I dedicate this book to my parents, Judy and Mack, whose endless generosity made possible my academic life.
—Geoff MacDonald

Over a decade ago, I dedicated my dissertation to my husband, Shaun Campbell, for his support. Shaun, looking back on it all, it was just the beginning of our long journey that has required your continued support, especially when dealing with our share of social pain such as the death of my mom and your baby niece, long drawn-out adoption processes, and our continuing parenting challenges. I am proud to call you my husband . . . as always. I could not have done this project without your love and encouragement. This dedication is only a small token of how much I continue to appreciate your love and understanding through the years.
—Lauri A. Jensen-Campbell

CONTENTS

CONTRIBUTORS

Andrew Baum, PhD, Department of Psychology, University of Texas at Arlington

Terry K. Borsook, MS, Department of Psychology, University of Toronto, Ontario, Canada

Zhansheng Chen, PhD, Department of Psychology, University of Hong Kong, Pokfulam, Hong Kong

Timothy Deckman, BS, Department of Psychology, University of Kentucky, Lexington

C. Nathan DeWall, PhD, Department of Psychology, University of Kentucky, Lexington

Sally S. Dickerson, PhD, Department of Psychology and Social Behavior, University of California, Irvine

Angela Liegey Dougall, PhD, Department of Psychology, University of Texas at Arlington

Naomi I. Eisenberger, PhD, Department of Psychology, University of California, Los Angeles

Robert J. Gatchel, PhD, Department of Psychology, College of Science, The University of Texas at Arlington

Haylie L. Gomez, MS, Department of Psychology, University of Texas at Arlington

Lauri A. Jensen-Campbell, PhD, Department of Psychology, University of Texas at Arlington

Nancy D. Kishino, OTR/L, CVE, West Coast Spine Restoration, Riverside, CA

Jennifer M. Knack, PhD, Faculty of Education, University of Ottawa, Ontario, Canada

Carroll Michelle Lee, BS, Department of Psychology, University of Texas at Arlington

Geoff MacDonald, PhD, Department of Psychology, University of Toronto, Ontario

Jaak Panksepp, PhD, College of Veterinary Medicine, Department of Veterinary Comparative Anatomy, Physiology and Pharmacology, Washington State University, Pullman

Richard S. Pond Jr., MA, Department of Psychology, University of Kentucky, Lexington

Stephanie S. Spielmann, MA, Department of Psychology, University of Toronto, Ontario

Shelley E. Taylor, PhD, Department of Psychology, University of California, Los Angeles

Baldwin M. Way, PhD, Department of Psychology, University of California, Los Angeles

Kipling D. Williams, PhD, Department of Psychological Sciences, Purdue University, West Lafayette, IN

Social
Pain

INTRODUCTION: EXPERIENCING THE ACHE OF SOCIAL INJURIES— AN INTEGRATIVE APPROACH TO UNDERSTANDING SOCIAL PAIN

LAURI A. JENSEN-CAMPBELL AND GEOFF MacDONALD

Maintaining belongingness, or feelings of social connection with others, is a fundamental human need (Baumeister & Leary, 1995). Individuals are thought to be driven to form and maintain positive, significant, lasting relationships. These interpersonal bonds, no matter what stage of the relationship, elicit some of the more intense human emotions (Bowlby, 1979). This volume focuses on the emotional experiences associated with the loss or disruption of these bonds. MacDonald and Leary (2005) defined *social pain* as "a specific emotional reaction to the perception that one is being excluded from desired relationships or being devalued by desired relationship partners or groups" (p. 202). Thus, social pain is a negative emotional state that arises from social injuries, or from perceptions of interpersonal rejection or loss, such as unrequited love, a relationship breakup, or the death of a loved one. Although such social injuries can lead to a range of emotional states, the experience of hurt feelings may be the key emotional marker of social pain (MacDonald, 2009). As the research in this volume demonstrates, this reference to painful feelings in response to social injury is not simply metaphorical. Research is quickly converging on the conclusion that social pain results from activation of pain affect, or the aspects of physical pain systems that promote feelings of unpleasantness in response to physical injury.

Although researchers in social, clinical, health, and developmental psychology have engaged in a disjointed dialogue about social pain (often using terms such as *emotional* or *psychological pain*), recent work from the neurosciences provides a coherent framework that promises a unifying platform for integrative research. This framework begins with the emerging recognition that social pain is a discrete emotional state whose causes, consequences, and functional value are only now being clarified. This volume is meant as a step in that direction.

This volume begins by providing a theoretical basis for the evolution of pain beyond contexts of physical injury. Pain, whether it is social or physical in nature, is important for survival because it alerts the organism that something is wrong. Pain signals allow the organism to change its circumstances to reduce or eliminate the pain or avoid similar situations that can cause pain. As such, pain serves as a protective mechanism from future damage or harm. The importance of maintaining social relationships and avoiding the possibility of social exclusion may have been vital to ancestral survival. Social relationships are so vital that threats to relationships may be processed as a basic survival threat (MacDonald & Leary, 2005). As such, pain from disruption of these relationships could have signaled our ancestors to change their behavior or the situation to reestablish belongingness.

Part I of this volume is titled Neurological and Physiological Bases of Social Pain. In Chapter 1, Jaak Panksepp provides an intense, engaging, and passionate review of both animal models and human neuroimaging data, arguing that the emotion system associated with social bonding may have developed as part of physical pain systems. The separation-distress PANIC/GRIEF system appears to be situated in similar areas of the brain across all mammalian species; for example, as Panksepp explains, the anterior cingulate is associated with separation-distress calls in mammals and feelings of sadness in humans. In addition, Panksepp provides evidence that this system evolved so that human beings could monitor social loss and seek social support when pain from social loss occurs (Panksepp, 2003, 2005). This chapter provides a wonderfully rich theoretical foundation for the volume.

Naomi Eisenberger (Chapter 2) outlines the neural mechanisms that are associated with the affective component of pain. She provides extensive evidence from both neuropsychological and neuroimaging studies that the dorsal anterior cingulate cortex is associated with pain distress and suffering, regardless of whether it is social or physical in nature. She then discusses some consequences associated with this overlap of social and physical pain affective systems. For example, the sensitivity to one type of pain (e.g., physical pain) should necessarily lead to sensitivity to the other pain (e.g., social pain) and vice versa. Moreover, regulatory and intensifying factors associated with one type of pain should have a similar influence on the other type of pain.

In Chapter 3, Sally Dickerson explores physiological responses to social pain, particularly in social evaluative situations. She theorizes how situations that lead to social evaluation can be interpreted as threats to social self-preservation and thus induce self-conscious emotions (e.g., guilt, pride, shame). Her work demonstrates that these self-conscious emotions that are associated with socially evaluative circumstances may be an integral part of physiological responses to social pain. Through a series of studies, she demonstrates that social evaluative circumstances are associated with increases in stress hormones (e.g., cortisol), stronger cardiovascular responses, and greater proinflammatory cytokine activity. Cortisol reactivity in particular was associated with the self-reported experience of self-conscious emotions. Moreover, individuals who feel greater social evaluative threat show greater increases in proinflammatory cytokine production.

Baldwin Way and Shelley Taylor (Chapter 4) provide additional evidence that the physiological mechanisms by which social pain functions involve the opioid, serotonin, dopamine, and oxytocin systems. In their chapter, these authors explore the genes that are responsible for signal control within these systems and how differences in the expression of these genes are associated with individual differences in responses to social pain processes. For example, the A118G polymorphism of the mu-opioid receptor gene (*OPRM1*) is associated with individual differences in physical pain perception in humans (Fillingim et al., 2005). Way and Taylor also report that the G allele, which is relatively more rare than the A allele, is also associated with greater self-reported sensitivity to rejection as well as greater cortisol reactivity when a social evaluative threat is faced, especially for women. Genetic evidence thus suggests an overlap in physical and social pain processes.

In Part II of this volume—Social Pain in Interpersonal Relationships—the authors incorporate the framework for social pain provided in the initial chapters into their analyses of the effect of social pain in interpersonal relationships. C. Nathan DeWall, Richard Pond Jr., and Timothy Deckman (Chapter 5) elucidate the overlap of physical and social pain systems by demonstrating in a cleverly designed short-term longitudinal study that pain relief medication can blunt hurt feelings. Because acetaminophen is a general analgesic that influences the central nervous system, DeWall et al. propose that it should reduce negative pain affect for both physical and social pain. Their findings suggest that persons who took acetaminophen (blindly) reported a reduction in hurt feelings over a 3-week period compared with those who took a placebo. They also discuss another neural pain region, the periaqueductal gray (PAG), which is closely coupled to the experience of both physical and social pain responses. The PAG has been associated with injury detection and pain reduction, and activation of the PAG is associated with the reduction of pain responses (e.g., Price, 1988).

Geoff MacDonald, Terry Borsook, and Stephanie Spielmann (Chapter 6) explore the effects of social pain in interpersonal relationships by examining the influence of social pain on perceptions of social reward and threat. They detail why individuals interested in the phenomenon of social pain should be cognizant of the distinction between social threats and rewards. In fact, their programmatic research suggests that because rejection and lost connections to others are painful, individuals may defensively manipulate the extent to which they perceive these events to be socially threatening or rewarding. The authors demonstrate that individuals with higher social threat perception are indeed less likely to expect enjoyment from future interactions. Conversely, individuals who perceive higher social rewards expect more enjoyment in future social interactions. These differences in threat and reward perception are reliably associated with important individual differences, such as attachment styles. This chapter provides a lucid argument for why it is important to understand the roles of both social threat and reward in that pain can come from both rejection and the loss of connection, which suggests two separate paths of influence on the regulation of social behavior.

Zhansheng Chen and Kipling Williams (Chapter 7) provide a unique perspective in demonstrating some possible boundary conditions for the overlap between physical and social pain. Their work highlights the importance of understanding aspects of social and physical pain that are distinct from each other. For example, previous research has found that believing that one will be at perpetual risk of social pain (i.e., alone) leads to greater cognitive deficits and a blunting of physical pain sensitivity than does thinking that one will be at perpetual risk of physical pain (e.g., become accident prone; Baumeister, Twenge, & Nuss, 2002; DeWall & Baumeister, 2006). As such, under certain circumstances social pain can lead to greater difficulties than can physical pain. The authors further explore these differences in social and physical pain by examining how people relive painful events: Although both types of pain were equally hurtful and did not differ in their recency, individuals reported that past social pains can actually be relived or reexperienced, unlike physical pain. The authors suggest that the mechanism for healing may be different for social and physical pain, causing social pains to "stay alive" under the surface while physical pains have long been mended. More research is needed to better understand the mechanisms underlying these possible differences. Discovering and better understanding boundary conditions for the overlap between social and physical pain should further help researchers and clinicians understand the scope of these pain systems.

In Part III, Health Consequences of Social Pain, the last three chapters of this volume focus on developmental and clinical consequences of social pain. Robert Gatchel and Nancy Kishino (Chapter 8) demonstrate how research on chronic physical pain may provide information about chronic social pain. They discuss the biopsychosocial perspective of pain and emotion and its implications for understanding social pain. For example, they demonstrate how social pain could potentially lead to heightened negative reactivity to a physically painful experience. The authors also provide evidence that chronic physical pain can lead to increases in psychopathological states that may further influence social interactions (e.g., anxiety, depression, personality disorders). Overall, this work suggests that insights into the mechanisms that link brain function with pain and emotion will lead to a better understanding of how physical and social pain are meshed together.

Andrew Baum, Carroll Michelle Lee, and Angela Liegey Dougall (Chapter 9) discuss how social pain can influence stress and health outcomes, focusing on one overlapping property of both physical and social pain—namely, that painful experiences are stressful. They then discuss how stress can influence neuroendocrine pathways and neural functioning to influence health outcomes. Focusing attention on the stress associated with social pain may suggest an important emerging area of inquiry—namely, that social pain can have serious negative consequences for health.

Finally, Jennifer Knack, Haylie Gomez, and Lauri Jensen-Campbell (Chapter 10) focus on how chronic social pain can lead to greater pain sensitivity over time. They provide evidence from several studies that individuals who are experiencing chronic social pain show greater insula activation, report more physical pain, and show different diurnal patterns in cortisol production. Indeed, the cortisol production of bullied adolescents resembles the pattern found in individuals with posttraumatic stress disorder. The authors provide further evidence from the clinical literature that chronic social pain influences biological systems and pain pathways in the brain, creating relatively permanent changes that make individuals more sensitive to pain, especially for individuals who may be initially more vulnerable to pain.

We conclude this volume by reemphasizing that the phenomenon under investigation has broad relevance for psychology but has never been given an integrative, scientific treatment. By involving internationally renowned scholars whose work has provided the foundation for this area of study and emerging researchers whose innovative approaches point to the future potential of work on social pain, we hope that the lessons of the volume provide a coherent picture of social pain as a starting point for new research.

REFERENCES

Baumeister, R. F., & Leary, M. R. (1995). The need to belong: Desire for interpersonal attachments as a fundamental human motivation. *Psychological Bulletin, 117*, 497–529. doi:10.1037/0033-2909.117.3.497

Baumeister, R. F., Twenge, J. M., & Nuss, C. K. (2002). Effects of social exclusion on cognitive processes: Anticipated aloneness reduces intelligent thought. *Journal of Personality and Social Psychology, 83,* 817–827. doi:10.1037/0022-3514.83.4.817

Bowlby, J. (1979). *The making and breaking of affectional bonds.* London, England: Tavistock.

DeWall, C. N., & Baumeister, R. F. (2006). Alone but feeling no pain: Effects of social exclusion on physical pain tolerance and pain threshold, affective forecasting, and interpersonal empathetic concern. *Journal of Personality and Social Psychology, 91,* 1–15. doi:10.1037/0022-3514.91.1.1

Fillingim, R. B., Kaplan, L., Staud, R., Ness, T. J., Glover, T. L., Campbell, C. M., . . . Wallace, M. R. (2005). The A118G single nucleotide polymorphism of the mu-opioid receptor gene (OPRM1) is associated with pressure pain sensitivity in humans. *The Journal of Pain, 6,* 159–167. doi:10.1016/j.jpain.2004.11.008

MacDonald, G. (2009). Social pain and hurt feelings. In P. Corr & G. Matthews (Eds.), *The Cambridge handbook of personality* (pp. 541–555). Cambridge, England: Cambridge University Press.

MacDonald, G., & Leary, M. R. (2005). Why does social exclusion hurt? The relationship between social and physical pain. *Psychological Bulletin, 131,* 202–223. doi:10.1037/0033-2909.131.2.202

Panksepp, J. (2003, October 10). Feeling the pain of social loss. *Science, 302,* 237–239. doi:10.1126/science.1091062

Panksepp, J. (2005). Feelings of social loss: The evolution of pain and the ache of a broken heart. In R. Ellis & N. Newton (Eds.), *Consciousness & emotions* (Vol. 1, pp. 23–55). Amsterdam, The Netherlands: John Benjamins.

Price, D. D. (1988). *Psychological and neural mechanisms of pain.* New York, NY: Raven Press.

I

NEUROLOGICAL AND PHYSIOLOGICAL BASES OF SOCIAL PAIN

1

THE NEUROBIOLOGY OF SOCIAL LOSS IN ANIMALS: SOME KEYS TO THE PUZZLE OF PSYCHIC PAIN IN HUMANS

JAAK PANKSEPP

Pain usually signals bodily injuries. However, some people experience painful bodily feelings even when there is no immediate environmental cause. In medical terms such pain would be considered *idiopathic*, sometimes *neurogenic*, probably reflecting some type of activity in brain sensory–affective systems closely related to the ability to feel physical pain. However, other types of psychogenic pain are more subtle, seemingly free-floating in the mind, with origins in humans' intrinsic, genetically ordained, social–emotional nature. There may be various evolutionary relationships among these forms of pain: A key relationship may be that certain sensory affects and emotional affects are evolutionarily related, even though emotional pain is a more profoundly existential, more viscerally self-referential affect than most sensory–affective forms of pain. In any event, pain and certain emotional–affective aspects of consciousness are intimately related (Chapman & Nakamura, 1999), providing a solid foundation for humans' social nature.

But what does it mean for humans to have a social–emotional nature, especially when most human social tendencies are learned? Lessons from cross-species affective neuroscience indicate that all mammals do have a limited set of innate (evolutionarily endowed) social–emotional circuits,

11

including those for male and female sexuality (LUST)[1] and nurturance (CARE), which eventually gets hormonally magnified into maternal urges); playfulness (PLAY); and, most important for this discussion and perhaps the earliest social development, the capacity to feel separation distress (PANIC/GRIEF), which serve as substrates for social bonding. In the emerging understanding of a core self, the primary-process emotional systems are key ingredients in the ancient viscerosomatic bodily representations that may be the groundwork for self-related, emotion-associated information processing within the brain (Northoff & Panksepp, 2008; Panksepp, 1998a, 1998b; Panksepp & Northoff, 2009).

The primary-process social–emotional systems are probably critically important for the developmental–epigenetic–cultural construction of higher social brain systems within the initially blank slate of the neocortex. The neocortex is largely a tabula rasa at birth. It is modularized by experience, which is most strikingly indicated by the emergence of a fine visual cortex even if the occipital tissues that would normally become visual cortex are surgically destroyed before birth (Sur & Leamey, 2001). On the basis of such findings, it may be surmised that all neocortical regions are dispositionally modularized by the way various subcortical systems differentially innervate the cortex and influence cortical specializations. Evolutionary psychological assertions notwithstanding, so far the postulation of genetically provided "modules" in higher regions of the brain has been advanced without any corroborating genetic or related neuroscientific data. My thesis is that psychic–social pain achieves its affective charge from genetically based lower subcortical emotional networks of the brain, which epigenetically and developmentally promote emotional specializations in higher regions of the brain. If so, scientific strategies that can illuminate the structural and functional details of those primary-process emotional circuits that allow social pain to exist and to spread memorial influences into higher regions of the brain need to be cultivated.

In this view of brain organization, the subcortical primary-process social–emotional systems are the foundations from which social bonds arise, and the PANIC/GRIEF networks that generate feelings of separation distress, as can be monitored by separation cries, may well be the unconditional wellspring for internal feelings of raw social pain. The diminutive forms of this emotion, such as shyness and social phobias, may arise from how painful social feelings motivate social learning.

---

[1]The capitalizations are used to minimize mereological fallacies (part–whole confusions) and to highlight the designation of specific brain networks that are critical components of the emotional wholes that can be observed only psychologically.

When social bonds are severed, all mammals experience emotional distress that has the affective quality of pain. In fact, one of the most difficult forms of pain that humans, as well as other mammals, can experience is that arising from social loss (Panksepp, 1981) and ostracism (Eisenberger et al., 2006; MacDonald & Leary, 2005). In this chapter, I explore how this primal emotional system for psychic pain and social bonding may have arisen from ancestral physical pain systems, and how the neuroanatomical and neurochemical underpinnings were first clarified through the use of animal models and more recently confirmed through human brain imaging. Now there are a variety of neurochemical regulators that could be evaluated in humans—from the role of endogenous opioids to oxytocin. The field is finally in a position to understand the nature of affect neuroscientifically.

THE EVOLUTION OF SUBJECTIVITY: FROM PHYSICAL PAIN TO EMOTIONAL PSYCHIC PAIN

Physical pain is nature's way of helping organisms escape and avoid environmental conditions that could destroy them. Without pain, it is hard to imagine how nature could have motivated organisms to escape stimuli that could harm them. Indeed, all the affect-generating state controls of the brain are ancestral or genetic "memories" that allow organisms to anticipate life-supporting and life-detracting events. They come in several varieties: *sensory affects*, such as taste and pain; *body-state changes* that trigger interoceptive–homeostatic affects, such as hunger and thirst; and *within-brain emotional affects*, such as joy and sadness. The likelihood that some of the earliest sensory affects, such as physical pain, served as substrates for the emergence of neuropsychic emotional affects such as the painful feeling of separation distress has led to the current understanding of the psychic pain that results from social loss— the feelings of grief and sadness that can, under the worst of circumstances, lead to depression, which at times is so awful that it promotes suicidal intent (Watt & Panksepp, 2009).

Thus, if one could decipher how the brain constructs the feeling of physical pain, one would have a solid beginning for understanding the ancestral sources of phenomenal consciousness and could begin to deal effectively with the large array of emotional feelings in which the sting of social loss is a cardinal feature, including separation distress, shyness, social phobias, feelings accompanying social exclusion, and suicidal ideation. For such reasons, I have long advocated the view that the separation-distress/PANIC/GRIEF system of the brain was evolutionarily designed to monitor social loss by engendering psychic pain that can be alleviated by social support (Panksepp, 1981, 2003a, 2005b, 2005d, 2005e).

These are admittedly subtle issues, and for most of its history neuroscience has not been well positioned, even with its increasingly impressive armamentarium of objective third-person observational tools, to study the nature of subjectivity, especially the affective states that arise from large-scale neurodynamics that control the instinctual–emotional psychobehavioral tendencies of the brain. Although such issues are scientifically daunting in humans, it was generally believed they were scientifically totally unworkable in other species. This has changed with the recognition that a dual-aspect monism ontology, which automatically implies new epistemological strategies, can break through the shell of subjectivity—that is, the instinctual–emotional actions of animals appear to be veridical indicators of primary-process or core emotional feeling states (Panksepp, 2008a).

Although the topic of emotional feelings has been perhaps the most difficult problem for the study of human consciousness, affective neuroscience now offers a way to cut through the Gordian knot (Panksepp, 1998a, 2005a). Certain brain systems are truly psychobehavioral, because affective neuroscience has demonstrated that whenever studies identify regions of the brain where localized electrical stimulation can provoke instinctual–emotional behavior patterns, such as anger or exploratory seeking, it is found that animals do have internal affective experiences as monitored by the empirical evaluation of whether animals like or dislike the stimulation (as can be done with conditioned place avoidance and preference tasks, among others). Decorticated animals can retain many such abilities. Such findings have rather uniformly supported the existence of emotional feelings in all other mammals that have been studied.

Because of such concordances, modern neuroscience is finally able to come to terms with those subtle mind–brain processes, even in other animals, appropriately called *affective states*—the internal world-valuative phenomenal experiences that arise directly from brain dynamics (Panksepp, 2005c, 2008a). The ability to finally deal with affective states of the brain objectively in animals, especially negative emotions that are distinct from fearfulness, is having increasingly profound implications for understanding a variety of human emotional and cultural problems as well as the nature of psychiatric disorders that contain feelings of social distress and pain at their core. The brain mechanisms that generate emotional feelings may eventually be used as endophenotypes in psychiatric practice to yield emotional symptom-based as opposed to the traditional conceptual syndrome–based therapies (Panksepp, 2006). Researchers finally have enough scientific understanding to coherently address aspects of such problems that transcend the purely biological realm. The emerging understanding of the neural nature of psychic pain in animals also has implications for understanding the nature of drug addiction and love in humans (Panksepp, 1998a). This kind of knowledge has abundant implications for psychiatric issues, especially depression and suicidality (Watt & Panksepp, 2009).

THE PANIC/GRIEF SYSTEM

The primary-process separation-distress system, an ancient emotional tool for social living and social bonding, homologous in all mammalian brains so far studied, is situated in the deep subneocortical midline regions of diencephalon and mesencephalon and projects upward to limbic regions, especially the anterior cingulate cortex (ACC). This emotional "gift of nature"— along with other social–emotional systems, especially social PLAY—probably helps regulate the higher attentional, motivational, and memorial processes that promote the developmental, epigenetic programming of the higher social brain by life experiences. This programming may perhaps include even neo-cortical cognitive specializations as useful as "mirror neurons" (Arbib, 2006; Rizzolatti & Sinigaglia, 2008) and as profound as capacities for cognitive empathy (for a theoretical overview and discussion, see Watt, 2007, along with commentaries).

One can observe the instinctual behavioral and affective manifestations of basic emotional brain networks more clearly in fellow mammals than in human beings. The human neocortex is adept at regulating and repressing the lower affect-generating regions of the brain (Liotti & Panksepp, 2004; Northoff et al., 2004). The PANIC/GRIEF system has been studied largely through the analysis of separation-distress vocalizations (also known as *isolation calls*). Species that have been used most effectively to study this neural system are chickens, dogs, guinea pigs, and primates but not laboratory rats (as I elaborate later). Such animals do not possess the neocortical ability to inhibit and modify primary-process emotional expressions of emotionality as do mature human beings. Indeed, the kind of brain intervention research that provides detailed knowledge about such circuits is unlikely to be done on humans (and some argue that it is unethical in animals as well).

In any event, more has been learned about the primary-process affective mechanisms of separation distress and psychic pain from the neurobiological study of separation calls in animal models—the premier indicator of the PANIC/GRIEF system—than will be learned from any foreseeable human research (Panksepp, 1981, 1998a, 2005b, 2005d, 2005e), although some neuroanatomical and neurochemical positron emission tomography (PET) imaging studies can confirm and extend principles first identified in animals (Damasio et al., 2000; Zubieta et al., 2003). Conversely, these foundational affective networks interact with many higher cognitive processes in humans that simply cannot be studied in animal models. Thus, the cognitive ramifications of these systems have been learned almost exclusively through human research (MacDonald & Leary, 2005).

The two levels of study need to be integrated. To do this well, one must recognize and discount myths advanced by nonbiologically oriented evolutionary psychologists: Most human cognitive complexities are not dictated genetically; they are largely products of developmental and epigenetic landscapes. The neocortex, so massively expanded in the human brain, is composed of highly repetitive self-similar columnar structures of about 3,000 neurons, on average. Because of their repetitive self-similarity, these columns resemble random access memory chips found in computers. With such a higher brain organization, it is highly likely that human neocortical modularization arises mostly through developmental landscapes (Sur & Rubenstein, 2005). Thus, those who believe such neocortical specializations emerged evolutionarily via natural selection need to support their beliefs with solid biological data from newborn humans.

Here I focus on the evolved cross-species subcortical brain mechanisms for separation distress that are indeed genetic endowments of most mammalian brains. I can be confident of this because in all mammals that have been studied using localized brain stimulation procedures, as well as other vertebrates such as domestic chickens, the separation-distress networks are situated in homologous regions of the brain (Bishop, 1984; Herman, 1979; Herman & Panksepp, 1981; Jürgens, 1998, 2002). The main regulatory neurochemistries are also the same (Newman, 1988; Panksepp, 1991, 1998a; Panksepp, Normansell, Herman, Bishop, & Crepeau, 1988). Thus, animal neuroscience provides general principles for understanding the foundations of the psychic pain that emerges in human minds from the loss of social support from loved ones. It permits a deeper and more detailed exploration of the underlying neuro-chemical, allowing cross-species translations up to the human level—the neurochemistries for affect seem to be conserved throughout mammalian lines. However, neuroevolutionary–psychobiological animal models do not advance the field's knowledge of the societal and cultural consequences of such ancestral tools for living.

The supposition that the separation-distress PANIC/GRIEF emotional system arose from sensory–affective pain networks is premised on their confluence in subcortical regions of the brain (Panksepp et al., 1988). For instance, from lower regions of the periaqueductal gray (PAG) and surrounding midbrain tissues, one can get pain vocalizations with localized electrical stimulation of the brain (ESB), whereas slightly further up in the midbrain, the vocalizations have the sound characteristics of natural separation calls

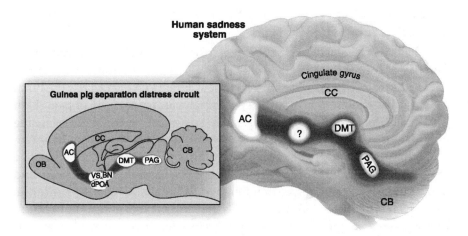

Figure 1.1. A schematic of human and mammalian separation distress systems. From "Feeling the Pain of Social Loss," by J. Panksepp, 2003, *Science, 302,* pp. 237–239. Copyright 2003 by the American Association for the Advancement of Science. Reprinted with permission.

(Panksepp, 1998a). In more rostral diencephalic subcortical regions, such as the dorsomedial thalamus, one continues to get separation calls, not pain squeals, all the way up to the anterior cingulate in some species (see Figure 1.1). PET imaging has implicated these same brain regions in the experience of human sadness (Damasio et al., 2000).

These same brain regions often "light up" during human brain imaging of the affective aspects of physical pain. Thus, the confluent anatomies and neurochemistries, especially endogenous opioids, suggest that these networks convey the affective qualities of pain. Because of such congruencies, the guiding premise for the past 3 decades has been that the emotional system for separation distress and sadness arose from the ancestral dynamics of physical pain (Panksepp, 1981; Panksepp, Herman, Vilberg, Bishop, & DeEskinazi, 1980). Indeed, with the emergence of such a primary-process emotional–affective system along with medial cortical self-related information processing (Northoff et al., 2006; Panksepp & Northoff, 2009), social-separation pain became as robust and sustained a feature of people's mental lives as sustained physical pain. However, before I discuss the psychobiology of psychic pain in some detail, I first consider the neural controls of physical pain.

A SYNOPSIS OF THE BRAIN MECHANISMS OF PHYSICAL PAIN

Pain is a useful feeling. It helps people survive. It helps people anticipate things that they should not do, thereby protecting them from further harm. Great progress has been made in the past few decades characterizing the brain systems that mediate the various experiential features of physical pain. Pain is typically defined as unpleasant sensory and affective experiences arising from potential or actual tissue damage—"potential" because the pain system is extremely good at anticipating forthcoming pain to the extent that one often withdraws one's hand from a hot stove before pain is experienced, and hence tissue damage is avoided or minimized. Whether this efficacy is intrinsic to the pain system or a reflection of early classical conditioning is not known. In any event, people can discriminate pain stimuli cognitively as well as affectively. There are clinical situations, for example, among people with frontal cortical damage, in which individuals can indicate that a stimulus is painful but claim that it does not affectively bother them.

Pain impulses from body surfaces below the neck, transmitted by specialized nociceptive fibers, enter the dorsal spinal cord and cross over promptly into ventral regions and ascend toward the thalamus via the spinothalamic tract. The neural pathways for the discriminative aspects of pain ascend from the thalamus to the somatosensory neocortex, just as the discriminative aspects of the other senses ascend from their thalamic relay nuclei to their respective cortical projection areas (except for olfaction, which does not need to project through the thalamus). Thus, pain impulses from thalamic nuclei to the somatosensory neocortex provide clear signals as to where pain is located on the body surface. The affective projections remain more diffusely organized in subcortical circuits. This divergence of control helps explain why an individual with somatosensory cortical damage subjected to laser stimulation of the skin cannot describe discrete pain sensation while still experiencing unpleasant feelings and making pain sounds after such stimulation (Ploner et al., 1999). Just the reverse can happen following cingulate cortex damage, which can dramatically reduce the affective sting of pain while leaving the discriminative–cognitive components intact (Foltz & White, 1962). This divergence of affective and cognitive aspects of pain follows patterns common in all sensory systems where they typically diverge into two branches when they enter the upper brain stem (from midbrain to the thalamus and the hypothalamus). The cognitive–discriminative branches sweep up to the cortex, whereas the affective aspects arise from subneocortical networks.

Following this general plan, the affective aspects of pain are mediated by poorly understood reticular fields of midline structures of the midbrain (e.g., lower PAG), medial thalamus, and various regions of the limbic forebrain—namely, older limbic–visceral cortices such as the insula (hidden under the massive swellings of the overlying auditory, somatosensory, and somatomotor cortices) as well as various anterior cingulate and other medial frontal cortical regions. It is largely within these latter visceral projections that most neurologists believe humans experience the affective sting of pain (Berthier et al., 1988). It is along these midline structures that one also sees the footprints of affective qualities of pain during human brain imaging (Casey, 2000).

This is pretty much the same plan for all other sensory affects and, to a lesser extent, the homeostatic affects, such as hunger and thirst, which remain almost exclusively subcortical (Denton, 2006), with fewer projections to orbitofrontal and insular regions farther forward. On the other hand, the emotional affects are integrated in very extensive longitudinal networks arising from centromedial midbrain regions such as the anterior PAG, with different systems ascending through the hypothalamus (SEEKING, RAGE, FEAR, LUST, and CARE) toward basal forebrain nuclei, the medial frontal cortex, and the amygdala, along with the surrounding temporal cortex. The remaining social emotions (PANIC/GRIEF and PLAY) ascend through medial thalamic and basal forebrain regions, to the higher visceral cortices, especially the anterior cingulate, but also to more rostral midline frontal cortical regions of the brain that subserve the processing of self-relevant information associated with emotionality (Northoff & Panksepp, 2008). These emotional systems share many attributes with pain.

Indeed, all of these affective midline structures have widespread brain effects. For instance, pain impulses already diverge widely in lower reticular regions of the dorsal pons and midbrain. There, pain impulses regulate major monoamine projections (especially norepinephrine and serotonin) that globally control all information processing in the cerebral cortices, with norepinephrine generally facilitating practically all aspects of psychological processing (by facilitating the signal-to-noise ratio in sensory and perceptual channels) and serotonin tending to dampen all forms of emotionality and associated cognitive arousals. For instance, when stressed, animals that are deficient in certain types of serotonin processing can go into a sympathetic crisis more easily and die, especially when they are young (Audero et al., 2008).

EVOLUTIONARY EMERGENCE OF SEPARATION DISTRESS

An important issue to consider is that the pain components that diverge into medial reticular areas, especially the PAG and surrounding tissues, served as a solid evolutionary foundation for separation distress. Through evolutionary utilization of these preexisting parts, new emotional pathways emerged that were tuned specifically to evaluating the presence of supportive social stimuli. As far as is known, this system engenders the psychological distress that arises from the absence of social support. This PANIC/GRIEF system of the mammalian brain arises from midbrain dorsal PAG regions. It is there where one first encounters brain sites, stimulation of which could generate sonographically normal separation calls (which are distinct from pain screeches). The ascending neural pathways fan out rostrally primarily to the medial thalamus and then on to various mid-diencephalic regions: At transitional zones where telencephalic expansions arise from the rostral diencephalon, separation-distress calls can be readily evoked with ESB from a series of transitional basal forebrain nuclei, especially the ventral septal area, dorsal preoptic area, and the intervening bed nuclei of the stria terminalis, and farther forward to the anterior cingulate (see Figure 1.1). This psychic-pain system is powerfully inhibited by endogenous opioids. This inhibition of psychic pain is not attributable simply to sedation because very modest doses yield these effects with no measureable motor impairments.

Still, to address this long-standing criticism of the discovery that my colleagues and I made that brain opioids were exquisitely effective in reducing the psychic pain of separation distress—namely, that we had only sedated animals (e.g., Winslow & Insel, 1991)—we conducted a study to validate opioid control of separation-distress circuitry completely within the brain. In a functional mapping study, it was found that the PAG sites that evoked analgesia, induced by stimulating PAG sites, activated endogenous opioid inhibition of separation-distress vocalizations (DVs) networks in the medial thalamus (Herman & Panksepp, 1981). This finding definitively indicated an intimate relationship between endogenous opioid pain-reducing systems and separation-distress circuitry. That is, the endogenous opioid pain-reducing systems inside the brain did regulate the thresholds of the brain circuits that promote separation DVs. PAG sites that yielded no analgesic effects did not modulate thresholds in separation-distress circuitry in the same way.

Several decades after our discovery, the introduction of modern functional brain imaging to monitor the dynamics of the human nervous system helped clarify the neuroanatomy of pain in the human brain (Craig, 2003a, 2003b; Rainville, 2002). Though I can provide here only a sketch of this enormous area of research, the classic idea that the brain makes a distinction between the cognitive–sensory aspects of pain and its affective intensity and unpleasantness is garnering ever more support from brain imaging studies (Tölle et al., 1999).

Brain imaging has indicated that opioid analgesia is achieved by dampening both the cortical and subcortical substrates of pain processing; for instance, the thalamic and higher anterior cingulate arousals seen during pain are almost completely obliterated with fentanyl (Casey, 2000). Indeed, pain itself sets in motion endogenous opioid release in an apparent attempt to regulate the intensity of aversive affect (Apkarian et al., 2005; Ribeiro et al., 2005). As is discussed in more detail later, placebo effects are substantially mediated through psychologically induced endogenous opioid release, with the psychological effects being evident in dorsolateral prefrontal cortical areas (bilaterally), the orbitofrontal cortex on the right side, and central regions of pontine–midbrain regions including ventral regions of the PAG (Benedetti et al., 2005; Wager et al., 2004). The socially sensitive psychic-pain system that runs from the PAG through the medial thalamus to the ACC (see Figure 1.1) provides a theoretically coherent rationale for the existence of placebo effects; this basic social circuit is designed so that supportive social stimuli release endogenous opioids. Such social-security effects may be the main cause of analgesic placebo effects in medicine, and because endogenous opioids regulate the strength of the immune system, other common placebo effects may have opioid triggers. Conversely, loss of social support should produce a low-opioid state within the brain, which could help explain interesting human clinical cases such as an individual with constitutional analgesia first experiencing pain after a very important social loss (Danziger & Willer, 2005).

DESCENDING PAIN CONTROL SYSTEMS AND PLACEBO EFFECTS

The brain regulates pain in various ways. For instance, the ventral PAG, where dorsal raphe serotonergic cells are concentrated, is part of a major descending pain control system that participates in placebo effects and the cognitive control of pain (Bingel et al., 2006; Fields, 2004). Thus, not only are brain opioids recruited during psychologically facilitated analgesia but the emotion-dampening influences of elevated serotonin activity can produce synergistic effects. Placebo effects can be reduced with opiate receptor antagonists (Grevert, Albert, & Goldstein, 1983; Petrovic et al., 2002); it remains to be seen whether other environmentally induced types of analgesia such as those induced via hypnosis and ritual folk-medical practices (also known as shamanism and "witch doctoring") are also under endogenous opioid control.

Now that more and more investigators recognize that the affective sting of social pain may share evolutionary relations to physical pain, many new avenues of understanding and clinically useful intervention may open up. The quality of social environments may contribute much not only to emotional feelings but also to one's ability to cope with pain (Gatchel & Turk, 1999). There has long been evidence that the pain of childbirth is eased with social support (Klaus et al., 1986) and substantial evidence that both cardiac and postoperative pain can be alleviated likewise (King et al., 1993; Kulik & Mahler, 1989).

The control of brain opioid dynamics by social contexts also allows one to conceptualize socially facilitated placebo-type effects in evolutionary psychological terms. Perhaps placebos gain their power from the evolutionary emergence of the "healing touch" partly mediated by opioid release in the brain. Contact comfort in animals clearly is partly mediated by release of opioids (Keverne, Nevison, & Martel, 1997; Panksepp, Bean, Bishop, Vilberg, & Sahley, 1980). Thus, various placebos, provided with conviction and care, may help ensure and calm distressed others through the induction of opioid-mediated comfort states. Indeed, placebos can reduce arousal of anterior cingulate regions of the brain, especially area 25, which are commonly overactive when people are depressed or in distress; ESB of these brain regions can produce antidepressant effects (Lozano et al., 2008; Mayberg et al., 2002, 2005). Indeed, perhaps brain-stimulation-induced antidepressant effects are due to opioid release that helps melt the sting of psychic pain, which is the residue of extended separation distress and loneliness that accompanies depression. If so, those antidepressant effects might be reversed by concurrent administration of opiate receptor antagonists.

The overall message is clear: There is still abundant room to use human empathy and the healing touch in the management of all forms of pain. This can take the form of music, which often quintessentially captures social feelings (Panksepp & Bernatzky, 2002; Panksepp & Trevarthen, 2008). In addition to development of ever better medications and other biological interventions to control pain, there is abundant room for the improvement of psychosocial approaches for all kinds of pain management. Even animals exhibit diminished vocal indices of emotional pain in response to nociceptive stimulation when they have abundant social companionship (e.g., Panksepp, 1980). There is also abundant room for evaluating whether analgesic and psychotropic drugs are more effective in supportive psychosocial contexts (see Panksepp & Harro, 2004). One reason opioids are so commonly used to treat the pain of terminal cancer is surely because such changes alleviate not just the physical pain but also the emotional pain of dying. This goal is both humane and appropriate. However, it would be a shame if humans did not continue to be the ultimate carriers of the healing touch.

NEUROCHEMISTRIES OF SOCIAL BONDING AND
THE PSYCHIC PAIN OF SEPARATION DISTRESS:
A SUMMARY OF THE RELEVANT ANIMAL DATA

Let me reiterate some of the key points made so far: To be a mammal is to have a variety of social–emotional needs from the first days of life, starting with loving touch; other social communications and connections, such as facial gestures and emotional prosodic language, are then added to create organisms that eventually have overwhelming needs for social attachments. The psychological pain that emerges from the loss of social connectedness— whether it be through the death of a loved one or simply losing contact with perceived social support—is a basic emotional response of mammalian brains. Scientific understanding of the underlying processes emerged from attempts to fathom the neurobiological nature of social bonds; we evaluated this idea initially by studying the effects of opiates on separation-distress vocalizations (Panksepp, 1981; Panksepp, Herman, et al., 1980). My colleagues and I now know that social bonding is mediated in part by the neurochemistries that regulate separation-distress systems that engender emotional pain when social bonds are severed, with relief cascading into delight when they are restored. When one is tuned in, one sees such processes operating as pervasive features of everyday adult social dynamics—from the pervasive use of the virtual connections of cell phones in today's society (to reach out and symbolically touch someone through sound) to the need to reach out and touch a loved one in the flesh.

Neuropharmacological Analysis of Separation Calls

Our work on the neurochemistry of separation calls in mammals started soon after the opiate receptor was discovered in the early 1970s, followed during the next decade by the discovery of a diverse range of opioid peptides within mammalian brains. The discovery of opioid neuropeptides finally explained how opioid alkaloids, down through the ages, had been such effective medicines for the control of pain and coughing centrally (within the brain) and diarrhea peripherally (the gastrointestinal system is enriched with opiate receptors). However, we promptly surmised that more subtle affective issues might be regulated by endogenous opioids, especially the way various rewards of the external world made animals feel good. Our own research focused on the positive affects arising from friendly social interactions and companionship. We hypothesized that brain opioids serve as major neuro-affective substrates for both narcotic addiction and social bonding in the brain, especially because they shared a comparable initial addictive or bonding phase, followed by tolerance or habituation to both opiates and social reward effects, which only amplified intense opponent-process withdrawal effect if either drugs or social rewards were not available.

One can now be confident that separation distress is a fundamental, primary-process emotional function of the mammalian brain that evolved from the brain mechanisms of physical pain. Thus, one reason social bonds are so long-lasting and robust, we surmised, was because the feelings of social security were reciprocally related to separation-induced psychic-pain mechanisms being active in the brain. The key empirical evidence was that the separation-distress circuitry is strongly inhibited by heightened endogenous opioid activity in the brains of dogs, guinea pigs, and young chickens, studied in that order (Herman & Panksepp, 1978; Panksepp, Herman, et al., 1978; Panksepp, Vilberg, et al., 1978). A corollary of this social-addiction idea was that feelings of loneliness increase the likelihood of becoming addicted to narcotic drugs (Panksepp, 1981; Panksepp, Herman, et al., 1980, Panksepp, Siviy, & Normansell, 1985). Many other psychotropic agents and brain neurochemistries were also evaluated (Panksepp et al., 1988), but only a few, such as oxytocin (Panksepp, 1992, 1998a), yielded robust and behaviorally specific inhibition of separation calls. It is interesting to note that in laboratory rodents eliminating oxytocin (as in knockout mice), animals actually exhibit fewer separation calls than normal (Winslow & Insel, 2002).

The opioid findings were replicated and extended by others (e.g., Kalin et al., 1988; Kehoe & Blass, 1986; Keverne et al., 1989, 1997). Now we know that social bonds are established and reinforced, in part, through addictive opioid dynamics in the brain. When opioid tone diminishes in the human brain, feelings of sadness increase (Zubieta et al., 2003). Such basic brain mechanisms for psychic pain provide unconditional neural substrates and affective urgencies for a host of higher mind–brain processes—secondary and tertiary emotional states that are dependent on learning and thought, respectively. They probably range from feelings of shyness and the resulting social phobias to distressing thoughts from being socially marginalized. Even though relevant human psychopharmacological work remains in its infancy, abundant predictions now exist from the preclinical work.

Because several other key neurochemistries have been implicated in the regulation of separation distress in animal models, a great deal of human work remains to be conducted. Besides all opioids that activate mu-receptors, oxytocin and prolactin need to be evaluated (Panksepp, 1992, 1998a). The norepinephrine (NE) alpha-2 receptor agonist clonidine is highly effective in animal models. This is not effected through autoreceptors on NE cell bodies that reduce brain NE signaling, but it is directly due to postsynaptic, NE-activating effects of the drug (Rossi, Sahley, & Panksepp, 1983). Nicotine is also quite effective (Sahley, Panksepp, & Zolovick, 1981), which may help explain certain qualitative aspects of smoking addictions.

A variety of separation-distress facilitators have been found. Among neuropeptides, Corticotropin Releasing Factor (CRF), an activator of the CRF-1 receptor, is especially potent in our avian models, and even the CRF-2 variant of the receptor, which responds selectively to urocortin, and is commonly thought not to provoke negative stress, arouses separation distress as much as CRF (Figure 1.2). Among the rapidly acting transmitters, glutamate is by far the most intense facilitator of separation distress (Panksepp, 1998a). Also, curare infused intracerebrally is incredibly potent (Panksepp, Siviy, & Normansell, 1985), an effect that may also be due to facilitation of glutamatergic transmission (Panksepp, 1998a). In any event, it is only among the neuropeptide systems that we currently anticipate development of new medicines that very strongly modulate the psychic pain of separation distress; opioids are preeminent candidates for development of a new generation of antidepressants and the treatment of all sorts of psychic pain, including excessive sadness and grief.

However, before proceeding to those topics, I wish to emphasize why certain species are better than others in this kind of research. This issue is not well appreciated among investigators who use animal models, even though it is thoroughly discussed in Panksepp, Newman, and Insel (1992). This issue is also important for human investigators who wish to evaluate the animal data critically, especially when so much of separation-distress research has recently shifted to the more convenient laboratory rat models. The data derived from those models are not as valid for understanding primary-process separation-distress circuitry as are data derived from primates, dogs, guinea pigs, and even domestic chickens.

Interlude: Why Separation Distress Cannot Be Well Studied in Laboratory Rats

To reiterate, in most mammalian species—especially those that develop strong mother–infant bonds among each other—social isolation engenders abundant and prolonged separation DVs, indicating an aversive experience that animals will do their utmost to avoid. It is clear that the underlying affective state is not just a feeling of fear, for fearful states actually reduce isolation calls (Davis, Gurski, & Scott, 1977). Although social-separation-induced distress may be the most robust form of psychic pain that exists, as a birthright, in most mammalian brains, such brain mechanisms are vestigial in some species. Species that give birth to a great number of very immature infants, essentially preemies (namely, rats and mice, especially of the "artificial" breeds used in most laboratories), are not ideal animal models for studying "real" separation distress (for full discussion, see

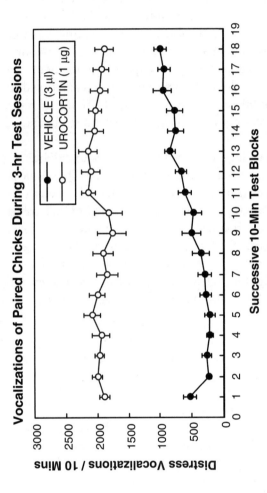

Figure 1.2. Vocalizations of Individual and Paired Chicks. The CRF1 receptor is typically thought to mediate stress, and placement of CRF into the ventricular system of young chickens dramatically elevates vocalizations when animals isolated from their flocks. The CRF2 receptor, which can be activated by a related peptide (urocortin) is typically not thought to be as stressful. As indicated below placement of 1 microgram of urocortin into the cerebrospinal fluid dramatically elevates distress vocalizations of two week old birds separated from their flock in pairs. This is as strong an effect as found in birds tested with 1 ug of CRF, and it lasts about as long (~5-6 hrs). When a much lower dose is injected (0.1 ug), the vocalizations are significantly elevated at about half of the maximal levels seen here, and the emotional state persists only for about 2 hours. Thus, in young birds, both CRF and urocortin dramatically elevate the emotion of separation distress (emotional protest) that is commonly thought to be an antecedent emotion to the despair of depression (Panksepp, 1998a). Data are means & SEMs, from Panksepp (1995, unpublished data).

Panksepp, 2003b). For instance, there is little clear evidence that robust, discrete social bonds exist between infants and mothers in laboratory rats and mice. As far as we know, such rodent mothers do not recognize their own infants nor do the young recognize their own mother. There is a simple evolutionary reason for this: These preemies, with eyes and ears closed until about 14 days of age, are pretty much stuck in the nest; they simply cannot get lost. They are more attached to the smell of their nest than to any specific mother. For such reasons we avoided the study of infant rats when we first wished to understand the neurobiology of the psychic pain that is activated when truly bonded young mammals get lost from their mothers.

Young rat pups certainly do show some isolation-type calls when they are separated from their nests (indeed, at times they do roll out of their nests and need to be retrieved and returned by mom), but these calls do not really have the character of true separation-distress vocalizations that the young of well-bonded species emit when they are lost. The bonded species cry for hours and hours if they are lost, and the sounds carry great distances. Nest-separated rats and mice vocalize just for a few minutes. The young of bonded species, like dogs, are not comforted simply by their being kept warm (Gurski, Davis, & Scott, 1980); they are fully comforted only by contact from their social caretakers. Infant rats, on the other hand, are substantially comforted simply by being kept warm, and the friendly presence of any female substantially reduces their modestly sustained ultrasonic "I'm out of the nest" vocalizations. Indeed, these ultrasonic vocalizations (USVs) do not carry any great distance, a requirement for a real separation call. They can be reflected by a leaf; they do not transmit around corners and would not inform mothers where their youngsters might be situated if they were lost at any substantial distance in the outside word. The rat USV simply alerts the mother to retrieve them when they have rolled out (or experimentally been placed outside) of the nest. Though young rat pups certainly do get attached to their nests and find maternal attention highly rewarding, when their eyes and ears open and they are finally reasonably mobile, their isolation-induced USVs cease. This is when real separation calls start in other altricial species (dogs, cats, humans).

Also, as is noted in the next section, many peculiarities have been found in the pharmacological control of these infant pup-out-of-nest calls, some of which are diametrically opposite of those found in well-bonded species that are mature enough to get seriously lost (Panksepp, 2003b). For instance, clonidine dramatically increases their USVs. It is clear that there are emotional strengths and weaknesses in each animal model, and one must remain sensitive to their ecological and evolutionary histories (especially when inadvertent human-guided breeding selection may have transpired in the confines of laboratory facilities for over 100 years).

THE DILEMMA OF PAIN AND EMOTIONAL FEELINGS
IN OTHER ANIMALS

It should be obvious to any sensitive observer of scientific progress that the details of how affective experiences such as the pleasantness and unpleasantness of certain psychological processes are generated within the brain must come from the study of animal models. The acceptance of this robust strategy is not wide because of the abundance of skeptics that claim animals do not have enough higher brain power to generate any states of mind, not even the experience of pain. For instance, one expert recently asserted that the anatomical "evidence indicates that they cannot, because the phylogenetically new pathway that conveys primary homeostatic afferent activity direct to thalamocortical levels in primates . . . is either rudimentary or absent in non-primates" (Craig, 2003a, p. 501).

Even though there must always remain some logical uncertainty as to whether other animals actually have affective experiences—and perhaps for the severest skeptics, whether even humans have affective experience in their brains—these views overlook a great deal of evidence. It is common for critics to assert that there is no proof that other animals have any feelings at all. However, not proof but the weight of evidence and issues of predictive validity must guide scientific thinking in this historically murky arena of thought. Through the blending of human and animal research, scientific strategies are emerging that allow the evaluation of the scientific substance behind many subtle processes, such as the neural causes of affective experiences, that have long been deemed beyond the pale of scientific analysis (Panksepp, 1998a, 2005a, 2005c, 2008a). However, because mixed feelings and opinions about the existence of painful experiences in other animals are still abundant, let me briefly pause to consider this contentious issue in some detail.

Animal investigators have traditionally been reticent to use terms such as *pain* in their empirical inquiries, preferring less affect-laden terms such as *nociceptive* responses, which are often accompanied by assertions that animal pain behaviors may be reflexive, with the implicit assumption that instinctual responses need not—perhaps could not—be accompanied by affective experiences. In fact, behavioral neuroscientists often choose to hide their ignorance about the nature of the primary-process neuromental apparatus under terms such as *reflexive* and *instinctual* responses. Meanwhile, every thoughtful human should know from personal histories that most of their affective experiences are gifts of nature—natural aspects of their brain and bodily functions. In fact, primary-process affects are ancestral "memories" that are intimately tied to associated emotional instinctual responses within mammalian brains. This fact is highlighted by the highly replicable fact that artificial electrical activation of the underlying circuits, always situated in similar subcortical regions, uniformly provoke internal states that can be used as rewards and punishments in a variety of learning and choice situations.

Even though such facts have been known for over half a century, because of behavioristic biases, the issue of subjective affective experience in other animals remains a problematic bone of contention among the majority of behaviorally oriented investigators. Most still prefer the "agnostic stance"—because animals cannot talk, and it cannot be known with absolute certainty what animals feel (or indeed, ultimately, what other humans feel), most neuroscientifically oriented investigators feel it is best to avoid such issues altogether. If coaxed to attend, they typically rise to the occasion by discussing the great sin of anthropomorphism, which in the current era is little more than whipping a dead horse. Arguments about evolutionary continuity and the weight of abundantly available functional data (Panksepp, 1998a, 2005a, 2005c) are more instructive and certainly the more valid ways to deal with the dilemma of understanding other minds.

The critical issue, of course, is the true nature of reality. Thus, to ignore the possibility that animal brains generate affects that may have class similarities to those of humans could be tantamount to discarding some of the key neuronal processes needed to make sense of what human and animal brains really do. Still, the skeptics do have one solid point: Feelings will never be observed any more directly than is the quantum world of subatomic particles. Feelings are an aspect of nature that has to be understood through the quality of predictions that can be made.

The time-honored scientific approach to revealing the more hidden aspects of the world scientifically has been the generation of novel predictions. Indeed, the human subjective responses to localized electrical brain stimulation of brain regions that yield instinctual emotional behaviors in animals are pretty much what one would expect if these behavioral systems were substrates for various basic emotional feelings (Heath, 1996; Panksepp, 1985). The empirical parallelisms between the human and animal data strongly suggest that animals do have comparable feelings when similar brain regions are stimulated.

In any event, as every pet owner or animal lover knows, the affective view generates an enormous number of predictions, which suggests that other animals, especially young ones, are bundles of experienced emotionality. Unfortunately, observations of "mere" behavior rarely generate robust novel predictions; that usually requires predictions that include neuroscience variables, especially neurochemical ones that can be employed in very similar ways in animals and humans.

Still, I would be remiss not to highlight some novel predictions at the behavioral level. For instance, sighing is often an indication of relief or exasperation in humans—a punctuation mark for a shift in affective state. In a remarkable experiment, Soltysik and Jelen (2005) monitored sighing in rats (operationalized as a double inspiration, with no intervening expiration) as a function of presumed feelings of relief. Rats were exposed to the pairing of a danger signal with foot shock, a well-studied approach to the classical conditioning of fear (LeDoux, 1996). After training, safety signals were inserted halfway between the onset of the danger signal and the usual onset of shock on some trials, heralding that no shock was forthcoming. At just that moment in time, the amount of sighing increased dramatically, more than tenfold over baseline levels. This is a prediction based on a priori consideration of the likelihood that animals did experience the shock as very aversive. There is no obvious alternative behavioristic interpretation.

Even more abundant predictions can be made once the neurochemical controls of certain brain processes are understood. The study of addiction is replete with such cross-species predictions. Let me just take just a few examples from the opioid social-bonding theory my colleagues and I have espoused for 30 years, making predictions from our understanding of human psychological dynamics to rats. It has long been known that the sting of physical pain can be reduced by social support, especially the provisions of supportive attention by a loving mother. We demonstrated that young rats are more sensitive to pain if they are individually housed as opposed to socially housed (Panksepp, 1980). Considering that opiates reduce physical as well as psychic pain of social isolation, we would predict that animals that have been food-hungry and companionship-hungry for 24 hr would make distinct social and food choices when given the opportunity under the affective states promoted by low doses of morphine, naloxone, or no-drug control injections. Indeed, young rats given 10 choices when under the influence of the very low 1 mg/kg dose of morphine that completely inhibits separation distress calls but that can increase playfulness run to a companion animal on only the first trial, and then run to food the subsequent nine trials. Their social motivation is clearly diminished. Under opioid blockade with 1 mg/kg naloxone, which should increase background psychic pain, after a few days of training, adolescent rats ran to companion animals on every trial. Under the control condition, they divided their choices about half and half (Panksepp, 1981).

This evidence suggests that opioids produce social confidence whereas opioid blockade produces social insecurity. When we followed up to test this prediction in terms of which animals become the winners and losers in a friendly social-competition situation (i.e., rough-and-tumble play, also known as *play fighting*), all other things being equal, the morphine-treated animals invariably became winners (on top at least nearly 70% of the time) and the naloxone ones always became losers (on top only about 30% of the time; Panksepp, Jalowiec, DeEskinazi, & Bishop, 1985). Indeed, when monitored with subtractive autoradiography, animals in the midst of joyous play are releasing abundant opioid in their brains (Panksepp & Bishop, 1981). To suggest that such patterns of results arise from reinforcement principles rather than affective changes is to choose an unreasonable conception of the natural world over a more reasonable one. Indeed, that great glue of behaviorism, that "phlogiston" of learning processes—reinforcement—may simply be an affectively neutral way of talking about how affective processes work in the brain to generate learning (Panksepp, 2005c).

So how might cross-species scientific approaches—the study of animal models—be facilitated to promote predictions at the human level? The focus will have to be on variables where useful translations are most likely. In my estimation, they will be found most abundantly within the realm of how evolutionarily created affective processes are controlled in the mammalian brain, especially by the underlying neurochemical variables. What proxy measures can be used to study the nature of emotional affects in animals? I advocate a naturalistic approach—the working hypothesis that the full patterns of many emotional–instinctual behaviors can be provisionally accepted as likely indicators of internal affective states (Panksepp, 1998a). Indeed, many findings have already been validated by various choice tasks such as conditioned place preferences and aversions and corresponding affective changes in humans. In other words, the inability to see clearly into the minds of other animals does not preclude the possibility of making predictions about changes in the affective tendencies of the human mind from studying the instinctual–emotional patterns and affective choices of other animals (Panksepp, 1999a, 1999b). This type of strategy continues to be a minority position, but it should become the majority position if such strategies lead to novel neuropsychological predictions at the human level, especially with respect to the wide varieties of psychiatric affective disorders (Panksepp, 2004, 2006).

Indeed, if the logic of the skeptics is extended to the logical limits, one should not accept the existence of pain in other humans. Such views were once common about human infants, leading to "minor" operations, especially circumcisions, without anesthesia soon after birth. This bioethical debate has not abated (e.g., Derbyshire, 2001 vs. Benatar & Benatar, 2001). As long as such skeptics prevail in the debate over the existence of affective experiences in animals, researchers will continue to neglect the enormous empirical riches about human emotions that could be harvested if they simply accepted the working assumption that affective experiences are a fundamental part of primary-process consciousness in all mammals. In short, separation distress in other animals is a highly aversive experience with many bodily consequences (Panksepp, 2003a), and it seems wiser to invest in the working hypothesis that other animals do have many affective experiences than to sustain the Cartesian bias that they do not. It is wise not only for potential ethical reasons but also because animal models may be the only efficient way to work out the underlying causal details. This is an arena of research where findings from animal models and the pursuit of human psychological research work well together.

EVOLUTION OF CONSCIOUSNESS: ANIMAL MODELS OF AFFECTIVE EXPERIENCES

Much of the earlier discussion is consistent with the conclusion that the experience of psychic pain does not emerge just from higher mental processes, but rather from the neurodynamics of quite ancient regions of the brain. Although the evolution of consciousness cannot yet be decoded with any confidence, it is certainly credible that among the most ancient forms of consciousness was the feeling of pain. Without pain, all organisms will die prematurely, for they have lost a major "anticipatory system" for survival. Being the courier of a most urgent survival concern—the need to stay out of harm's way—pain is surely a substantial part of primary-process consciousness, along with a diversity of hypothalamic systems that monitor bodily or homeostatic needs such as hunger and thirst. Likewise, the various other primary-process emotional systems that anticipate other major survival concerns are built in as ancestral memories—essential tools for living—as opposed to something organisms picked up through individual learning. The evidence for the existence of primary-process SEEKING, FEAR, RAGE, LUST, CARE, PANIC/GRIEF, and PLAYfulness systems is so substantial that only diehard behaviorists or social constructivists seem to have difficulty accepting the evidence.

However, how do the lower reaches of the nervous system have the right stuff to create internal feelings? At present many lines of evidence point toward the conclusion that raw affective feelings are constitutive aspects of a core self (Northoff & Panksepp, 2008; Panksepp & Northoff,

2009) and that psychic pain and emotional feelings exist in the brain as far down as the PAG (Panksepp, 1998b). Our working hypothesis is that primary-process emotional feelings are created by the neurodynamics of these self-same brain systems that coordinate various emotional–instinctual behavior patterns (Panksepp, 2005b, 2005e, 2008a). For instance, the separation-distress vocalization system, in the current view, is the very neural substrate for psychic pain that lies at the heart of the affective experiences of many higher order social travails, from feelings of social defeat and the resulting shame to internal experiences of ostracism and shyness—all of which lead to social phobias. Such psychic pain may lie at the heart of melancholic depression. This hypothesis has many clinical implications (Panksepp, 2004, 2006), and I focus here on treatment of depression, social phobias, and suicidal crises.

NEUROPSYCHOLOGICAL LANGUAGES OF SADNESS AND PAINFUL GRIEF

In many cultures, people experience their anguish following the loss of a loved one in terms of painful feelings. One can now be confident that such terms are more than semantic metaphors, but one cannot be certain about how many types of psychic emotional pain might exist in the brain and how these emotional states figure in psychiatric disorders. Until demonstrated otherwise, I suggest that although there is a single kind of underlying primary-process form of psychic pain (namely, that arising from separation-distress circuitry), such a core feeling can diversify enormously as a function of learning (secondary processes) as well as human capacity of thought and perhaps other complex cognitive processes (tertiary processes). Because of the relevance of such feelings for mental health issues, I now consider how the brain substrates of psychic pain emerging from separation-distress mechanisms might interface with psychiatric problems such as depression and suicide.

The psychological pain that often accompanies depression (Bair, Robinson, & Eckert, 2004; Broggi, 2008) is currently deemed to be idiopathic, medically unexplained. Not much more is known about the heightened levels of physical pain that often accompany depression (Katona, Peveler, & Dowrick, 2005), even though it is known that both types of pain, especially when occurring together, herald the most costly, troublesome, and treatment-resistant kinds of depression (Greenberg, Leong, & Birnbaum, 2003). These may be the kinds of depressive episodes that are promoted by the most severe early childhood adversities such as the loss of parents (Gilmer & McKinney, 2003), which straightforwardly implicates excessive and sustained arousal of separation-distress circuitry and the ensuing phase of sustained despair. Thereby the cascade of separation distress to despair, as Bowlby (1973, 1980) first described it, may become a sustained mood state, leading perhaps to the most treatment-resistant forms of depression (Watt & Panksepp, 2009).

As might be inferred from the neuroanatomy of separation-distress circuitry, this cascade of events may be closely related to neural substrates reaching from mesencephalic PAG regions up to the ACC (see Figure 1.1), with opioid modulation throughout the course of the circuitry. Not only have higher regions of this neural trajectory been implicated in the genesis of painful ostracized feelings arising from social exclusion (Eisenberger, Lieberman, & Williams, 2003), but this circuitry is also aroused during auto-biographically evoked sadness, which is accompanied by diminished brain opioid levels, as monitored by PET imaging of carfentanil binding in human subjects (Zubieta et al., 2003).

Thus, a growing brain imaging literature indicates that separation distress and sadness, feelings of dejection following perceived social rejection, and depression share neural substrates. The affective distress of painful feelings is associated with anterior cingulate arousal (Rainville, Duncan, Price, Carrier, & Bushnell, 1997), as are sadness (Damasio et al., 2000; Liotti & Panksepp, 2004) and the distress of social exclusion (Eisenberger, Jarcho, Lieberman, & Naliboff, 2006; Eisenberger, Lieberman, & Williams, 2003; for details, see Chapter 2, this volume). Abnormal activity levels in slightly more anterior subgenual cingulate regions have been implicated in the genesis of depression (Mayberg, 2004) as well as placebo- and antidepressant-drug-induced allevi-ation of depression (Mayberg et al., 2002). Indeed, the antidepressant effects of localized brain stimulation near anterior cingulate area 25 may be due to direct disruption of psychic-pain processing in area 25, putting essentially a functional lesion in the higher reaches of the psychic-pain system. If so, the antidepressant effects that have at times been observed by surgical lesioning of this region may directly reflect a selective lesion in the brain system that mediates psychic pain.

These emotional regions of the ACC are clearly critical for the regulation of emotional feelings that are relevant for both depression and psychological pain. What are the evolutionary foundations for these findings?

PHARMACOLOGICAL MANIPULATION OF PSYCHIC PAIN

Perhaps an understanding of specific emotions at the primary-process level will lead to better treatment of mental disorders through the targeting of specific emotional symptoms rather than syndromes. Psychic pain can already be treated through the recognition that a substantial aspect of this concept is the arousal of separation distress/PANIC circuitry and the fact that this emotional network is powerfully regulated by various other neurochemistries shared by all mammals. Because brain opioids and oxytocin dramatically reduce separation distress in animal models, they currently remain the most testable ideas at the human level. As is seen in the next section, other brain facilitators such as glutamate transmission are yielding new antidepressant modalities in ongoing human clinical research. Also as summarized in Chapter 5 of this volume, over-the-counter analgesics such as acetaminophen can gradually reduce the intensity of hurt feelings. However, here my focus is primarily on opioids that are exquisitely and rapidly effective in quelling separation distress in animal models.

There exists a large array of opioid agents that could currently be evaluated in various psychic-pain disorders, with perhaps social phobia, the grief and sadness following loss of a loved one, and depression being optimal target symptoms for focused investigation. At present oxytocin can be causally manipulated only with intranasal administration of the peptide, but recently nonpeptide congeners have been developed by several drug firms that may eventually allow investigators to evaluate changes in social-loss-induced psychic pain following more global systemic manipulation of oxytocinergic dynamics. They also may be very effective agents for diminishing shyness and social phobias. Also, certain depressive syndromes (e.g., those induced by social loss) that do not respond optimally to conventional antidepressants might benefit, as I explain later, from medications such as buprenorphine that can help recalibrate brain opioid functions without addictive side effects.

PSYCHOPHARMACOLOGICAL TREATMENTS OF DEPRESSION AND SUICIDAL IDEATION

In part, clinical depression reflects imbalanced positive and negative affective chemistries within the brain, and there are many candidates to consider (Watt & Panksepp, 2009). Recent advances in psychiatrically relevant neuropeptide research in animal models suggest that diminished pleasure chemistries and elevated distress chemistries do contribute substantially to clinical depression (e.g., Panksepp, 2007; Watt & Panksepp, 2009). Novel treatments may emerge from this knowledge.

Because social losses, especially during childhood, predispose individuals to chronically elevated levels of psychic pain and heightened susceptibility to depression for the rest of their lives (see Heim & Nemeroff, 1999), homeostatic imbalances in affective neuropeptide systems are prime candidates for generating the psychic pain of depression. For instance, it is possible that chronic melancholia arises substantially from overactivity of brain separation-distress circuitry (Watt & Panksepp, 2009). Because endogenous brain opioids facilitate all pleasures of life, from food to play to sex (Panksepp, 1998a), chronic opioid "pleasure deficits" could promote depression.

Indeed, it has long been known that depressive pain is dramatically heightened during opiate as well as psychostimulant withdrawal, and certainly opiate addiction is sustained largely by the desire of the addict to cover up the psychic pain that emerges during withdrawal. Indeed, many eventual addicts begin to take opiates to self-medicate the negative feelings inherited from constitutional and childhood insecurities as well as the slings and arrows of adult misfortunes (Khantzian, 2003). If these emotional dynamics were better understood, might there be a greater willingness to consider using opiates, especially "safe" ones like buprenorphine, to treat depression once again?

In the present context, it is noteworthy that before the era of modern psychiatric medicines, depression was most effectively treated, in the short term, with pleasure-producing opiates. However, as drug tolerance, dependence, and addictive urges emerged, opiate withdrawal intensified negative affect and depression. Only continued use of opiates could sustain emotional homeostasis. The "cure" was often worse than the disease.

With the emergence of nonopiate antidepressants half a century ago, some enhancing norepinephrine, others serotonin, the pleasure deficit concept of depression faded almost into oblivion. The new medicines were not pleasure-producing molecules; they did not robustly modify affective states in nondepressed individuals. Because they were not addictive, the pleasure principle was shelved. However, because most forms of depression are predisposed by various social losses, especially early in life, and opioids are very important in regulating such affective states, the role of opioids in treating drug-resistant depressions (a substantial subset of all cases) needs to be again put on the table. This need is indicated by the power of opioids in controlling separation distress in animal models, along with the human brain imaging indicating that some of these neurochemical systems, especially low levels of brain opioids, figure prominently in ordinary human sadness (Zubieta et al., 2003) and depression (Kennedy, Koeppe, Young, & Zubieta, 2006).

If psychic pain contributes substantially to depressive affects, then the aforementioned understanding of separation-distress circuitry should have clear implications for the treatment of depression. Not only do abundant preclinical data indicate that practically every pleasure is facilitated by brain opioids (Panksepp, 1998a), but narcotic addicts often consume opiates to alleviate psychic pain, depressive feelings arising from social insecurities, or actual social loss and the resulting despair. It is well known that social isolation tends to increase intake of practically all addictive drugs in animal models. Although addiction liability has precluded use of opioids in depression now, "safe" opioids such as buprenorphine can probably be used as highly effective, rapidly acting antidepressants with little danger of debilitating addiction.

Buprenorphine stimulates mu-opioid receptors (those that promote pleasure and satisfaction) at very low doses. Conversely, it blocks those same receptors at slightly higher doses (hence it is called a *partial agonist*). Thus, it has practically no risk of overdose. Buprenorphine is exceptionally useful for narcotic detoxification. It alleviates feelings of dysphoria when addicts are in withdrawal. It was used as the front-line treatment for narcotic detoxification in Europe for several decades, before being approved by the United States Food and Drug Administration in 2003. One useful characteristic of buprenorphine is its long duration of action, with no acute euphoric effects, stimulating mu-opioid receptors just enough to alleviate feelings of stress and provide affective homeostasis. Another is that it blocks kappa-receptors, which mediate the kind of dysphoria provoked by stress and drug withdrawal (Land et al., 2008), and thereby should help further reduce the psychic pain of depression.

There are many individual case studies in the medical literature describing the remarkable efficacy of buprenorphine in treating depression. Although no gold-standard double-blind, placebo-controlled (DBPC) studies have yet been conducted, several open trials indicate that buprenorphine at remarkably low doses can sustain robust antidepressant effects in patients who have received no sustained relief from traditional medications (Bodkin, Zornberg, Lukas, & Cole, 1995). These effects have been achieved without precipitating dose-escalating addictive urges.

The open clinical trial by Bodkin and colleagues (1995) dramatically affirmed how rapidly and effectively low doses of buprenorphine can reverse the negative affect of depression. They evaluated the efficacy of buprenorphine in 10 people with lifelong depression, starting with miniscule 0.15 mg doses (about 2% of the 10 mg typically used for narcotic detoxification), followed by modest increments as needed, with eventual therapeutic doses ranging from 0.6 to 3.6 mg/day. Most had never obtained stable relief from traditional antidepressants. Three clients withdrew early from the trial because of nausea, a common side effect of all mu-receptor stimulants in opiate-naive individuals (antinausea medications were not attempted). One elderly woman obtained temporary relief, but feelings of despair returned. The remaining six clients obtained dramatic antidepressant effects within a few days, and benefits were sustained indefinitely in most clients, with the average therapeutic dose being a very modest 1.26 mg/day. Let me share one of the dramatic cases described by Bodkin et al., 1995: "A 41-year-old, married, white, male, high-level computer programmer with two young children. A very religious man. . . . His first episode of depression was at age 15" (p. 52). He had no sustained benefits from desipramine, amoxapine, bupropion, or fluoxetine. He felt better after the first intranasal 0.15 mg of buprenorphine, and at the end of 6 weeks his Hamilton Rating Scale for Depression had dropped from 21 to 4, and "at the end of a week . . . he reported himself to be 90% recovered . . . [and] was no longer lethargic. His demeanor changed completely; he conversed spontaneously, with a full range of affect. . . . By the end of two weeks he felt completely recovered" (p. 53).

Such striking observations highlight the need for fully controlled, DBPC trials. However, that is a challenge in an opiate-phobic culture, especially when little profit can be made from old, off-patent drugs. A case could be made for orphan drug status, if future work confirms such agents can reduce severe depressive despair—a state often accompanied by suicidal intent—for which no effective medicines exist. Because sustained psychological pain is a common symptom in individuals who attempt or contemplate suicide, it is reasonable to consider at least part of this psychic pain to reflect low endogenous brain opioid activity. For instance, brain opioid receptors have been found to be massively elevated in many individuals who committed suicide (Gross-Isseroff, Biegon, Voet, & Wezman, 1998). Such receptor proliferations (i.e., also known as *receptor supersensitivity*) typically occur when transmitter levels for a receptor have been diminished for long periods. If suicidal ideation is promoted by diminished pleasure chemistries within the brain, perhaps opioids could provide islands of affective relief, during which suicidal ideation might be further ameliorated with psychotherapy.

There are currently no accepted medications to abort suicidal tendencies. Might buprenorphine replenish satisfaction resources sufficiently well to allow psychotherapeutic interventions more time to help such individuals choose life over death? Might the gentle feeling of opiate-induced peacefulness even facilitate efficacy of social interventions? When suicidal clients realize that their dark nights of the soul are provoked, in part, by neurochemical imbalances, could they use that knowledge to help restore affective balance into their daily living? Under the leadership of psychiatrist Yoram Yovell at the University of Haifa, we are currently evaluating such interventions, and three of four clients have so far exhibited reductions in suicidal ideation when treated with low doses of buprenorphine.

In the context of antidepressant medicinal development, let me share a final striking parallelism between the animal and emerging human data. Another likely neurochemical dimension for psychic pain is glutamatergic transmission within the brain. To some extent this should be uncontroversial because of the high likelihood that every experience has glutamatergic components: Glutamate is the most widespread, universal excitatory transmitter in the brain. The relevant animal observation is that the separation-distress call can be dramatically activated by N-methyl-D-aspartic acid (NMDA)-type glutamate receptor stimulants while NMDA antagonists strongly block such indices of psychic pain (see Panksepp, 1998a, pp. 269–270). This linkage is exciting from a clinical perspective because recent therapeutic work highlights that glutamate antagonists such as ketamine can be rapidly acting antidepressants (Zarate et al., 2006). Indeed, more recent work has found that individuals with sustained arousal in anterior cingulate regions that have been implicated in the affective distress of depression (Mayberg, 2004) are especially likely to exhibit rapid therapeutic effects with ketamine (Salvadore et al., 2009). Those who do not exhibit sustained arousal in this depressogenic brain region during exposure to aversive stimuli typically do not obtain robust antidepressant benefits from ketamine. Thus, again a remarkable convergence is found between animal studies of separation-distress circuitry and clinical applicability to human emotional disorders.

SYNOPSIS OF THEORETICAL PERSPECTIVES

Could there be endogenous feelings of social pain in human brains if they did not have various intrinsic social–emotional circuits that are shared with other mammals? I doubt it. The brain system that figures most heavily in such feelings—although it may diversify into various higher social and cognitive emotions with maturation (e.g., shyness, guilt, shame, grief, and social phobia as well as the distress of social exclusion)—is the ancient system that mediates separation distress. To lose social support is a painful experience, and perhaps it is most painful to lose a devoted, loving mother when a child is young and relatively helpless. A robust emotional system was evolutionarily constructed in midline subcortical regions, reaching upward into medial cortical regions, especially of the anterior cingulate, which mediates the painful distress of being lost and alone. It is noteworthy that these medial cortical and subcortical brain regions are implicated in the construction of the core SELF down below and self-related information processing up above (Northoff et al., 2006; Northoff & Panksepp, 2008; Panksepp & Northoff, 2009).

There is no evidence that other higher regions of the neocortex participate in actively generating affective feelings, except perhaps by cognitive triggering. For instance, higher cognitive activities can surely generate thoughts that will activate the PANIC/GRIEF circuitry as well as other primary-process emotional systems of the brain. However, typically cortical–cognitive activity, if anything, tends to reduce emotionality (Damasio et al., 2000; Northoff et al., 2009). Strong emotions are typically disruptive of cool cortical processing. Still, with emotional tutelage, the cortex can create emotionally moving art—from poetry and songs of love and loss to great orchestral scores, dance, and literature.

It is obvious that the cortex works most efficiently when it is not buffeted by emotional storms (Liotti & Panksepp, 2004). Modern brain imaging that is sensitive to the fact that cognitive judgments made in the midst of brain scanning can markedly affect results has some chance of seeing which brain regions actually generate emotional feelings. Indeed, if experimenters minimize cognitive biases during scanning sessions and harvest affective judgments following scanning, then positive correlations are evident between subcortical brain arousal and affective intensity and negative correlations between neo-cortical arousal and affective emotional intensity (Northoff et al., 2009). Similarly, the best PET scanning of basic affective states shows that emotional affects are elaborated by subcortical brain systems that overlap with the emo-tional circuits worked out in animal models (e.g., Damasio et al., 2000). This information is not meant to suggest that the cortex does not cognitively dwell and elaborate on emotional feelings. It surely does.

The PANIC/GRIEF system, the great motivator of social bonds, caressed by endogenous opioids and oxytocin released by loving others, can effectively quell feelings of psychic pain and endow the cortex with great human riches through social learning. The higher human brain, the neocortex, has little of that social heritage as a birthright. As far as is known, the mammalian neocortex is largely a tabula rasa at birth. Evolutionary psychologists who believe otherwise still need to provide some compelling neuropsychological and genetic data for any intrinsic modules within the neocortex of the human brain. Until they do, it remains most reasonable to conclude that most of the higher aspects of the human social brain—from mirror neurons to language, from empathy and romantic love to enmity and hatred—are grounded in and developmentally arise from the intrinsic social capacities of humans' ancient mammalian brains. An evolutionary analysis of psychic pain requires that one gets the foundational issues right. Then, only through the meticulous study of the brains of fellow mammals can one ever get a clear image of where human emotional nature comes from. How these psychic energies can be nurtured into new forms within the neocortex, strange and beautiful, is a project for the many artists and social constructivists devoted to existential and cultural complexities.

CONCLUSIONS

It has long been common in diverse human cultures for people to talk about the loss of a loved one in terms of painful feelings. It is now known that this is more than poetic license, more than a semantic metaphor (Panksepp, 2003b, 2005b, 2005d, 2005e). The emotional pain that accompanies grief and intense loneliness shares some of the same neural pathways that generate the affective sting of physical pain. The strongest neuroscience evidence (i.e., causal as opposed to just correlational) comes from animal brain research. Localized electrical stimulation of a network of interconnected medial sub-cortical and cortical brain areas implicated in the production and regulation of physical pain also regulates the affective sting of psychological pain, as is most clearly exemplified by the brain circuits that generate separation cries.

In addition to the anterior cingulate, these circuits include the deep subcortical sources of basic social–emotional urges arising from the PAG, the dorsomedial thalamus, the bed nucleus of the stria terminalis, and the ventral septal and dorsal preoptic areas. The PAG and medial thalamus have long been implicated in the control of physical pain. The PAG is the premier brain region from which emotional distress is most easily evoked by the lowest intensities of brain stimulation, in both animals and humans. The fact that physical pain and social-emotional pain share regulatory neurochemistries such as glutamate, endogenous opioids, and oxytocin provides the most compelling link between the affective distress of physical and psychological pain, pain as subtle as social ostracism that may be impossible to study in animal models (Eisenberger et al., 2003, 2006; Williams, 2001; Williams et al., 2000). Social loss, grief, and intense loneliness are registered here and imbued with the sting of painful affect. As far as can be told by peering back into evolutionary time, these social-pain systems arose as exaptations from physical pain systems at a remote time in humanity's ancestral past.

A growing human psychosocial literature is beginning to indicate that the social environment can modulate the affective intensity of pain (e.g., Brown et al., 2003; Eisenberger et al., 2003; Leary & Springer, 2000), an effect long recognized in animal studies. Likewise, recent brain imaging is remarkably consistent with the idea that certain brain areas, such as the ACC, long implicated in the processing of pain responses (Rainville, 2002), also participate in the genesis of distressful social feelings (Eisenberger et al., 2003, 2006), including depressive affect (Mayberg, 2004), but also in many other social–emotional processes, such as sexual arousal (Redouté et al., 2000). Animal brain research also highlights the importance of the anterior cingulate in social processes such as maternal behavior, social bonding, and separation calls, as well as the urge to talk to others (MacLean, 1990; Panksepp, 1998a). From a more cognitive, decision-making perspective it has been shown how heart rate variability during various behavioral and cognitive tasks is correlated with anterior cingulate arousal, suggesting "that a principal function of the ACC is the regulation of bodily states of arousal to meet concurrent behavioral demand" (Critchley et al., 2003, p. 2149).

Of course, correlative findings such as the many functional magnetic resonance imaging studies cited earlier need to now be linked to causal analyses. One critical test would be to include opioid manipulations. The animal work would predict that participants given opiates or oxytocin or glutamate antagonists should exhibit dampening of the medial cortical and subcortical regions, accompanied by diminished distress whether the distress is provoked by being shunned or as a result of endogenous social phobias or depression.

It is obvious that most causal mind–brain dissections can never be done in humans, and continued progress will require animal models, especially if researchers in the field can credibly address the underlying affective processes (Panksepp, 1998a, 2005b).

An enormous stumbling block to future progress in this as well as many areas of psychologically meaningful emotion research is the continuing unwillingness of most neuroscientifically oriented investigators to discuss brain-affective processes in the animals they study. Although it is unlikely that animal brains can elaborate high-level forms of self-awareness evident in most humans, there is now a mass of evidence that animals do experience their primary-process emotional states as intensely as humans do—perhaps more intensely because they have less cortical inhibition. Why prominent investigators still argue that animals have only emotional behaviors while humans have emotional feelings remains a puzzling aspect of the current intellectual scene.

Abundant evidence now indicates that all mammals experience the affective sting of physical pain, which, as in humans, may have been the foundation for the evolution of psychic-pain circuits such as the separation-distress systems that ascend to anterior cingulate regions. Separation distress is very aversive to other animals, and it is scientifically wiser to work from the premise that all mammals share many emotional experiences, homologous to those of humans, than to sustain the Cartesian bias that they do not. Sensitive brain research on other animals may really be the only way to illuminate the underlying causal details.

It is gratifying that human brain imaging highlights similar affective substrates of separation distress in animals and humans (e.g., Freed & Mann, 2007; Lorberbaum et al., 2002; Swain et al., 2007). Such conjunctions reveal the evolutionary commonalities between human and animal emotions better than ever before. As it becomes clear that the details of primary-process emotional systems can be revealed only through detailed neuroscientific work on animal models, more and more investigators, with clinical expertise, may begin to work on the details of these systems. Indeed, I left clinical training in the 1960s because I realized there was really no other way than cross-species evolutionary perspectives to truly understand the foundations of human emotions. This deeply Darwinian approach is still massively underrepresented within the psychological sciences.

REFERENCES

Apkarian, A. V., Bushnell, M. C., & Zubieta, J. K. (2005). Human brain mechanisms of pain perception and regulation in health and disease. *European Journal of Pain*, 9, 463–484. doi:10.1016/j.ejpain.2004.11.001

Arbib, M. A. (Ed.). (2006). *Action to language via the mirror neuron system*. Cambridge, England: Cambridge University Press. doi:10.1017/CBO9780511541599

Audero, E., Coppi, E., Mlinar, B., Rossetti, T., Caprioli, A., Banchaabouchi, M. A., . . . Gross, C. (2008, July 4). Sporadic autonomic dysregulation and death associated with excessive serotonin autoinhibition. *Science, 321*, 130–133. doi:10.1126/science.1157871

Bair, M., Robinson, R., & Eckert, G. (2004). Impact of pain and depression treatment response in primary care. *Psychosomatic Medicine, 66*, 17–22. doi:10.1097/01.PSY.0000106883.94059.C5

Benatar, D., & Benatar, M. (2001). A pain in the fetus: Toward ending confusion about fetal pain. *Bioethics, 15*, 57–76. doi:10.1111/1467-8519.00212

Benedetti, F., Mayberg, H. S., Wager, T. D., Stohler, C. S., & Zubieta, J. K. (2005). Neurobiological mechanisms of the placebo effect. *The Journal of Neuroscience, 25*, 10390–10402. doi:10.1523/JNEUROSCI.3458-05.2005

Berthier, M., Starkstein, S., & Leiguarda, R. (1988). Asymbolia for pain: A sensory-limbic disconnection syndrome. *Annals of Neurology, 24*, 41–49. doi:10.1002/ana.410240109

Bingel, U., Lorenz, J., Schoell, E., Weiller, C., & Büchel, C. (2006). Mechanisms of placebo analgesia: rACC recruitment of a subcortical antinociceptive network. *Pain, 120*, 8–15. doi:10.1016/j.pain.2005.08.027

Bishop, P. (1984). *Brain and opiate modulation of avian affective vocalizations* (Unpublished doctoral dissertation). Bowling Green State University, Bowling Green, OH.

Bodkin, J. L., Zornberg, G. L., Lukas, S. E., & Cole, J. O. (1995). Buprenorphine treatment of refractory depression. *Journal of Clinical Psychopharmacology, 15*, 49–57. doi:10.1097/00004714-199502000-00008

Bowlby, J. (1973). *Attachment and loss: Vol. 2. Separation: Anxiety and anger*. New York, NY: Basic Books.

Bowlby, J. (1980). *Loss: Sadness and depression*. New York, NY: Basic Books.

Broggi, G. (2008). Pain and psycho-affective disorders. *Neurosurgery, 62*, SHC901–SHC920. doi:10.1227/01.neu.0000333760.53748.9e

Brown, J. L., Sheffield, D., Leary, M. R., & Robinson, M. E. (2003). Social support and experimental pain. *Psychosomatic Medicine, 65*, 276–283. doi:10.1097/01.PSY.0000030388.62434.46

Casey, K. L. (2000). Concepts of pain mechanisms: The contribution of functional imaging of the human brain. *Progress in Brain Research, 129*, 277–287. doi:10.1016/S0079-6123(00)29020-1

Chapman, C. R., & Nakamura, Y. (1999). A passion of the soul: An introduction to pain for consciousness researchers. *Consciousness and Cognition, 8*, 391–422. doi:10.1006/ccog.1999.0411

Craig, A. D. (2003a). Interoception: The sense of the physiological condition of the body. *Current Opinion in Neurobiology, 13*, 500–505. doi:10.1016/S0959-4388(03)00090-4

Craig, A. D. (2003b). Pain mechanisms: Labeled lines versus convergence in central processing. *Annual Review of Neuroscience, 26,* 1–30. doi:10.1146/annurev.neuro.26.041002.131022

Critchley, H. D., Mathias, C. J., Josephs, O., O'Doherty, J., Zanini, S., Dewar, B.-K., . . . Dolan, R. (2003). Human cingulate cortex and autonomic control: Converging neuroimaging and clinical evidence. *Brain, 126,* 2139–2152. doi:10.1093/brain/awg216

Damasio, A. R., Grabowski, T. J., Bechara, A., Damasio, H., Ponto, L. L. B., Parvizi, J., & Hichwa, R. D. (2000). Subcortical and cortical brain activity during the feeling of self-generated emotions. *Nature Neuroscience, 3,* 1049–1056. doi:10.1038/79871

Danziger, N., & Willer, J.-C. (2005). Tension headache as the unique pain experience of a patient with congenital insensitivity to pain. *Pain, 117,* 478–483. doi:10.1016/j.pain.2005.07.012

Davis, K. L., Gurski, J. C., & Scott, J. P. (1977). Interaction of separation distress with fear in infant dogs. *Developmental Psychobiology, 10,* 203–212. doi:10.1002/dev.420100304

Denton, D. (2006). *The primordial emotions: The dawning of consciousness.* New York, NY: Oxford University Press.

Derbyshire, S. W. G. (2001). Fetal pain: An infantile debate. *Bioethics, 15,* 77–84. doi:10.1111/1467-8519.00213

Eisenberger, N., Jarcho, J., Lieberman, M., & Naliboff, B. (2006). An experimental study of shared sensitivity to physical pain and social rejection. *Pain, 126,* 132–138. doi:10.1016/j.pain.2006.06.024

Eisenberger, N. I., Lieberman, M. D., & Williams, K. D. (2003, October 10). Does rejection hurt? An fMRI study of social exclusion. *Science, 302,* 290–292. doi:10.1126/science.1089134

Fields, H. (2004). State-dependent opioid control of pain. *Nature Reviews. Neuroscience, 5,* 565–575. doi:10.1038/nrn1431

Foltz, E. L., & White, E. W. (1962). Pain relief by frontal cingulotomy. *Journal of Neurosurgery, 19,* 89–100. doi:10.3171/jns.1962.19.2.0089

Freed, P. J., & Mann, J. J. (2007). Sadness and loss: A neurobiopsychosocial model. *The American Journal of Psychiatry, 164,* 28–34. doi:10.1176/appi.ajp.164.1.28

Gatchel, R., & Turk, D. (Eds.). (1999). *Psychosocial factors in pain: Critical perspectives.* New York, NY: The Guilford Press.

Gilmer, W., & McKinney, W. (2003). Early experience and depressive disorder: Human and non-human primate studies. *Journal of Affective Disorders, 75,* 97–113.

Greenberg, P., Leong, S., & Birnbaum, H. (2003). The economic burden of depression with painful symptoms. *The Journal of Clinical Psychiatry, 64,* 17–23.

Grevert, P., Albert, L. H., & Goldstein, A. (1983). Partial antagonism of placebo analgesia by naloxone. *Pain, 16,* 129–143. doi:10.1016/0304-3959(83)90203-8

Gross-Isseroff, R., Biegon, A., Voet, H., & Wezman, A. (1998). The suicide brain: A review of postmortem receptor/transporter binding studies. *Neuroscience and Biobehavioral Reviews, 22*, 653–661. doi:10.1016/S0149-7634(97)00061-4

Gurski, J. C., Davis, K., & Scott, J. P. (1980). Interaction of separation discomfort with contact comfort and discomfort in the dog. *Developmental Psychobiology, 13*, 463–467. doi:10.1002/dev.420130504

Heath, R. G. (1996). *Exploring the mind-body relationship.* Baton Rouge, LA: Moran Printing.

Heim, C., & Nemeroff, C. B. (1999). The impact of early adverse experiences on brain systems involved in the pathophysiology of anxiety and affective disorders. *Biological Psychiatry, 46*, 1509–1522. doi:10.1016/S0006-3223(99)00224-3

Herman, B. H. (1979). *An exploration of brain social attachment substrates in guinea pigs.* Unpublished doctoral dissertation, Bowling Green State University, Bowling Green, OH.

Herman, B. H., & Panksepp, J. (1978). Effects of morphine and naloxone on separation distress and approach attachment: Evidence for opiate mediation of social affect. *Pharmacology, Biochemistry, and Behavior, 9*, 213–220. doi:10.1016/0091-3057 (78)90167-3

Herman, B. H., & Panksepp, J. (1981, March 6). Ascending endorphin inhibition of distress vocalization. *Science, 211*, 1060–1062. doi:10.1126/science.7466377

Jürgens, U. (1998). Neuronal control of mammalian vocalization with special reference to the squirrel monkey. *Naturwissenschaften, 85*, 376–388. doi:10.1007/ s001140050519

Jürgens, U. (2002). Neural pathways underlying vocal control. *Neuroscience and Biobehavioral Reviews, 26*, 235–258. doi:10.1016/S0149-7634(01)00068-9

Kalin, N. H., Shelton, S. E., & Barksdale, C. M. (1988). Opiate modulation of separation-induced distress in non-human primates. *Brain Research, 440*, 285–292. doi:10.1016/0006-8993(88)90997-3

Katona, C., Peveler, R., & Dowrick, C. (2005). Pain symptoms in depression; definition and clinical significance. *Clinical Medicine, 5*, 390–395.

Kehoe, P., & Blass, E. M. (1986). Opioid-mediation of separation distress in 10-day-old rats: Reversal of stress with maternal stimuli. *Developmental Psychobiology, 19*, 385–398. doi:10.1002/dev.420190410

Kennedy, S. E., Koeppe, R. A., Young, E. A., & Zubieta, J. K. (2006). Dysregulation of endogenous opioid emotion regulation circuitry in major depression in women. *Archives of General Psychiatry, 63*, 1199–1208. doi:10.1001/archpsyc.63.11.1199

Keverne, E. B., Martensz, N., & Tuite, B. (1989). β-Endorphin concentrations in CSF of monkeys are influenced by grooming relationships. *Psychoneuroendocrinology, 14*, 155–161. doi:10.1016/0306-4530(89)90065-6

Keverne, E. B., Nevison, C. M., & Martel, F. L. (1997). Early learning and the social bond. *Annals of the New York Academy of Sciences, 807*, 329–339. doi:10.1111/ j.1749-6632.1997.tb51930.x

Khantzian, E. J. (2003). Understanding addictive vulnerability: An evolving psycho-dynamic perspective (With commentaries by J. Panksepp, B. Johnson, G. F. Koob, V. Morrison, and C. Yorke and response by E. J. Khantzian). *Neuropsychoanalysis, 5*, 5–69.

King, K. B., Reis, H. T., Porter, L. A., & Norsen, L. H. (1993). Social support and long-term recovery from coronary artery surgery: Effects on patients and spouses. *Health Psychology, 12*, 56–63. doi:10.1037/0278-6133.12.1.56

Klaus, M. H., Kennel, J. H., Robertson, S. S., & Rosa, R. (1986). Effects of social support during parturition on maternal and infant mortality. *British Medical Journal, 293*, 585–587. doi:10.1136/bmj.293.6547.585

Kulik, J. A., & Mahler, H. I. (1989). Social support and recovery from surgery. *Health Psychology, 8*, 221–238. doi:10.1037/0278-6133.8.2.221

Land, B. B., Bruchas, M. R., Melief, E., Xu, M., Lemos, J. C., & Chavkin, C. (2008). The dysphoric component of stress is encoded by activation of the dynorphin-kappa opioid system. *The Journal of Neuroscience, 28*, 407–414. doi:10.1523/JNEUROSCI. 4458-07.2008

Leary, M. R., & Springer, C. A. (2000). Hurt feelings: The neglected emotion. In R. Kowalski (Ed.), *Aversive behaviors and interpersonal transgression* (pp. 151–175). Washington, DC: American Psychological Association.

LeDoux, J. (1996). *The emotional brain.* New York, NY: Simon & Schuster.

Liotti, M., & Panksepp, J. (2004). Imaging human emotions and affective feelings: Implications for biological psychiatry. In J. Panksepp (Ed.), *Textbook of biological psychiatry* (pp. 33–74). New York, NY: Wiley.

Lorberbaum, J. P., Newman, J. D., Horwitz, A. R., Dubno, J. R., Lydiard, R. B., Hamner, M. B., . . . George, M. S. (2002). A potential role for thalamocingulate circuitry in human maternal behavior. *Biological Psychiatry, 51*, 431–445. doi:10.1016/S0006-3223(01)01284-7

Lozano, A. M., Mayberg, H. S., Giacobbe, P., Hamani, C., Craddock, R. C., & Kennedy, S. H. (2008). Subcallosal cingulate gyrus deep brain stimulation for treatment-resistant depression. *Biological Psychiatry, 64*, 461–467. doi:10.1016/ j.biopsych.2008.05.034

MacDonald, G., & Leary, M. R. (2005). Why does social exclusion hurt? The relationship between social and physical pain. *Psychological Bulletin, 131*, 202–223. doi:10.1037/0033-2909.131.2.202

MacLean, P. D. (1990). *The triune brain in evolution.* New York, NY: Plenum Press.

Mayberg, H. S. (2004). Depression: A neuropsychiatric perspective. In J. Panksepp (Ed.), *A textbook of biological psychiatry* (pp. 197–229). New York, NY: Wiley.

Mayberg, H. S., Lozano, A. M., Voon, V., McNeely, H. E., Seminowicz, D., Hamani, C., . . . Kennedy, S. H. (2005). Deep brain stimulation for treatment-resistant depression. *Neuron, 45*, 651–660. doi:10.1016/j.neuron.2005.02.014

Mayberg, H. S., Silva, J. A., Brannan, S. K., Tekell, J., Mahurin, R., McGinnis, S., & Jerabek, P. A. (2002). The functional neuroanatomy of the placebo effect. *The American Journal of Psychiatry, 159*, 728–737. doi:10.1176/appi.ajp.159.5.728

Newman, J. D. (Ed.). (1988). *The physiological control of mammalian vocalizations*. New York, NY: Plenum Press.

Northoff, G., Heinzel, A., Bermpohl, F., Niese, R., Pfennig, A., Pascual-Leone, A., & Schlaug, G. (2004). Reciprocal modulation and attenuation in the prefrontal cortex: An fMRI study on emotional-cognitive interaction. *Human Brain Mapping, 21*, 202–212. doi:10.1002/hbm.20002

Northoff, G., Heinzel, A., de Greck, M., Bermpohl, F., Dobrowolny, H., & Panksepp, J. (2006). Self-referential processing in our brain—a meta-analysis of imaging studies on the self. *NeuroImage, 31*, 440–457. doi:10.1016/j.neuroimage.2005.12.002

Northoff, G., & Panksepp, J. (2008). The trans-species concept of self and the subcortical-cortical midline system. *Trends in Cognitive Sciences, 12*, 259–264. doi:10.1016/j.tics.2008.04.007

Northoff, G., Schneider, F., Walter, M., Bermpohl, F., Heinzel, A., Tempelmann, C., . . . Panksepp, J. (2009). Differential parametric modulation of self-relatedness and emotions in different brain regions. *Human Brain Mapping, 30*, 369–382. doi:10.1002/hbm.20510

Panksepp, J. (1980). Brief social isolation, pain responsivity, and morphine analgesia in young rats. *Psychopharmacology, 72*, 111–112. doi:10.1007/BF00433816

Panksepp, J. (1981). Brain opioids: A neurochemical substrate for narcotic and social dependence. In S. Cooper (Ed.), *Progress in theory in psychopharmacology* (pp. 149–175). London, England: Academic Press.

Panksepp, J. (1985). Mood changes. In P. J. Vinken, G. W. Bruyn, & H. L. Klawans (Eds.), *Handbook of clinical neurology: Vol. 1(45). Clinical neuropsychology* (pp. 271–285). Amsterdam, Holland: Elsevier Science.

Panksepp, J. (1991). Affective neuroscience: A conceptual framework for the neuro-biological study of emotions. In K. Strongman (Ed.), *International reviews of emotion research* (pp. 59–99). Chichester, England: Wiley.

Panksepp, J. (1992). Oxytocin effects on emotional processes: Separation distress, social bonding, and relationships to psychiatric disorders. *Annals of the New York Academy of Sciences, 652*, 243–252. doi:10.1111/j.1749-6632.1992.tb34359.x

Panksepp, J. (1998a). *Affective neuroscience: The foundations of human and animal emotions*. London, England: Oxford University Press.

Panksepp, J. (1998b). The periconscious substrates of consciousness: Affective states and the evolutionary origins of the SELF. *Journal of Consciousness Studies, 5*, 566–582.

Panksepp, J. (1999a). Emotions as viewed by psychoanalysis and neuroscience: An exercise in consilience, and accompanying commentaries. *Neuropsychoanalysis. 1*, 15–89.

Panksepp, J. (1999b). Neural systems: From animals to humans. In D. Levinson, J. J. Ponzetti Jr., & P. F. Jorgensen (Eds.), *Encyclopedia of emotions* (Vol. 2, pp. 475–478). New York, NY: Macmillan.

Panksepp, J. (2003a, October 10). Feeling the pain of social loss. *Science, 302,* 237–239. doi:10.1126/science.1091062

Panksepp, J. (2003b). Can the anthropomorphic analysis of "separation calls" in other animals inform us about the emotional nature of social loss in humans? *Psychological Review, 110,* 376–388. doi:10.1037/0033-295X.110.2.376

Panksepp, J. (Ed.). (2004). *A textbook of biological psychiatry.* New York, NY: Wiley.

Panksepp, J. (2005a). Affective consciousness: Core emotional feelings in animals and humans. *Consciousness and Cognition, 14,* 30–80. doi:10.1016/j.concog.2004.10.004

Panksepp, J. (2005b). Feelings of social loss: The evolution of pain and the ache of a broken heart. In R. Ellis & N. Newton (Eds.), *Consciousness & emotions* (Vol. 1, pp. 23–55). Amsterdam, Holland: John Benjamins.

Panksepp, J. (2005c). On the embodied neural nature of core emotional affects. *Journal of Consciousness Studies, 12,* 158–184.

Panksepp, J. (2005d). Social support and pain: How does the brain feel the ache of a broken heart? *Journal of Cancer Pain & Symptom Palliation, 1,* 59–65. doi:10.1300/J427v01n01_08

Panksepp, J. (2005e). Why does separation-distress hurt? A comment on MacDonald and Leary. *Psychological Bulletin, 131,* 224–230. doi:10.1037/0033-2909.131.2.224

Panksepp, J. (2006). Emotional endophenotypes in evolutionary psychiatry. *Progress in Neuro-Psychopharmacology & Biological Psychiatry, 30,* 774–784. doi:10.1016/j.pnpbp.2006.01.004

Panksepp, J. (2007). Affective consciousness. In M. Velmans & S. Schneider (Eds.), *The Blackwell companion to consciousness* (pp. 114–129). Malden, MA: Blackwell Publishing.

Panksepp, J. (2008a). The affective brain and core-consciousness: How does neural activity generate emotional feelings? In M. Lewis, J. M. Haviland, & L. F. Barrett (Eds.), *Handbook of emotions* (pp. 47–67). New York, NY: Guilford Press.

Panksepp, J. (2008b, May). *The neuroscience of primary-process emotionality: Implications for psychiatry and affective well-being.* Presidential address at the Society of Biological Psychiatry's 63rd Annual Scientific Convention and Meeting, Washington, DC.

Panksepp, J., Bean, N. J., Bishop, P., Vilberg, T., & Sahley, T. L. (1980). Opioid blockade and social comfort in chicks. *Pharmacology, Biochemistry, and Behavior, 13,* 673–683. doi:10.1016/0091-3057(80)90011-8

Panksepp, J., & Bernatzky, G. (2002). Emotional sounds and the brain: The neuro-affective foundations of musical appreciation. *Behavioural Processes, 60,* 133–155. doi:10.1016/S0376-6357(02)00080-3

Panksepp, J., & Bishop, P. (1981). An autoradiographic map of ³H diprenorphine binding in the rat brain: Effects of social interaction. *Brain Research Bulletin, 7,* 405–410. doi:10.1016/0361-9230(81)90038-1

Panksepp, J., & Harro, J. (2004). Future of neuropeptides in biological psychiatry and emotional psychopharmacology: Goals and strategies. In J. Panksepp (Ed.), *Textbook of biological psychiatry* (pp. 627–659). New York, NY: Wiley.

Panksepp, J., Herman, B., Conner, R., Bishop, P., & Scott, J. P. (1978). The biology of social attachments: Opiates alleviate separation distress. *Biological Psychiatry, 13*, 607–618.

Panksepp, J., Herman, B. H., Vilberg, T., Bishop, P., & DeEskinazi, F. G. (1980). Endogenous opioids and social behavior. *Neuroscience and Biobehavioral Reviews, 4*, 473–487. doi:10.1016/0149-7634(80)90036-6

Panksepp, J., Jalowiec, J., DeEskinazi, F. G., & Bishop, P. (1985). Opiates and play dominance in juvenile rats. *Behavioral Neuroscience, 99*, 441–453. doi:10.1037/0735-7044.99.3.441

Panksepp, J., Newman, J. D., & Insel, T. R. (1992). Critical conceptual issues in the analysis of separation distress systems of the brain. In K. T. Strongman (Ed.), *International review of studies on emotion* (Vol. 2, pp. 51–72). Chichester, England: Wiley.

Panksepp, J., Normansell, L. A., Herman, B., Bishop, P., & Crepeau, L. (1988). Neural and neurochemical control of the separation distress call. In J. D. Newman (Ed.), *The physiological control of mammalian vocalizations* (pp. 263–299). New York, NY: Plenum Press.

Panksepp, J., & Northoff, G. (2009). The trans-species core SELF: The emergence of active cultural and neuro-ecological agents through self-related processing within subcortical-cortical midline networks. *Consciousness and Cognition, 18*, 193–215. doi:10.1016/j.concog.2008.03.002

Panksepp, J., Siviy, S. M., & Normansell, L. A. (1985). Brain opioids and social emotions. In M. Reite & T. Fields (Eds.), *The psychobiology of attachment and separation* (pp. 3–49). New York, NY: Academic Press.

Panksepp, J., & Trevarthen, C. (2008). Motive impulse and emotion in acts of musicality and in sympathetic emotional response to music. In S. Maloch & C. Trevarthen (Eds.), *Communicative musicality* (pp. 105–146). Oxford, England: Oxford University Press.

Panksepp, J., Vilberg, T., Bean, N. J., Coy, D. H., & Kastin, A. J. (1978). Reduction of distress vocalization in chicks by opiate-like peptides. *Brain Research Bulletin, 3*, 663–667. doi:10.1016/0361-9230(78)90014-X

Petrovic, P., Kalso, E., Petersson, K. M., & Ingvar, M. (2002, February 7). Placebo and opioid analgesia: Imaging a shared neuronal network. *Science, 295*, 1737–1740. doi:10.1126/science.1067176

Ploner, M., Freund, H. J., & Schnitzler, A. (1999). Pain affect without pain sensation in a patient with a postcentral lesion. *Pain, 81*, 211–214. doi:10.1016/S0304-3959(99)00012-3

Rainville, P. (2002). Brain mechanisms of pain affect and pain modulation. *Current Opinion in Neurobiology, 12*, 195–204. doi:10.1016/S0959-4388(02)00313-6

Rainville, P., Duncan, G., Price, D., Carrier, B., & Bushnell, M. (1997, August 15). Pain affect encoded in human anterior cingulate but not somatosensory cortex. *Science, 277*, 968–971. doi:10.1126/science.277.5328.968

Redouté, J., Stoléru, S., Grégoire, M.-C., Costes, N., Cinotti, L., Lavenne, F., . . . Pujol, J.-F. (2000). Brain processing of visual sexual stimuli in human males. *Human Brain Mapping, 11*, 162–177. doi:10.1002/1097-0193(200011)11:3<162:: AID-HBM30>3.0.CO;2-A

Ribeiro, S. C., Kennedy, S. E., Smith, Y. R., Stohler, C. S., & Zubieta, J. K. (2005). Interface of physical and emotional stress regulation through the endogenous opioid system and mu-opioid receptors. *Progress in Neuro-Psychopharmacology & Biological Psychiatry, 29*, 1264–1280. doi:10.1016/j.pnpbp.2005.08.011

Rizzolatti, G., & Sinigaglia, C. (2008). *Mirrors in the brain: How our minds share actions and emotions.* Oxford, England: Oxford University Press.

Rossi, J., III, Sahley, T. L., & Panksepp, J. (1983). The role of brain norepinephrine in clonidine suppression of isolation-induced distress in the domestic chick. *Psychopharmacology, 79*, 338–342. doi:10.1007/BF00433414

Sahley, T. L., Panksepp, J., & Zolovick, A. J. (1981). Cholinergic modulation of separation distress in the domestic chick. *European Journal of Pharmacology, 72*, 261–264. doi:10.1016/0014-2999(81)90283-1

Salvadore, G., Cornwell, B. R., Colon-Rosario, V., Coppola, R., Grillon, C., Zarate, C. A., Jr., & Manji, H. (2009). Increased anterior cingulate cortical activity in response to fearful faces: A neurophysiological biomarker that predicts rapid antidepressant response to ketamine. *Biological Psychiatry, 65*, 289–295.

Soltysik, S., & Jelen, P. (2005). In rats, sighs correlate with relief. *Physiology & Behavior, 85*, 598–602. doi:10.1016/j.physbeh.2005.06.008

Sur, M., & Leamey, C. A. (2001). Development and plasticity of cortical areas and networks. *Nature Reviews. Neuroscience, 2*, 251–262. doi:10.1038/35067562

Sur, M., & Rubenstein, J. L. (2005, November 4). Patterning and plasticity of the cerebral cortex. *Science, 310*, 805–810. doi:10.1126/science.1112070

Swain, J. E., Lorberbaum, J. P., Kose, S., & Strathearn, L. (2007). Brain basis of early parent-infant interactions: Psychology, physiology, and in vivo functional neuro-imaging studies. *Journal of Child Psychology and Psychiatry, and Allied Disciplines, 48*, 262–287. doi:10.1111/j.1469-7610.2007.01731.x

Tölle, T. R., Kaufmann, T., Siessmeier, T., Lautenbacher, S., Berthele, A., Munz, F., . . . Bartenstein, P. (1999). Region-specific encoding of sensory and affective components of pain in the human brain: A positron emission tomography correlation analysis. *Annals of Neurology, 45*, 40–47. doi:10.1002/1531-8249(199901)45: 1<40::AID-ART8>3.0.CO;2-L

Wager, T. D., Rilling, J. K., Smith, E. E., Sokolik, A., Casey, K. L., Davidson, R. J., . . . Cohen, J. D. (2004, February 20). Placebo-induced changes in fMRI in the anticipation and experience of pain. *Science, 303*, 1162–1167. doi:10.1126/ science.1093065

Watt, D. F. (2007). Toward a neuroscience of empathy: Integrating affective and cognitive perspectives (with commentaries by L. Biven & J. Panksepp, V. Gallese, I. Morrison, and L. S. Sandberg & F. N. Busch and response by D. F. Watt). *Neuropsychoanalysis*, 9, 119–172.

Watt, D. F., & Panksepp, J. (2009). Depression: An evolutionarily conserved mechanism to terminate separation-distress? A review of aminergic, peptidergic, and neural network perspectives. *Neuropsychoanalysis*, 11(11), 5–104.

Williams, K. D. (2001). *Ostracism: The power of silence*. New York, NY: Guilford Press.

Williams, K. D., Cheung, C. K. T., & Choi, W. (2000). Cyberostracism: Effects of being ignored over the Internet. *Journal of Personality and Social Psychology*, 79, 748–762. doi:10.1037/0022-3514.79.5.748

Winslow, J. T., & Insel, T. R. (1991). Endogenous opioids: Do they modulate the rat pup's response to social isolation? *Behavioral Neuroscience*, 105, 253–263. doi:10.1037/0735-7044.105.2.253

Winslow, J. T., & Insel, T. R. (2002). The social deficits of the oxytocin knockout mouse. *Neuropeptides*, 36, 221–229. doi:10.1054/npep.2002.0909

Zarate, C. A., Jr., Singh, J. B., Carlson, P. J., Brutsche, N. E., Ameli, R., Luckenbaugh, D. A., . . . Manji, H. K. (2006). A randomized trial of an N-methyl-D-aspartate antagonist in treatment-resistant major depression. *Archives of General Psychiatry*, 63, 856–864. doi:10.1001/archpsyc.63.8.856

Zubieta, J. K., Ketter, T. A., Bueller, J. A., Xu, Y., Kilbourn, M. R., Young, E. A., & Koeppe, R. A. (2003). Regulation of human affective responses by anterior cingulate and limbic mu-opioid neurotransmission. *Archives of General Psychiatry*, 60, 1145–1153. doi:10.1001/archpsyc.60.11.1145

2

THE NEURAL BASIS OF SOCIAL PAIN: FINDINGS AND IMPLICATIONS

NAOMI I. EISENBERGER

According to most studies, people's number one fear is public speaking. Number two is death. Death is number two. Does that sound right? This means that to the average person, if you go to a funeral, you're better off in the casket than doing the eulogy.

—Jerry Seinfeld

Many would agree with the notion that public speaking is frightening, and some would do nearly anything to avoid it. Indeed, public speaking is often cited as people's number-one fear. However, in the preceding quote, comedian Jerry Seinfeld highlights one of the stranger truths about human beings—namely, that the fear of public speaking is right up there with the fear of death. How can that be possible? When directly compared with the fear of death, the fear of public speaking seems trivial. Death, after all, is the end of one's existence, the termination of all relationships, life, and experience. Public speaking is, well, just that—getting up in front of a group of people and talking. Yet, for many people, just the thought of speaking in front of an audience can make the stomach turn. How is it that the fear of public speaking could even be mentioned in the same discussion as the fear of death?

Research from social psychology suggests that one of the reasons that public speaking may be so feared is because of the evolutionary importance of social inclusion for survival and the increased risk of rejection that comes with speaking to a group (Baumeister & Leary, 1995). The fear of public speaking stems, in part, from the fear of being evaluated negatively and rejected by the people to whom one is speaking. Throughout the evolution of humans and other mammalian species, maintaining close social ties, and thus minimizing opportunities for social rejection and social isolation, has been critical for survival. From birth, mammals rely on the care and nurturance of a caregiver because of their inability to survive on their own. Later in life, being connected to a social group increases chances of survival by providing shared resources and protection from predators. Thus, over the course of evolutionary history, being separated from a caregiver or from the social group significantly decreased chances of survival. Because of this, even though social rejection may no longer be such a dangerous proposition, modern-day fears of public speaking may be a remnant of human beings' evolutionary past, in which rejection from the social group typically resulted in death.

People's need for social connection not only has left its mark on their most intense fears but also has shaped their underlying neural makeup. My colleagues and I have previously argued that the need for social connection is so important and that the threat of social rejection is so severe that the experience of social rejection is actually processed by some of the same neural machinery that processes physical pain (Eisenberger & Lieberman, 2004), which gives support to the notion that rejection hurts. In fact, some have suggested that over the course of mammalian evolution, the social attachment system, which keeps people connected to close others, may have piggybacked directly onto the physical pain system, borrowing the pain signal to indicate when social ties are threatened or lost (Panksepp, 1998). From an evolutionary standpoint, feeling pain upon social rejection makes a lot of sense. If broken social ties are experienced as painful, individuals will be more likely to avoid situations that might threaten social ties or lead to rejection (e.g., public speaking), hence increasing one's likelihood of inclusion in the group and one's chances of survival. Thus, one of the mechanisms for ensuring social connection may be through the experience of pain during social rejection, and this may be instantiated, in part, through an overlap in the neural systems underlying physical and social pain.

In this chapter, I explore the notion that physical and social pain share similar neurocognitive substrates and discuss what this overlapping neural circuitry means for the experience of social relationships and the dread and pain that come with the possibility or actuality of losing these social bonds. To do this, I examine whether social and physical pain rely on shared neural circuitry and summarize findings from some of my own work that has examined the neural correlates of socially painful experience in humans. I then highlight several studies that have tested novel questions stemming from the hypothesis that physical and social pain processes overlap, such as (a) Are individuals who are more sensitive to physical pain also more sensitive to social pain? and (b) Do factors that increase or decrease social pain (social rejection vs. social support) alter physical pain in a parallel manner? To conclude, I extend the field's understanding of the neural systems underlying physical and social pain experience by examining related issues such as aggression and race-based rejection.

IS THERE EVIDENCE FOR A PHYSICAL–SOCIAL PAIN OVERLAP?

One reason to believe that physical and social pain share overlapping mechanisms is that they share a common vocabulary. When individuals describe what it feels like to be rejected or left out, they describe their experience with physical pain words, complaining of hurt feelings, broken hearts, or the pain of rejection. In fact, there are no direct synonyms for the painful feelings that result from broken social bonds other than these physical pain words. It is notable that the use of physical pain words to describe a socially painful experience is a phenomenon that is common to many different languages—not just English (MacDonald & Leary, 2005). However, linguistic evidence alone does not substantiate the claim that physical and social pain processes overlap. A broken heart could simply be a figure of speech and might not actually be experienced as painful.

One way to more convincingly demonstrate an overlap in the mechanisms that support physical and social pain processes is to show that they rely on shared neural circuitry. Here, I review neuropsychological and neuroimaging research suggesting that the dorsal anterior cingulate cortex (dACC), a large structure on the medial wall of the frontal lobe, is one of the key neural structures involved in physical and social pain processes. Though undoubtedly many other neural structures are involved in this overlap, such as the insula, periaqueductal gray (PAG), and dorsomedial thalamus (Panksepp, 2003; see also Chapter 1, this volume), I focus primarily on the dACC, both because of the role that it plays in the distressing experience of physical pain in humans and because of the role that it plays in separation-distress behaviors in nonhuman mammals and social pain experience in humans.

The dACC and Physical Pain in Humans

Painful experience can be divided into two components: the sensory and affective components (Price, 2000). The sensory component of pain has to do with the intensity of the painful stimulus. Asking about the sensory component of pain can be likened to asking, "How loud is the volume on the radio?" The affective component of pain has to do with the perceived unpleasantness of the painful stimulus, which should be dissociable, at least in part, from the intensity of the painful stimulus. Asking about the affective component of pain can be likened to asking, "How much does the volume of the radio bother you?" The answers to these questions will often be correlated, but each addresses distinct features of experience.

Both neuropsychological and neuroimaging studies demonstrate that the dACC is involved in the affective or distressing component of painful experience, as opposed to the sensory component. Chronic pain patients who have undergone cingulotomy, a surgical procedure in which a portion of the dACC is removed, often report that though they can still identify the source location of the painful stimuli, the pain no longer bothers them (Foltz & White, 1968). Such evidence highlights the unique role that this neural region plays in the distressing or what is sometimes referred to as the "suffering" component of pain experience.

Similarly, neuroimaging studies have shown that the activity of the dACC tracks the affective component of pain experience. Subjects who were hypnotized so as to selectively increase the unpleasantness of noxious stimuli (affective component) without altering the intensity (sensory component) showed increased activity in the dACC without changing activity in primary somatosensory cortex (Rainville, Duncan, Price, Carrier, & Bushnell, 1997). Likewise, self-reports of pain unpleasantness correlate specifically with dACC activity (Peyron et al., 2000; Ploghaus et al., 1999; Sawamoto et al., 2000) and those with greater pain sensitivity show greater dACC responses to painful stimuli (Coghill, McHaffie, & Yen, 2003).

The dACC and Separation Distress in Nonhuman Mammals

In addition to its role in physical pain, the dACC is also involved in separation-distress behaviors in nonhuman mammals, which suggests that it may also play a role in some forms of social pain experience. Across many mammalian species, infants emit distress vocalizations when separated from their mothers. These vocalizations are thought to reflect separation distress in the infants and serve the purpose of cueing the mother to retrieve the infant to prevent prolonged separation between the two.

With regard to the role that the dACC plays in distress vocalizations specifically, it has been shown that ablation of the dACC in squirrel monkeys leads to decreases in distress vocalizations but not other kinds of vocalizations (Kirzinger & Jürgens, 1982; MacLean & Newman, 1988), whereas electrical stimulation of the dACC in rhesus monkeys leads to the spontaneous production of distress vocalizations (Jürgens & Ploog, 1970; Ploog, 1981; Smith, 1945). In addition, highlighting the specific role of the dACC rather than other neural regions in producing distress vocalizations, stimulation of the area corresponding to Broca's area, an area known to be involved in speech production, elicits movement of the vocal chords but no distress vocalizations in monkeys and apes (Leyton & Sherrington, 1917; Ploog, 1981). Thus, distress vocalizations seem to be distinctly related to dACC activation and not to the activation of neural regions involved in speech production more generally.

On the basis of the involvement of the dACC in physical pain in humans and separation-distress behaviors in nonhuman mammals, the remaining link to be examined is whether this same neural region also plays a role in social pain in human populations. In a series of studies, we examined whether this and other pain-related neural regions were involved in the feelings associated with being socially excluded.

The dACC and Social Pain in Humans

In the first neuroimaging study of social exclusion in humans (Eisenberger, Lieberman, & Williams, 2003), participants were led to believe that they would be scanned while playing an interactive ball-tossing game—called Cyberball (Williams, Cheung, & Choi, 2000)—over the Internet with two other individuals who were also in functional magnetic resonance imaging (fMRI) scanners. Unbeknownst to participants, they were actually playing with a pre-set computer program. Participants completed one round of the ball-tossing game in which they were included for the entire game and a second round in which they were excluded by the other players, partway through the game (see Figure 2.1). After completing the game, participants exited the scanner and filled out self-report measures of how much social distress they felt in response to being left out (e.g., "I felt rejected," "I felt meaningless").

Upon being excluded from the game, compared with when being included, participants reported feeling significant levels of social distress and showed increased activity in a region of the dACC, very similar to the region of the dACC associated with the unpleasantness of physical pain. Moreover, the magnitude of dACC activity correlated strongly with self-reports of social distress felt during the exclusion episode, such that individuals who showed greater dACC activity in response to social rejection also reported feeling more distressed by the rejection episode. Participants also showed increased activity in the insula, a region known to be involved in processing visceral sensation (e.g., visceral pain) as well as negative affective states (Aziz, Schnitzler, & Enck, 2000; Cechetto & Saper, 1987; Lane, Reiman, Ahern, Schwartz, & Davidson, 1997; Phan, Wager, Taylor, & Liberzon, 2004; Phillips et al., 1997); however, insular activity did not correlate significantly with self-reported social distress in this study.

In addition, in response to social exclusion relative to inclusion, participants showed significant activity in the right ventral prefrontal cortex (RVPFC), a region of the brain typically associated with regulating physical pain experience or negative affect (Hariri, Bookheimer, & Mazziotta, 2000; Lieberman et al., 2004, 2007; Ochsner & Gross, 2005; Petrovic & Ingvar, 2002; Wager et al., 2004). Consistent with this region's role in emotion regulatory processes, greater RVPFC activity was associated with lower levels of

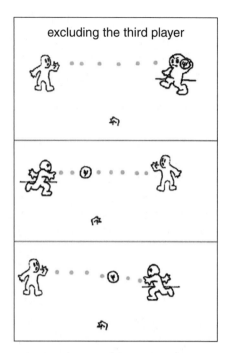

Figure 2.1. Illustration of the Cyberball game during the social inclusion condition (left) and social exclusion condition (right). The subject ("the third player") is represented by the hand at the bottom of the screen. From "Why Rejection Hurts: A Common Neural Alarm System for Physical and Social Pain," by Naomi I. Eisenberger and Matthew D. Lieberman, 2004, *Trends in Cognitive Sciences, 8,* p. 296. Copyright 2004 by Elsevier. Reprinted with permission.

self-reported social distress in response to social exclusion, which suggests that this region may be involved in regulating the distress of being socially excluded. Last, it was found that the dACC was a significant mediator of the RVPFC–distress relationship, such that RVPFC may relate to lower levels of social distress by down-regulating the activity of the dACC.

Thus, neural responses to an episode of social exclusion recruited some of the same neural regions that are involved in the distress (dACC) and regulation (RVPFC) of physical pain experience. In fact, when comparing the neural activations in this study of social pain with those from a study of physical pain in irritable bowel syndrome patients (Lieberman et al., 2004), one notices very similar regions of activation in the dACC and RVPFC (see Figure 2.2; the left panel displays social pain, and the right panel displays physical pain). Moreover, these two studies demonstrate similar patterns of correlations between neural activity and pain distress, such that, in both cases, greater dACC activity was associated with greater reports of social pain or physical pain distress, whereas greater RVPFC activity was associated with

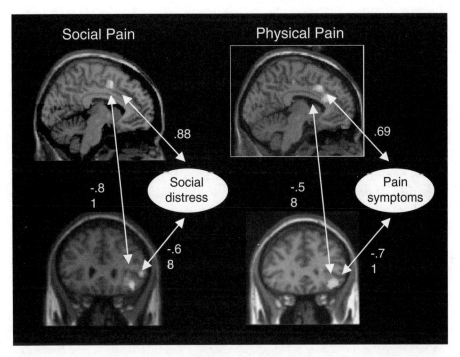

Figure 2.2. The left side of the panel displays the neural activity during social exclusion (compared with social inclusion) that correlates with self-reported social distress. The right side of the panel displays the neural activity during painful visceral stimulation (compared with baseline) that correlates with self-reported pain experience. Data from Eisenberger, Lieberman, and Williams (2003) and Lieberman et al. (2004).

lower reports of distress and less dACC activity. Thus, not only do physical and social pain recruit some of the same neural regions, but, for both types of pain, these neural regions relate to painful or distressing experience in similar ways.

We subsequently demonstrated that individuals who tend to feel more rejected in their everyday social interactions also showed greater activity in pain-related neural regions in response to social rejection (Eisenberger, Gable, & Lieberman, 2007). In this study, participants completed a 10-day experience-sampling study in which they were randomly signaled at different times during their daily lives and were asked to report on their feelings of social distress in their most recent social interaction (momentary social distress: e.g., "I felt accepted/rejected by my interaction partner"). We then examined how individual differences in real-world momentary social distress related to neural responses to the Cyberball social exclusion task.

Results revealed that individuals who reported feeling greater momentary social distress during their real-world social interactions across this 10-day period also showed greater dACC activity in response to being rejected in the Cyberball social exclusion task. In addition, individuals who reported greater momentary social distress in their daily lives also showed greater activity (in response to social exclusion) in the amygdala, a neural region involved in affective processing (Davis & Whalen, 2001), and in the PAG, a neural region involved in pain processing and attachment-related behaviors (Bandler & Shipley, 1994). Thus, even real-world experiences of social rejection seem to relate to greater activity in pain-related regions of the brain.

As further evidence that social pain stimuli activate pain-related neural circuitry, we examined neural activity as individuals watched short film clips of actors making "disapproving" facial expressions (Burklund, Eisenberger, & Lieberman, 2007). A disapproving facial expression connotes that one has done something wrong or inappropriate and that one risks being rejected because of it. To the extent that disapproving facial expressions signify the possibility of social rejection, participants, particularly those who are rejection-sensitive (Downey & Feldman, 1996), should show greater activity in regions such as the dACC in response to watching these facial expressions unfold.

In this study, participants watched a series of 3-s film clips in which targets displayed specific facial expressions. Participants watched blocks of disapproving facial expressions, in which the actor raised one side of the upper lip, lowered the inner corners of the brow in a fashion similar to that displayed when expressing confusion, and slightly tilted or pulled the head backwards—similar to the "contempt" faces described by Darwin (1872/1998) and Matsumoto and Ekman (2004). Participants also watched blocks of anger expressions, blocks of disgust expressions, and blocks of a neutral crosshair fixation. Anger and disgust expressions were included to contrast with the disapproving expressions because they share both similar and distinguishing features. Like disapproval, anger and disgust are negative emotional expressions. However, although anger and disgust expressions typically signify physical and contamination threats, respectively (although, in some cases, they can also signify threats to social connection), a disapproving face signifies only a threat to social connection and has no alternative meaning.

As in previous studies of neural responses to emotional faces (Fitzgerald, Angstadt, Jelsone, Nathan, & Phan, 2006; Morris et al., 1996; Phillips et al., 1997; Whalen et al., 2001), participants showed significant activity in the amygdala and various regions of the prefrontal cortex in response to viewing each of these emotional expressions compared with when viewing a neutral crosshair fixation. However, when examining individual differences in rejection sensitivity, we found that individuals who scored higher in rejection sensitivity showed greater dACC activity while viewing the disapproving faces but not while viewing the anger or disgust faces, highlighting a specific role for the dACC in responding to disapproving faces among rejection-sensitive individuals. Moreover, rejection sensitivity correlated specifically with activity in the dACC in response to viewing disapproving faces but not with the activity of other limbic regions (e.g., amygdala, insula), which suggests that dACC activity, rather than limbic system activity more generally, may be specifically responsive to these cues of rejection.

Summary

Across diverse languages, individuals use the same words to describe the negative feelings associated with physical injury and social rejection. Moreover, neural data from both animal and human subjects converge to show that some of the same neural regions support both physical and social pain experience. One of these regions, the dACC, has been shown to be involved in the experienced unpleasantness of physical pain, the elicitation of separation-distress behaviors in nonhuman mammals, and the experience of distress following social rejection in humans. Other regions that have also been shown to play a role in these pain processes include the insula and PAG, which encode physical pain experience (Aziz et al., 2000; Bandler & Shipley, 1994; Cechetto & Saper, 1987), as well as the RVPFC, which has been involved in regulating painful as well as generally negative affective experience (Hariri et al., 2000; Lieberman et al., 2004, 2007; Petrovic & Ingvar, 2002; Wager et al., 2004).

Taken together, these data provide solid evidence for a physical–social pain overlap. In the next section, I highlight some of the research that has examined the consequences of such a functional overlap in these pain systems. For example, one implication of a physical–social pain overlap is that individuals who are more sensitive to one type of pain should also be more sensitive to the other. I examine this hypothesis and others in the next section. It should be noted, however, that even though there is evidence to support a functional overlap in physical and social pain processes, these processes certainly do not overlap completely. This fact can be known intuitively because one can differentiate between pain resulting from a relationship snub and pain resulting from physical injury. Moreover, research has identified specific differences between these two types of pain experience. For example, Chen, Williams, Fitness, and Newton (2008) showed that individuals can easily relive the pain of previous relationship breakups or other socially painful events; however, it is much harder, and sometimes impossible, to relive the pain of physical injury. Thus, even though there are certainly ways in which physical and social pain experiences are different, this next section focuses on ways in which these pain processes are similar and the consequences of this similarity.

WHAT ARE THE CONSEQUENCES OF
A PHYSICAL–SOCIAL PAIN OVERLAP?

To the extent that physical and social pain processes overlap, one can generate novel hypotheses regarding some of the functional consequences of such an overlap. One hypothesis is that if physical and social pain sensitivity are governed by the same underlying system, then individuals who are more sensitive to one type of pain should also be more sensitive to the other. A second hypothesis is that regulating or potentiating one type of pain should influence the other type of pain in a similar manner, because influencing one type of pain process should alter the underlying neural system that supports both types of painful experience. I review evidence for each of these hypotheses here.

Hypothesis 1

Individual differences in sensitivity to one kind of pain should relate to individual differences in sensitivity to the other.

To examine whether individual differences in physical and social pain sensitivity correlate with each other, my colleagues and I conducted a behavioral study that measured the extent to which baseline sensitivity to physical pain correlated with sensitivity to a socially painful experience (Eisenberger, Jarcho, Lieberman, & Naliboff, 2006). Participants in this study provided a baseline measure of physical pain sensitivity by rating the temperature at which they perceived a painful heat stimulus delivered to their forearm to be very unpleasant ("pain threshold"). After this, participants were randomly assigned to play one round of the Cyberball game in which they were either included for the entire game or excluded midway through the game and were then asked to rate how rejected they felt during the game.

Results demonstrated that individuals who were more sensitive to physical pain at baseline (e.g., lower baseline pain thresholds) were also more distressed by the social rejection episode (but not by the inclusion episode). Moreover, this relationship remained significant after controlling for neuroticism, which suggests that this relationship cannot be explained solely by a general tendency to report higher levels of negative experience. Thus, as predicted, those who were more sensitive to physical pain at baseline were also more sensitive to the pain of social rejection.

As another test of this hypothesis, we investigated whether genetic differences in opioid-related activity, known for its role in physical pain processes, were also associated with differences in social pain sensitivity (Way, Taylor, Lieberman, & Eisenberger, 2008). In this study, 30 subjects were genotyped so we could examine functional differences in a mu-opioid receptor gene polymorphism (*OPRM1*; A118G), which has been shown to relate to individual differences in physical pain sensitivity (Fillingim et al., 2005). Each subject also completed the Cyberball social exclusion task in the scanner so we could examine neural sensitivity to social exclusion and filled out several self-report measures assessing individual differences in traits related to social pain sensitivity.

Results demonstrated that individuals with one or more of the minor G alleles, compared with those homozygous for the A allele, scored higher in self-reported trait rejection sensitivity (Mehrabian, 1976). In addition, in response to social exclusion, individuals with one or more of the minor G alleles showed greater activity in the dACC and anterior insula, neural regions involved in processing physical pain stimuli. These findings map nicely onto recent work showing that infant rhesus monkeys with the minor G allele, compared with those with the common allele, exhibit higher levels of distress vocalizations when separated from their mothers (Barr et al., 2008). Thus, individual differences in a pain-related genetic polymorphism also predicted individual differences in trait social pain sensitivity, evidenced by greater rejection-sensitivity scores, as well as individual differences in state social pain sensitivity, evidenced by greater pain-related neural activity in response to social rejection.

Hypothesis 2

Factors that regulate or potentiate one type of pain should have a similar effect on the other type of pain.

To the extent that physical and social pain processes overlap, factors that reduce or enhance one type of painful experience should affect the other type of pain in a similar manner. Few studies have directly examined this hypothesis because it is not necessarily intuitive to measure feelings of social and physical pain in the same study. However, some studies have shown these types of effects, and the number of studies that have explicitly tested this notion is increasing.

Pain-Regulation Effects

Pharmacological studies provide strong evidence for the notion that regulating one type of pain can inadvertently regulate the other type of pain in a complementary manner. For example, opiate-based medications, known primarily for their powerful analgesic properties, have also been shown to reduce the pain of social separation in nonhuman mammals (Panksepp, 1998); infants treated with opiates demonstrated fewer distress vocalizations when separated from their mothers than did those treated with saline (Herman & Panksepp, 1978; Kalin, Shelton, & Barksdale, 1988; Panksepp, 1998; Panksepp, Herman, Conner, Bishop, & Scott, 1978).

Although it is more difficult to experimentally examine opioid-related processes in humans, it is known anecdotally that opiates reduce social pain in humans, potentially contributing to their powerfully addictive nature (Panksepp, 1998). Moreover, an experimental study has shown that acetaminophen, another pain-reducing drug, can reduce social pain in a human sample (DeWall et al., in press). In this study, a daily dose of acetaminophen (i.e., Tylenol), compared with placebo, led to a significant reduction in daily "hurt feelings" over the course of a 3-week period. Moreover, in a subsequent study, participants who took acetaminophen for a 3-week period, compared with those who took placebo, showed reduced pain-related neural activity (dACC, anterior insula) in response to a scanner-based episode of social exclusion.

In a similar fashion, drugs that are primarily thought to reduce social pain have been shown to reduce physical pain as well. For example, antidepressants (e.g., selective serotonin reuptake inhibitors, or SSRIs), known for their capacity to reduce depression and anxiety, which often result from social stressors, have also been shown to alleviate physical pain in humans (Nemoto et al., 2003; Shimodozono et al., 2002; Singh, Jain, & Kulkarni, 2001). In fact, antidepressants are now commonly prescribed to treat chronic pain conditions (e.g., Fishbain, Cutler, Rosomoff, & Rosomoff, 1998).

In addition to pharmacological studies, studies of social support have also demonstrated the regulatory effects of social factors on physical pain. Across numerous studies, social support, a variable that should primarily relate to reduced social pain, also relates to reduced physical pain experience. For example, correlational evidence shows that individuals with more social support also reported feeling less pain during childbirth (Chalmers, Wolman, Nikodem, Gulmezoglu, & Hofmeyer, 1995; Kennell, Klaus, McGrath, Robertson, & Hinkley, 1991), following coronary artery bypass surgery (King, Reis, Porter, & Norsen, 1993; Kulik & Mahler, 1989), and during cancer (Zaza & Baine, 2002). More convincing, however, is experimental evidence that has shown that individuals who were randomly assigned to receive social support from a friend or stranger, compared with those who received no support, reported experiencing less pain during a cold pressor task, a painful task that involves submerging one's arm in ice water (Brown, Sheffield, Leary, & Robinson, 2003). Moreover, merely viewing a picture of one's significant other while receiving a painful heat stimulus led to lower reports of pain unpleasantness than did viewing a picture of a stranger or neutral object (Master et al., 2009).

Pain-Potentiation Effects

To date, no experimental studies have examined whether potentiating physical pain also increases social pain; however, correlational evidence suggests that the two experiences are related. For example, Bowlby (1969) noted that when children experience physical pain, they become much more sensitive to the whereabouts of their caregiver, experiencing distress more frequently and easily upon noting distance from the caregiver. Similarly, compared with healthy controls, adults with chronic pain are more likely to have an anxious attachment style, characterized by a heightened sense of concern with their partner's relationship commitment (Ciechanowski, Sullivan, Jensen, Romano, & Summers, 2003).

A few studies have started to examine the reverse—namely, that experiences that increase social pain can increase physical pain experience too. For example, we tested the notion that feeling socially excluded would lead to an increase in sensitivity to physical pain (Eisenberger et al., 2006). Participants in this study were randomly assigned to play one round of the Cyberball game in which they were either included during the game or excluded midway through the game. During the last 30 s of the Cyberball game (when participants were being either included or excluded), participants were exposed to three painful heat stimuli and were asked to rate the unpleasantness of each. This was done to determine whether being included or excluded changed physical pain sensitivity. After completing this task, participants were asked to rate how rejected they felt during the Cyberball game.

Although there was no main effect of exclusion on pain sensitivity (i.e., rejected subjects did not become more pain-sensitive than did included subjects), results demonstrated that individuals who felt the most distressed by the social rejection episode also reported the highest pain ratings to the heat stimuli that were delivered at the end of the rejection episode, and this effect remained significant after controlling for neuroticism. Thus, even though this finding is correlational, it suggests that augmented sensitivity to one type of pain is related to augmented sensitivity to the other.

It should be noted that these findings are somewhat different from those of another study that examined the effect of social exclusion (using a different manipulation) on physical pain sensitivity (DeWall & Baumeister, 2006). This study was based on the observation that extreme physical pain can sometimes turn off the pain system itself, leading to temporary analgesia or numbness (Gear, Aley, & Levine, 1999). On the basis of this observation, it was hypothesized that, to the extent that physical and social pain overlap, extreme forms of social exclusion should lead to numbness, not only to negative social experiences but to physical pain as well.

DeWall and Baumeister (2006) manipulated social exclusion by telling participants that they would be alone in the future. Participants in this "future alone" condition, compared with those who were given no feedback or who were told that they would have satisfying relationships in the future, showed a reduced (rather than an increased) sensitivity to physical pain. Differences between these two sets of findings could be due to the underlying nature of the pain system, such that mild pain (e.g., being excluded by strangers during the Cyberball game) augments pain sensitivity, whereas more intense pain (e.g., being told that one will be alone in the future) leads to analgesia (Gear et al., 1999; Price, 2000). It is also possible that the "future alone" manipulation may have induced more depression-like affect, which in some cases has been associated with reduced experimental pain sensitivity (Adler & Gattaz, 1993; Dickens, McGowan, & Dale, 2003; Orbach, Mikulincer, King, Cohen, & Stein, 1997), whereas the Cyberball manipulation may have induced more anxiety-like affect, which has been linked with increased experimental pain sensitivity (Cornwall & Donderi, 1988; Lautenbacher & Krieg, 1994; Melzack & Wall, 1999). Nonetheless, it is important to note that in both studies, physical and social pain sensitivity still seem to be working in parallel. In the first study, greater sensitivity to social rejection was correlated with greater sensitivity to physical pain; in the second, an extreme form of social exclusion resulted in general emotional insensitivity to both social and physical pain.

A final example of the effect of social pain potentiation on physical pain is Gray and Wegner's (2008) examination of whether an intentional interpersonal transgression (i.e., stepping on someone's toe on purpose), which is typically more emotionally hurtful than an accidental transgression, was also more physically painful. Participants believed that another subject, who was actually a confederate, was going to choose which of two tasks the participant was going to complete. In the intentional transgression condition, the confederate chose a task that involved the participant receiving electric shock; in the unintentional transgression condition, the confederate chose a pitch judgment task for the participant to complete, but the participant still received shock as a result of study constraints. Participants were told which task the confederate chose for them and then rated pain unpleasantness as they received a series of electric shocks.

Results revealed that physical pain ratings following the intentional transgression were higher than were those following the unintentional transgression. In addition, though participants in the unintentional transgression condition showed habituation to repeated painful stimulation, those in the intentional transgression condition did not. Thus, social factors that are primarily thought to increase emotional pain seem to affect physical pain in a congruent manner.

Summary

Identification of an overlap in the neural substrates that underlie physical and social pain leads to several novel hypotheses regarding the ways in which these two types of painful experiences interact. For example, the studies reviewed here demonstrated that those more sensitive to physical pain were also more sensitive to social pain and that factors that regulate or potentiate one kind of pain have similar effects on the other. There are likely many other consequences of this functional overlap, and it will be interesting to watch as new hypotheses are developed and explored.

WHAT CAN BE LEARNED FROM UNDERSTANDING THE NEURAL CORRELATES OF SOCIAL PAIN?

Understanding the shared neural circuitry that underlies physical and social pain allows one not only to make novel predictions about how one type of painful experience may influence the other but also to answer questions about other social processes that are challenging to assess with self-reports alone. For example, it is known that aggressive behavior can be either the product of blunted emotional sensitivity, leading an individual to aggress because he or she cares little about the feelings of others, or the product of enhanced emotional sensitivity, leading an individual to aggress defensively in response to negative social treatment (Berkowitz, 1993). Which type of aggressive behavior occurs among those who are predisposed to aggressive behavior on the basis of their underlying genetic makeup?

As a second example, racial discrimination is one form of negative social treatment that some have to deal with on a daily basis. Are experiences of racial discrimination just as painful as the sting of social rejection, or does attributing negative social treatment to race change the dynamics of these events? Later in this section, I review two studies that begin to answer these questions by using neuroimaging tools to investigate the experiential substrates that underlie these social events.

Understanding a Genetic Precursor to Aggression

Previous work has demonstrated a link between aggressive behavior and a specific genetic polymorphism that encodes monoamine oxidase-A (MAOA), an enzyme that degrades monoamines such as serotonin (Caspi et al., 2002). MAOA-deficient men from a single Dutch kindred demonstrated elevated levels of impulsive aggression, arson, and attempted rape (Brunner, Nelen, Breakefield, Ropers, & van Oost, 1993). In addition, when exposed to early adversity, men with the low expression allele (MAOA-L) of the 30-bp variable number tandem repeats polymorphism in the MAOA promoter region (MAOA-uVNTR) were more likely to develop antisocial behavior than were men with the high expression allele (MAOA-H; Caspi et al., 2002). Despite mounting evidence suggesting a relationship between the MAOA-uVNTR and aggressive behavior, it is unclear how this genetic polymorphism predisposes individuals to aggressive behavior.

Many possible mechanisms might help to explain the functional relationship between the MAOA polymorphism and aggressive behavior. One possibility is that MAOA-L individuals show blunted socioemotional sensitivity, making them less concerned with the feelings of others, less empathic, and thus more likely to commit violent crimes because they care less about harming others or the repercussions of doing so (Blair, 2007). Another possibility is that MAOA-L individuals show heightened socioemotional sensitivity, making them more sensitive to negative social experiences such as social rejection and more likely to respond to these experiences with defensively aggressive behavior (Crick & Dodge, 1996; Dodge et al., 2003; Dodge & Pettit 2003; Twenge, 2005; Twenge, Baumeister, Tice, & Stucke, 2001).

To investigate the underlying socioemotional experience that links this genetic polymorphism with aggression, we examined how different allelic variants in the MAOA polymorphism related to neural responses to social rejection (using the Cyberball game) as well as self-report measures of trait aggression (Eisenberg, Way, Taylor, Welch, & Lieberman, 2007). To the extent that the link between MAOA and aggression is a function of blunted socioemotional sensitivity, MAOA-L individuals should show less dACC activity to social rejection (less social pain) than do MAOA-H individuals. On the other hand, to the extent that the link between MAOA and aggression is a function of heightened socioemotional sensitivity, MAOA-L individuals should show greater dACC activity to social rejection (more social pain) than do MAOA-H individuals. In either case, MAOA-L individuals should report higher levels of trait aggression than do MAOA-H individuals.

Consistent with previous work, we found that MAOA-L individuals reported higher levels of trait aggression than did MAOA-H individuals. More important, results indicated that MAOA-L individuals, compared with MAOA-H individuals, showed greater dACC responses to social rejection (see Figure 2.3), which suggests that the relationship between MAOA and trait aggression may be due to heightened, rather than blunted, socioemotional sensitivity, fitting with previous findings (Meyer-Lindenberg et al., 2006). Moreover, the relationship between the MAOA polymorphism and trait aggression was partially mediated by dACC responses to social rejection.

Thus, using knowledge of the neural systems underlying social pain experience, we were able to show that MAOA-related aggression was a function of heightened socioemotional sensitivity—a finding that may have been difficult to assess with self-reports alone, given the sensitive and personal nature of the underlying psychological experience. Clarifying the underlying socioemotional mechanisms that link MAOA to aggression is critical for both

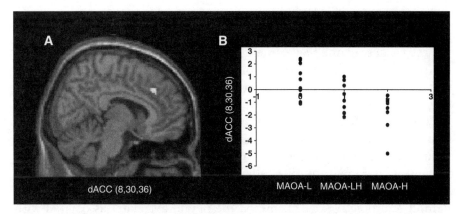

Figure 2.3. dACC activity (8,30,36) that varies as a function of the MAOA polymorphism. (A) Activity in the dACC, during social exclusion versus inclusion, that correlates with individual differences in the MAOA polymorphism (maximum activation at 8,30,36) and shows greater activity for MAOA-L, compared with MAOA-H or MAOA-LH (females with one low expression and one high expression allele) individuals. (B) Scatterplot showing the relationship between the MAOA polymorphism and dACC (8,30,36) responses to social exclusion versus inclusion. From "Understanding Genetic Risk for Aggression: Clues from the Brain's Response to Social Exclusion," by N. I. Eisenberger, B. M. Way, S. E. Taylor, W. T. Welch, and M. D. Lieberman, 2007, *Biological Psychiatry, 61*, p. 1105. Copyright 2007 by Elsevier. Reprinted with permission.

understanding the experience of individuals at risk for aggression and for identifying appropriate interventions for treating these aggressive behaviors. Moreover, identifying a genetic correlate of social pain sensitivity may aid not only in the identification and treatment of aggressive disorders but also in the identification and treatment of other clinical disorders that relate closely to sensitivity to social pain as well (e.g., social anxiety, depression).

Exploring the Neural Correlates of Racial Discrimination

In some ways, racial discrimination can be conceptualized as the routine experience of social rejection. Those who experience racial discrimination perceive that they are being treated unfairly—rejected from a social group, not granted a promotion, or given poorer treatment—because of their race. In light of these hardships, it is natural to ask about the psychological consequences of racial discrimination. In other words, does the repeated experience of rejection, unfair treatment, and disadvantage have negative psychological consequences for the person who is experiencing these events? One would think that it must. Research, however, has debated whether attributing unfair treatment to race makes the experience better or worse.

It is not surprising that some have suggested that attributing negative social treatment to race can be psychologically harmful; if one is maltreated because of one's race, one is likely to continue to be a target of such maltreatment (Schmitt & Branscombe, 2002). However, others have suggested the counterintuitive notion that perceptions of racial discrimination may actually serve a "self-protective" function (Crocker & Major, 1989). To the extent that negative social treatment is due to one's race and not something personal about one's character, the cause of the negative social treatment is external to one's self and thus less psychologically damaging. Because it is inherently difficult to ask individuals who are the target of racial discrimination about whether perceptions of discrimination are painful or protective, we examined the neural correlates associated with feeling that one is the target of racial discrimination. Using neuroimaging tools, one can examine the feelings associated with racial discrimination in a more covert way that is less subject to demand characteristics or self-presentational concerns.

In this study (Masten, Telzer, & Eisenberger, 2008), we examined the neural correlates of felt racial discrimination by investigating the neural regions that are involved when one judges a rejection episode to be due to one's race as opposed to some other factor (e.g., one's personality, one's behavior). African American (AA) subjects (n = 18, nine female) completed the Cyberball social exclusion task. Each participant was greeted by a Caucasian American (CA) experimenter and two CA confederates, and participants were led to believe that they would be playing the ball-tossing game with the two CA confederates. The subject and confederates were instructed in how to play the game and then spent a few minutes introducing themselves to each other. Race was never mentioned during this meeting session, nor was it mentioned in any of the recruitment materials. Each participant was then scanned while supposedly playing the Cyberball game with the two CA players. In reality, however, participants played with a preset computer game. As in previous studies, the participant was included during the first round of the game and excluded partway through the second round (thus all AA subjects were ultimately rejected by two CA players).

Immediately following the game, participants rated how upset they felt in response to the rejection episode (social distress: e.g., "I felt rejected," "I felt meaningless"). They also rated the extent to which they thought they were rejected because of their race. After completing these self-report measures, each participant completed a face-to-face interview with the experimenter. Here, each participant was asked about his or her thoughts and feelings about the rejection episode as well as his or her possible reasons for why the rejection occurred. Again, race was never mentioned by the experimenter unless the participant spontaneously brought it up, in which case the experimenter asked the participant to elaborate on his or her thoughts. This interview was video-taped for later analysis.

Consistent with previous work on social pain, AA participants who were judged to be the most distressed during their videotaped interviews showed the most pain-related neural activity (dACC, anterior insula) in response to the social rejection episode and the least emotion regulatory activity (right ventrolateral prefrontal cortex). However, to the extent that AA participants believed that they were rejected because of their race, they showed significantly less activity in the dACC and more activity in prefrontal regions associated with regulating negative affect (medial prefrontal cortex, rostral anterior cingulate cortex; Petrovic & Ingvar, 2002; Phelps, Delgado, Nearing & LeDoux, 2004).

Thus, although observed distress following social exclusion was associated with greater pain-related neural activity, attributing rejection to race was associated with less pain-related neural activity, consistent with the counter-intuitive notion that perceiving discrimination can, in some cases, protect one's well-being (Crocker & Major, 1989). Findings such as these would have been difficult to assess with self-reports alone and have important implications for understanding the experiences of those who have to face negative social treatment on a daily basis.

CONCLUSIONS

Taken together, the research presented here puts forth a strong case for the notion that being rejected hurts. Not only do people use physical pain words to describe rejection experiences, but some of the same neural regions that process physical pain process social pain too. One of the implications of these findings is that episodes of rejection or relationship dissolution can be just as damaging and debilitating to the person experiencing those events as can episodes of physical pain. Thus, even though physical pain conditions may be treated more seriously and regarded as more valid ailments, the pain of social loss can be equally as distressing, as demonstrated by the activation of pain-related neural circuitry to social disconnection as well.

It is important not to forget, though, that though painful in the short term, feelings of distress and heartache following broken social relationships also serve a valuable function—namely, to ensure the maintenance of close social ties. To the extent that being rejected hurts, individuals are motivated to avoid situations in which rejection is likely. Over the course of evolutionary history, avoiding social rejection and staying socially connected to others likely increased chances of survival, because being part of a group provided additional resources, protection, and safety. Thus, the experience of social pain, while distressing and hurtful in the short term, is an evolutionary adaptation that promotes social bonding and ultimately survival.

REFERENCES

Adler, G., & Gattaz, W. F. (1993). Pain perception threshold in major depression. *Biological Psychiatry, 34,* 687–689. doi:10.1016/0006-3223(93)90041-B

Aziz, Q., Schnitzler, A., & Enck, P. (2000). Functional neuroimaging of visceral sensation. *Journal of Clinical Neurophysiology, 17,* 604–612. doi:10.1097/00004691-200011000-00006

Bandler, R., & Shipley, M. T. (1994). Columnar organization in the midbrain periaqueductal gray: Modules for emotional expression? *Trends in Neurosciences, 17,* 379–389. doi:10.1016/0166-2236(94)90047-7

Barr, C. S., Schwandt, M. L., Lindell, S. G., Higley, J. D., Maestripieri, D., Goldman, D., . . . Heilig, M. (2008). Variation at the mu-opioid receptor gene (OPRM1) influences attachment behavior in infant primates. *Proceedings of the National Academy of Sciences of the United States of America, 105,* 5277–5281. doi:10.1073/pnas.0710225105

Baumeister, R. F., & Leary, M. R. (1995). The need to belong: Desire for interpersonal attachments as a fundamental human motivation. *Psychological Bulletin, 117,* 497–529. doi:10.1037/0033-2909.117.3.497

Berkowitz, L. (1993). *Aggression: Its causes, consequences and control.* Philadelphia, PA: Temple University Press.

Blair, R. J. R. (2007). The amygdala and ventromedial prefrontal cortex in morality and psychopathy. *Trends in Cognitive Sciences, 11,* 387–392. doi:10.1016/j.tics.2007.07.003

Bowlby, J. (1969). *Attachment and loss: Vol. 1. Attachment.* New York, NY: Basic Books.

Brown, J. L., Sheffield, D., Leary, M. R., & Robinson, M. E. (2003). Social support and experimental pain. *Psychosomatic Medicine, 65,* 276–283. doi:10.1097/01.PSY.0000030388.62434.46

Brunner, H. G., Nelen, M., Breakefield, X. O., Ropers, H. H., & van Oost, B. A. (1993, October 22). Abnormal behavior associated with a point mutation in the structural gene for monoamine oxidase A. *Science, 262,* 578–580. doi:10.1126/science.8211186

Burklund, L. J., Eisenberger, N. I., & Lieberman, M. D. (2007). Rejection sensitivity moderates dorsal anterior cingulate activity to disapproving facial expressions. *Social Neuroscience, 2,* 238–253. doi:10.1080/17470910701391711

Caspi, A., McClay, J., Moffitt, T. E., Mill, J., Martin, J., Craig, I. W., . . . Poulton, R. (2002, August 2). Role of genotype in the cycle of violence in maltreated children. *Science, 297,* 851–854. doi:10.1126/science.1072290

Cechetto, D. F., & Saper, C. B. (1987). Evidence for a viscerotopic sensory representation in the cortex and thalamus in the rat. *The Journal of Comparative Neurology*, *262*, 27–45. doi:10.1002/cne.902620104

Chalmers, B., Wolman, W. L., Nikodem, V. C., Gulmezoglu, A. M., & Hofmeyer, G. J. (1995). Companionship in labour: Do the personality characteristics of labour supporters influence their effectiveness? *Curationis*, *18*, 77–80.

Chen, Z., Williams, K. D., Fitness, J., & Newton, N. (2008). When hurt will not heal: Exploring the capacity to relive social and physical pain. *Psychological Science*, *19*, 789–795.

Ciechanowski, P., Sullivan, M., Jensen, M., Romano, J., & Summers, H. (2003). The relationship of attachment style to depression, catastrophizing and health care utilization in patients with chronic pain. *Pain*, *104*, 627–637. doi:10.1016/S0304-3959(03)00120-9

Coghill, R. C., McHaffie, J. G., & Yen, Y. F. (2003). Neural correlates of interindividual differences in the subjective experience of pain. *Proceedings of the National Academy of Sciences of the United States of America*, *100*, 8538–8542. doi:10.1073/pnas.1430684100

Cornwall, A., & Donderi, D. C. (1988). The effect of experimentally induced anxiety on the experience of pressure pain. *Pain*, *35*, 105–113. doi:10.1016/0304-3959(88)90282-5

Crick, N. R., & Dodge, K. A. (1996). Social information-processing mechanisms on reactive and proactive aggression. *Child Development*, *67*, 993–1002. doi:10.2307/1131875

Crocker, J., & Major, B. (1989). Social stigma and self-esteem: The self-protective properties of stigma. *Psychological Review*, *96*, 608–630. doi:10.1037/0033-295X.96.4.608

Darwin, C. (1998). *The expression of the emotions in man and animals*. New York, NY: Oxford University Press. (Original work published 1872) doi:10.1037/10001-000

Davis, M., & Whalen, P. J. (2001). The amygdala: Vigilance and emotion. *Molecular Psychiatry*, *6*, 13–34. doi:10.1038/sj.mp.4000812

DeWall, C. N., & Baumeister, R. F. (2006). Alone but feeling no pain: Effects of social exclusion on physical pain tolerance and pain threshold, affective forecasting, and interpersonal empathy. *Journal of Personality and Social Psychology*, *91*, 1–15. doi:10.1037/0022-3514.91.1.1

DeWall, C. N., MacDonald, G., Webster, G. D., Masten, C., Baumeister, R. F., Powell, C., . . . Eisenberger, N. I. (in press). Tylenol reduces social pain: Behavioral and neural evidence. *Psychological Science*.

Dickens, C., McGowan, L., & Dale, S. (2003). Impact of depression on experimental pain perception: A systematic review of the literature with meta-analysis. *Psychosomatic Medicine*, *65*, 369–375. doi:10.1097/01.PSY.0000041622.69462.06

Dodge, K. A., Lansford, J. E., Salzer Burks, V., Bates, J. E., Pettit, G. S., Fontaine, R., & Price, J. M. (2003). Peer rejection and social information-processing factors in the development of aggressive behavior problems in children. *Child Development, 74*, 374–393. doi:10.1111/1467-8624.7402004

Dodge, K. A., & Pettit, G. S. (2003). A biopsychosocial model of the development of chronic conduct problems in adolescence. *Developmental Psychology, 39*, 349–371. doi:10.1037/0012-1649.39.2.349

Downey, G., & Feldman, S. I. (1996). Implications of rejection sensitivity for intimate relationships. *Journal of Personality and Social Psychology, 70*, 1327–1343. doi:10.1037/0022-3514.70.6.1327

Eisenberger, N. I., Gable, S. L., & Lieberman, M. D. (2007). fMRI responses relate to differences in real-world social experience. *Emotion (Washington, D.C.), 7*, 745–754. doi:10.1037/1528-3542.7.4.745

Eisenberger, N. I., Jarcho, J. M., Lieberman, M. D., & Naliboff, B. D. (2006). An experimental study of shared sensitivity to physical pain and social rejection. *Pain, 126*, 132–138. doi:10.1016/j.pain.2006.06.024

Eisenberger, N. I., & Lieberman, M. D. (2004). Why rejection hurts: The neurocognitive overlap between physical and social pain. *Trends in Cognitive Sciences, 8*, 294–300. doi:10.1016/j.tics.2004.05.010

Eisenberger, N. I., Lieberman, M. D., & Williams, K. D. (2003, October 10). Does rejection hurt? An fMRI study of social exclusion. *Science, 302*, 290–292. doi:10.1126/science.1089134

Eisenberger, N. I., Way, B. M., Taylor, S. E., Welch, W. T., & Lieberman, M. D. (2007). Understanding genetic risk for aggression: Clues from the brain's response to social exclusion. *Biological Psychiatry, 61*, 1100–1108. doi:10.1016/j.biopsych.2006.08.007

Fillingim, R. B., Kaplan, L., Staud, R., Ness, T. J., Glover, T. L., Campbell, C. M., . . . Wallace, M. R. (2005). The A118G single nucleotide polymorphism of the mu-opioid receptor gene (OPRM1) is associated with pressure pain sensitivity in humans. *The Journal of Pain, 6*, 159–167. doi:10.1016/j.jpain.2004.11.008

Fishbain, D. A., Cutler, R., Rosomoff, H. L., & Rosomoff, R. S. (1998). Do antidepressants have an analgesic effect in psychogenic pain and somatoform pain disorder? A meta-analysis. *Psychosomatic Medicine, 60*, 503–509.

Fitzgerald, D. A., Angstadt, M., Jelsone, L. M., Nathan, P. J., & Phan, K. L. (2006). Beyond threat: Amygdala reactivity across multiple expressions of facial affect. *NeuroImage, 30*, 1441–1448. doi:10.1016/j.neuroimage.2005.11.003

Foltz, E. L., & White, L. E. (1968). The role of rostral cingulotomy in "pain" relief. *International Journal of Neurology, 6*, 353–373.

Gear, R. W., Aley, K. O., & Levine, J. D. (1999). Pain-induced analgesia mediated by mesolimbic reward circuits. *The Journal of Neuroscience, 19*, 7175–7181.

Gray, K., & Wegner, D. M. (2008). The sting of intentional pain. *Psychological Science, 19*, 1260–1262.

Hariri, A. R., Bookheimer, S. Y., & Mazziotta, J. C. (2000). Modulating emotional response: Effects of a neocortical network on the limbic system. *Neuroreport, 11*, 43–48.

Herman, B. H., & Panksepp, J. (1978). Effects of morphine and naloxone on separation distress and approach attachment: Evidence for opiate mediation of social affect. *Pharmacology, Biochemistry, and Behavior, 9*, 213–220. doi:10.1016/0091-3057(78)90167-3

Jürgens, U., & Ploog, D. (1970). Cerebral representation of vocalization in the squirrel monkey. *Experimental Brain Research, 10*, 532–554. doi:10.1007/BF00234269

Kalin, N. H., Shelton, S. E., & Barksdale, C. M. (1988). Opiate modulation of separation-induced distress in non-human primates. *Brain Research, 440*, 285–292. doi:10.1016/0006-8993(88)90997-3

Kennell, J., Klaus, M., McGrath, S., Robertson, S., & Hinkley, C. (1991). Continuous emotional support during labor in US hospital: A randomized control trial. *JAMA, 265*, 2197–2201. doi:10.1001/jama.265.17.2197

King, K. B., Reis, H. T., Porter, L. A., & Norsen, L. H. (1993). Social support and long-term recovery from coronary artery surgery: Effects on patients and spouses. *Health Psychology, 12*, 56–63. doi:10.1037/0278-6133.12.1.56

Kirzinger, A., & Jürgens, U. (1982). Cortical lesion effects and vocalization in the squirrel monkey. *Brain Research, 233*, 299–315. doi:10.1016/0006-8993(82)91204-5

Kulik, J. A., & Mahler, H. I. (1989). Social support and recovery from surgery. *Health Psychology, 8*, 221–238. doi:10.1037/0278-6133.8.2.221

Lane, R. D., Reiman, E. M., Ahern, G. L., Schwartz, G. E., & Davidson, R. J. (1997). Neuroanatomical correlates of happiness, sadness, and disgust. *The American Journal of Psychiatry, 154*, 926–933.

Lautenbacher, S., & Krieg, J. C. (1994). Pain perception in psychiatric disorders: A review of the literature. *Journal of Psychiatric Research, 28*, 109–122. doi:10.1016/0022-3956(94)90023-X

Leyton, A. S. F., & Sherrington, C. S. (1917). Observations of the excitable cortex of the chimpanzee, orangutan, and gorilla. *Quarterly Journal of Experimental Physiology (Cambridge, England), 11*, 135–222.

Lieberman, M. D., Eisenberger, N. I., Crockett, M. J., Tom, S. M., Pfeifer, J. H., & Way, B. M. (2007). Putting feelings into words: Affect labeling disrupts amygdala activity to affective stimuli. *Psychological Science, 18*, 421–428. doi:10.1111/j.1467-9280.2007.01916.x

Lieberman, M. D., Jarcho, J. M., Berman, S., Naliboff, B. D., Suyenobu, B. Y., Mandelkern, M., & Mayer, E. A. (2004). The neural correlates of placebo effects: A disruption account. *NeuroImage, 22*, 447–455. doi:10.1016/j.neuroimage.2004.01.037

MacDonald, G., & Leary, M. R. (2005). Why does social exclusion hurt? The relationship between social and physical pain. *Psychological Review, 131*, 202–223.

MacLean, P. D., & Newman, J. D. (1988). Role of midline frontolimbic cortex in production of the isolation call of squirrel monkeys. *Brain Research, 450*, 111–123. doi:10.1016/0006-8993(88)91550-8

Masten, C., Telzer, E., & Eisenberger, N. I. (2008). *An fMRI investigation of attributing negative social treatment to racial discrimination*. Unpublished manuscript.

Master, S. L., Eisenberger, N. I., Taylor, S. E., Naliboff, B. D., Shirinyan, D., & Lieberman, M. D. (2009). A picture's worth: Partner photographs reduce experimentally induced pain. *Psychological Science, 20*, 1316–1318.

Matsumoto, D., & Ekman, P. (2004). The relationship among expressions, labels, and descriptions of contempt. *Journal of Personality and Social Psychology, 87*, 529–540. doi:10.1037/0022-3514.87.4.529

Mehrabian, A. (1976). Questionnaire measures of affiliative tendency and sensitivity to rejection. *Psychological Reports, 38*, 199–209.

Melzack, R., & Wall, D. (1999). *Textbook of pain*. Edinburgh, Scotland: Churchill Livingstone.

Meyer-Lindenberg, A., Buckholtz, J. W., Kolachana, B. R., Hariri, A., Pezawas, L., Blasi, G., . . . Weinberger, D. R. (2006). Neural mechanisms of genetic risk for impulsivity and violence in humans. *Proceedings of the National Academy of Sciences of the United States of America, 103*, 6269–6274.

Mitchell, J. P., Banaji, M. R., & Macrae, C. N. (2005). General and specific contributions of the medial prefrontal cortex to knowledge about mental states. *NeuroImage, 28*, 757–762. doi:10.1016/j.neuroimage.2005.03.011

Morris, J. S., Frith, C. D., Perrett, D. I., Rowland, D., Young, A. W., Calder, A. J., & Dolan, R. J. (1996). A differential neural response in the human amygdala to fearful and happy facial expressions. *Nature, 383*, 812–815. doi:10.1038/383812a0

Nemoto, H., Toda, H., Nakajima, T., Hosokawa, S., Okada, Y., Yamamoto, K., . . . Goto, F. (2003). Fluvoxamine modulates pain sensation and affective processing of pain in human brain. *Neuroreport, 14*, 791–797. doi:10.1097/00001756-200305060-00003

Ochsner, K. N., & Gross, J. J. (2005). The cognitive control of emotion. *Trends in Cognitive Sciences, 9*, 242–249. doi:10.1016/j.tics.2005.03.010

Orbach, I., Mikulincer, M., King, R., Cohen, D., & Stein, D. (1997). Thresholds and tolerance of physical pain in suicidal and nonsuicidal adolescents. *Journal of Consulting and Clinical Psychology, 65*, 646–652. doi:10.1037/0022-006X.65.4.646

Panksepp, J. (1998). *Affective neuroscience*. New York, NY: Oxford University Press.

Panksepp, J. (2003, October 10). Neuroscience. Feeling the pain of social loss. *Science, 302*, 237–239. doi:10.1126/science.1091062

Panksepp, J., Herman, B., Conner, R., Bishop, P., & Scott, J. P. (1978). The biology of social attachments: Opiates alleviate separation distress. *Biological Psychiatry, 13*, 607–618.

Petrovic, P., & Ingvar, M. (2002). Imaging cognitive modulation of pain processing. *Pain, 95*, 1–5. doi:10.1016/S0304-3959(01)00467-5

Peyron, R., Laurent, B., & Garcia-Larrea, L. (2000). Functional imaging of brain responses to pain. A review and meta-analysis. *Neurophysiologie Clinique, 30*, 263–288. doi:10.1016/S0987-7053(00)00227-6

Phan, K. L., Wager, T. D., Taylor, S. F., & Liberzon, I. (2004). Functional neuroimaging studies of human emotions. *CNS Spectrums, 9,* 258–266.

Phelps, E. A., Delgado, M. R., Nearing, K. I., & LeDoux, J. E. (2004). Extinction learning in humans: Role of the amygdala and vmPFC. *Neuron, 43,* 897–905.

Phillips, M. L., Young, A. W., Senior, C., Brammer, M., Andrew, C., Calder, A. J., . . . David, A. S. (1997). A specific neural substrate for perceiving facial expressions of disgust. *Nature, 389,* 495–498. doi:10.1038/39051

Ploghaus, A., Tracey, I., Gati, J. S., Clare, S., Menon, R. S., Matthews, P. M., & Rawlins, J. N. P. (1999, June 18). Dissociating pain from its anticipation in the human brain. *Science, 284,* 1979–1981. doi:10.1126/science.284.5422.1979

Ploog, D. (1981). Neurobiology of primate audio-vocal behavior. *Brain Research, 3,* 35–61. doi:10.1016/0165-0173(81)90011-4

Price, D. D. (2000, June 9). Psychological and neural mechanisms of the affective dimension of pain. *Science, 288,* 1769–1772. doi:10.1126/science.288.5472.1769

Rainville, P., Duncan, G. H., Price, D. D., Carrier, B., & Bushnell, M. D. (1997, August 15). Pain affect encoded in human anterior cingulate but not somatosensory cortex. *Science, 277,* 968–971. doi:10.1126/science.277.5328.968

Sawamoto, N., Honda, M., Okada, T., Hanakawa, T., Kanda, M., Fukuyama, H., . . . Shibasaki, H. (2000). Expectation of pain enhances responses to nonpainful somatosensory stimulation in the anterior cingulate cortex and parietal operculum/posterior insula: An event-related functional magnetic resonance imaging study. *The Journal of Neuroscience, 20,* 7438–7445.

Schmitt, M. T., & Branscombe, N. R. (2002). The internal and external causal loci of attributions to prejudice. *Personality and Social Psychology Bulletin, 28,* 620–628. doi:10.1177/0146167202288006

Shimodozono, M., Kawahira, K., Kamishita, T., Ogata, A., Tohgo, S., & Tanaka, N. (2002). Reduction of central poststroke pain with the selective reuptake inhibitor fluvoxamine. *The International Journal of Neuroscience, 112,* 1173–1181. doi:10.1080/00207450290026139

Singh, V. P., Jain, N. K., & Kulkarni, S. K. (2001). On the antinociceptive effect of fluoxetine, a selective serotonin reuptake inhibitor. *Brain Research, 915,* 218–226. doi:10.1016/S0006-8993(01)02854-2

Smith, W. (1945). The functional significance of the rostral cingular cortex as revealed by its responses to electrical excitation. *Journal of Neurophysiology, 8,* 241–255.

Twenge, J. M. (2005). When does social rejection lead to aggression? The influences of situations, narcissism, emotion, and replenishing connections. In K. D. Williams, J. P. Forgas, & W. von Hippel (Eds.), *The social outcast: Ostracism, social exclusion, rejection, and bullying* (pp. 201–212). New York, NY: Cambridge University Press.

Twenge, J. M., Baumeister, R. F., Tice, D. M., & Stucke, T. S. (2001). If you can't join them, beat them: Effects of social exclusion on aggressive behavior. *Journal of Personality and Social Psychology, 81,* 1058–1069. doi:10.1037/0022-3514.81.6.1058

Wager, T. D., Rilling, J. K., Smith, E. E., Sokolik, A., Casey, K. L., Davidson, R. J., . . . Cohen, J. D. (2004, February 20). Placebo-induced changes in fMRI in the anticipation and experience of pain. *Science, 303,* 1162–1167. doi:10.1126/ science.1093065

Way, B. M., Taylor, S. E., & Eisenberger, N. I. (2009). Variation in the mu-opioid receptor gene (OPRM1) is associated with dispositional and neural sensitivity to social rejection. *Proceedings of the National Academy of Sciences, 106,* 15079–15084.

Whalen, P. J., Shin, L. M., McInerney, S. C., Fischer, H., Wright, C. I., & Rauch, S. L. (2001). A functional MRI study of human amygdala responses to facial expressions of fear versus anger. *Emotion (Washington, DC), 1,* 70–83. doi:10.1037/ 1528-3542.1.1.70

Williams, K. D., Cheung, C. K. T., & Choi, W. (2000). Cyberostracism: Effects of being ignored over the Internet. *Journal of Personality and Social Psychology, 79,* 748–762. doi:10.1037/0022-3514.79.5.748

Zaza, C., & Baine, N. (2002). Cancer pain and psychosocial factors: A critical review of the literature. *Journal of Pain and Symptom Management, 24,* 526–542. doi:10.1016/ S0885-3924(02)00497-9

3

PHYSIOLOGICAL RESPONSES TO EXPERIENCES OF SOCIAL PAIN

SALLY S. DICKERSON

Children who are consistently teased or ostracized, or are always the last ones chosen for the team; people who make fools of themselves in public presentations, or are ridiculed by superiors; and individuals who are put down, criticized, or rejected by relationship partners or because they possess devalued characteristics or social stigmas often experience *social evaluative threat* (SET), which occurs when the self could be negatively judged by others (Dickerson & Kemeny, 2004). Social evaluative experiences can lead to *social pain*—the emotional response to the perception that one is being excluded, rejected, or devalued by a significant individual or group (MacDonald & Leary, 2005). A growing body of evidence suggests that SET is accompanied by specific physiological responses, including changes in the cardiovascular, neuroendocrine, and immune systems (e.g., Dickerson, 2008; Dickerson, Gruenewald, & Kemeny, 2004). Therefore, social evaluative events that induce social pain are capable of eliciting not only intense emotional responses but physiological responses as well. Though the acute experience of social pain may produce short-term changes in physiological parameters, more chronic or prolonged experiences could result in dysregulation of physiological systems, which could lead to negative health outcomes.

Why might social pain be associated with physiological responses? Humans have a fundamental need to belong and to be socially accepted by others (e.g., Baumeister & Leary, 1995; Bowlby, 1969; James, 1890/1950; Maslow, 1987), and preserving the social self is integral to maintaining one's well-being and survival. Conditions with the potential for evaluation and rejection jeopardize this fundamental goal. Threats to other central goals, such as threats to physical self-preservation (e.g., safety, survival), are associated with coordinated psychological and physiological responses, which are elicited to deal with the demands of the situation. As with threats to physical self-preservation, threats to the goal of social self-preservation may also elicit a coordinated psychobiological response (for a review, see Dickerson, Gruenewald, & Kemeny, 2009). Indeed, theorists have argued that experiences of physical and social pain share neural, cognitive, emotional, and behavioral components (Eisenberger & Lieberman, 2004; MacDonald & Leary, 2005). Therefore, both physical and social threats may be capable of eliciting certain physiological responses.

SOCIAL EVALUATIVE THREAT AND SOCIAL PAIN

Self-conscious emotions, including shame, embarrassment, and humiliation, can arise from beliefs that others are negatively evaluating the self or judging one's social acceptability (e.g., Leary, 2007); therefore, these emotions have been proposed as a central emotional response to SET (for a review, see Dickerson, Gruenewald, & Kemeny, 2004; Gruenewald, Dickerson, & Kemeny, 2007). This proposal draws on a rich theoretical tradition in which self-conscious emotions are associated "almost exclusively to the judgment of others" (Darwin, 1871/1899, p. 114) and with assessments of low or declining status, acceptance, or social attention (e.g., Gilbert, 2000; Leary, 2007).

Empirical studies have also documented the linkages between self-conscious emotion and social evaluation (e.g., Keltner & Buswell, 1996; R. H. Smith, Webster, Parrott, & Eyre, 2002). For example, Gruenewald, Kemeny, Aziz, and Fahey (2004) randomly assigned participants to complete math and speech tasks either alone in a room (non-SET condition) or in front of an evaluative audience (SET condition). Those performing under SET showed greater increases in self-conscious emotions than did those in the non-SET condition; however, there were no significant differences between conditions for other emotional states (e.g., anxiety). The effect was recently replicated (Dickerson, Mycek, & Zaldivar, 2008) and suggests a specific link between self-conscious emotions and SET.

This linkage between self-conscious emotion and SET has direct consequences for the conditions under which social pain may be experienced. Self-conscious emotions (along with other emotions, such as hurt feelings) are aspects of social pain because they are part of the emotional response to exclusion or devaluation by others (MacDonald & Leary, 2005); thus, social evaluative experiences, which induce self-conscious emotional states, are therefore also experiences of social pain. Consequently, the physiological effects of SET also could be categorized as the physiological effects of social pain.

CORTISOL RESPONSES TO SOCIALLY PAINFUL EXPERIENCES

Stressors can elicit a number of physiological changes, which are thought to be important in the short term for modulating a wide range of somatic functions that may be needed to respond appropriately to the threat. Following certain stressors, cortisol is released as part of a hormone cascade that begins when the hypothalamic–pituitary–adrenocortical (HPA) axis is activated by neural inputs from the central nervous system. In specific terms, the hypothalamus releases corticotropin-releasing hormone, which in turn stimulates the anterior pituitary to secrete adrenocorticotropic hormone (ACTH), which triggers the adrenal cortex to release cortisol into the bloodstream. Cortisol is an important regulatory hormone that can affect other physiological systems (e.g., sympathetic nervous system, immune system). Cortisol also has a primary role in metabolic functioning and is capable of mobilizing energy resources (e.g., glucose) to provide the necessary "fuel" for the body (Lovallo & Thomas, 2000; Sapolsky, Romero, & Munck, 2000).

Laboratory Performance Stressor Studies

There is growing evidence that SET can elicit increases in cortisol. In a meta-analytic review of 208 acute psychological stressor studies (Dickerson & Kemeny, 2004), stressors that included elements of social evaluation (e.g., audience present) were associated with greater increases in cortisol compared with stressors without this component; in fact, the effect size for the social evaluative stressors ($d = 0.67$) was nearly three times the size of those lacking this characteristic ($d = 0.21$). This effect was heightened when SET was coupled with uncontrollability. Stressors with both components were associated with large increases in cortisol ($d = 0.92$), whereas those without either component did not activate this system ($d < 0.00$). Social evaluative, uncontrollable stressors not only were capable of eliciting substantial increases in cortisol but also were associated with slower times to recovery (i.e., participants returned to prestressor baseline levels less quickly). Taken together, this evidence indicates that stressors capable of inducing social pain (i.e., SET) elicit substantial and prolonged increases in cortisol, particularly when compared with other nonsocial stressor tasks.

Several experimental studies have directly compared cortisol reactivity in conditions with and without social evaluation, consequently also manipulating the experience of social pain. Gruenewald and colleagues (2004) randomly assigned participants to deliver a speech and complete a computerized math task either alone in a room (non-SET condition) or in front of an evaluative audience panel (SET condition). Participants in both conditions rated the task as equally demanding, difficult, and effortful, indicating that the task was similarly "stressful" for the two conditions. However, only the social evaluative condition elicited a significant cortisol response. Those in the non-SET condition showed no changes in cortisol from pre- to posttask. Furthermore, participants who showed greater increases in self-conscious emotions in response to the speech and math stressor also showed greater increases in cortisol, which demonstrates that the emotional and physiological responses to SET were elicited in parallel. This result suggests that conditions that induce social pain also trigger cortisol reactivity and that this effect may hinge on the experience of self-conscious emotions.

Recent research has focused on understanding the specific components of the social evaluative context that are capable of eliciting cortisol reactivity. My colleagues and I recently tested whether it is the mere presence of others that triggers cortisol responses or whether explicit social evaluation is necessary (Dickerson, Mycek, & Zaldivar, 2008). Participants were randomly assigned to deliver a speech in one of three conditions: in front of an evaluative audience (SET), alone in a room (non-SET), or in the presence of an inattentive confederate (who was not paying attention to the participant during the speech, or PRES). We found that only the SET condition elicited a significant cortisol response; the PRES and non-SET conditions were not associated with increases in this hormone. This finding indicates that simply having others present during a stressful experience may not elicit cortisol responses. Instead, the perception that others are explicitly evaluating performance may be the active ingredient responsible for eliciting cortisol reactivity under SET.

In addition, we found that among those in the social evaluative condition, self-conscious cognitive and emotional responses and cortisol responses were correlated (Dickerson, Mycek, & Zaldivar, 2008); those with higher levels of posttask self-conscious states showed greater reactivity to the task. There was no relationship between cortisol reactivity and other negative emotions such as fear or sadness. This finding again suggests that an emotional component of social pain is tied to cortisol responses under SET.

A subsequent study further examined the "active ingredient" of the social evaluative context that is responsible for increases in cortisol. Many social evaluative stressor protocols involve both real-time social evaluation (e.g., audience present) and the potential for subsequent evaluation by others (e.g., performance is videotaped; Kirschbaum, Pirke, & Hellhammer, 1993).

Therefore, we tested whether the potential for future evaluation is capable of eliciting cortisol reactivity and is the element driving cortisol reactivity under SET (Robbins, Dickerson, Epstein, & Zaldivar, 2009). Participants were instructed to deliver a speech alone in the room (similar to the non-SET condition described earlier), except that they were told that their performance would be videotaped and later evaluated by two individuals for content and delivery; thus, there was not explicit social evaluation (e.g., audience present) but only the potential for subsequent evaluation (with the videotape). Consistent with hypotheses, this videotaped performance context did not elicit increases in cortisol; in fact, the cortisol trajectories were identical to the non-SET condition in the Dickerson, Mycek, and Zaldivar (2008) study. In addition, the video and non-SET contexts showed similarly low levels of posttask self-conscious cognitions and emotions, suggesting that the potential for evaluation (a) is not sufficient for eliciting cortisol levels and (b) is not strongly associated with social pain. This finding further underscores that cortisol reactivity (and the experience of social pain) to SET may be contingent on explicit social evaluation.

Other studies have used different performance tasks to compare cortisol reactivity under social evaluative and non–social evaluative contexts. Rohleder, Beulen, Chen, Wolf, and Kirschbaum (2007) found that ballroom dancing competitions—which are inherently social evaluative—triggered greater increases in cortisol compared with nonevaluative practice sessions. This result extends the experimental laboratory findings to naturally occurring stressors and demonstrates that social evaluative performance tasks outside of the lab are also capable of eliciting increases in cortisol.

Taken together, these studies document that social evaluative stressors—which elicit social pain—can also reliably elicit strong and substantial increases in cortisol under laboratory and naturalistic performance conditions. In addition, the cortisol responses to SET occur in concert with self-conscious emotions, which suggests an integrated emotional and physiological response to experiences of social pain.

Interpersonal Conflict and Rejection

The studies described earlier have all examined SET in the context of performance tasks, both within and outside of the laboratory. However, other research has demonstrated that negative interpersonal interactions that involve evaluation, conflict, or rejection can also lead to the experience of social pain—and can elevate cortisol levels.

Several studies have used laboratory social rejection paradigms to test whether exclusion or ostracism can elicit cortisol responses. Blackhart, Eckel, and Tice (2007) found that participants who were told after a 15-min conversation period that "nobody wants to work with you" on a subsequent task (i.e., rejection condition) showed elevated cortisol levels compared with participants who were told that everyone wanted to work with them (i.e., acceptance condition). This result is aligned with earlier findings from a Stroud and colleagues (Stroud, Tanofsky-Kraff, Wilfley, & Salovey, 2000) study, in which women who were increasingly ignored and ostracized by two confederates during a "getting to know you" discussion task showed increases in cortisol, which demonstrated that negative interpersonal interactions characterized by rejection can activate the cortisol system. It is interesting that this cortisol response to social rejection was observed primarily among women (Stroud, Salovey, & Epel, 2002), with men showing little to no cortisol reactivity. This finding suggests that women may be particularly sensitive or responsive physiologically to experiences of social pain. However, there were no differences between men and women in cortisol responses to social rejection in the Blackhart et al. (2007) study, which indicates that future research on gender differences is warranted.

Other research has looked at cortisol responses to social rejection in children. Gunnar, Sebanc, Tout, Donzella, and van Dulmen (2003) obtained sociometric assessments of peer rejection by having 3- to 5-year-olds nominate their classmates who they especially liked and did not like at preschool; salivary cortisol samples were collected during the school day. Those who were more disliked (e.g., peer rejected) had higher levels of cortisol compared with the other more socially accepted children, which indicates that rejection is capable of increasing cortisol activity among young children as well.

Social evaluative and hostile communication patterns within the context of close relationships have also been examined to test the effects of conflict on physiological parameters. When married couples are asked to discuss a major problem in their relationship in the laboratory, wives who are on the receiving end of criticism, disapproval, and other social evaluative and rejecting behaviors show increases in HPA activity, including elevations in ACTH and cortisol levels (Kiecolt-Glaser et al., 1997; Malarkey, Kiecolt-Glaser, Pearl, & Glaser, 1994). This effect has been observed among both newlywed samples (Malarkey et al., 1994) and older adults who have been married on average more than 40 years (Kiecolt-Glaser et al., 1997). It is interesting that in both samples of married couples, the effect of abrasive communication styles during conflict emerged only among women, mirroring the gender differences in the physiological effects of social rejection reviewed earlier, which again suggests women may be more physiologically vulnerable under conditions of social pain.

Summary and Future Directions: Cortisol and Social Pain

A body of evidence now demonstrates that social evaluative and rejecting contexts provide one set of conditions capable of eliciting cortisol responses.

This has been shown using a variety of different paradigms, ranging from social evaluative laboratory performance tasks to incidents of rejection, ostracism, or conflict. In addition, cortisol responses to SET and rejection have been documented across the life span, from preschool-age children (e.g., Gunnar et al., 2003) to older adults (e.g., Kiecolt-Glaser et al., 1997). However, the vast majority of these studies have been conducted in the laboratory (cf. Gunner et al., 2003; Rohleder et al., 2007); future research should examine how SET and rejection influence cortisol reactivity in more naturally occurring situations. Studies that use daily diary methodology and salivary cortisol assessment could examine these important questions of generalizability. In addition, few studies have examined SET within ongoing interpersonal relationships (cf. Kiecolt-Glaser et al., 1997) but instead have used strangers or new acquaintances to induce evaluation or rejection in the participants. It will also be important to continue to examine these processes as they unfold in developing and established interpersonal relationships.

Furthermore, studies should continue to explore the affective correlates of cortisol reactivity. The self-conscious emotions associated with social pain, which are elicited under SET, may be linked to cortisol responses; a growing number of studies have reported a correlation between self-conscious cognitive and emotional responses and cortisol activity (Dickerson, Mycek, & Zaldivar, 2008; Gruenewald et al., 2004; Lewis & Ramsay, 2002). In addition, more general measures of distress or negative emotion have not been associated with cortisol responses (e.g., Dickerson & Kemeny, 2004), which suggests a specific association between the self-conscious emotions and cortisol under SET. Taken together, these studies provide evidence that the conditions that trigger social pain trigger increases in cortisol, and the emotions associated with social pain are linked with this physiological response.

CARDIOVASCULAR RESPONSES TO SOCIALLY PAINFUL EXPERIENCES

Cortisol is not the only physiological parameter that can be elevated in response to experiences of social pain. Acute stressors can activate the sympathetic nervous system (SNS), which elicits elevations in heart rate, systolic blood pressure (SBP), diastolic blood pressure (DBP), and secretion of the catecholamines epinephrine, and norepinephrine. These changes help induce arousal, activation, and vigilance during a threatening situation that would facilitate the fight-or-flight response.

Many investigations have shown that social evaluative performance stressors, such as giving a speech in front of an evaluative audience, can lead to substantial increases in heart rate and blood pressure (e.g., Kirschbaum et al.,

1993). These changes are typically observed rapidly (e.g., upon initiation of the stressor) and tend to dissipate quickly after the threat is removed (e.g., fast recovery), especially when compared with cortisol trajectories in similar situations. Besides social evaluative performance stressors, other types of social threats can elicit cardiovascular reactivity as well; social rejection or hostile social conflict can also lead to elevations in heart rate and blood pressure (e.g., Kiecolt-Glaser et al., 1993; Stroud et al., 2000).

Although SET can certainly increase cardiovascular parameters, the effects appear to not be as specific to SET compared with cortisol. In the Gruenewald et al. (2004) study, there were increases in heart rate, SBP, and DBP under both SET and non-SET conditions; in other words, participants showed cardiovascular reactivity regardless of whether they were alone in a room or in front of an evaluative audience. This effect was recently replicated in a study using similar methodology (Dickerson, Gable, Irwin, Aziz, & Kemeny, 2009). However, the Gruenewald et al. (2004) study found that cortisol was elicited only under the SET condition. This suggests that the cardiovascular system may be responsive to a wide variety of different "stressful" situations, whereas other parameters, such as cortisol, may be more sensitive to the social milieu of the threat. Nevertheless, it is clear that experiences of social pain often elicit increases in heart rate and blood pressure along with activation of the HPA axis.

Although both social and nonsocial stressors may elicit increases in cardiovascular markers, the magnitude of the experience of social pain may moderate responses to social threat. For example, the Gruenewald et al. (2004) study found marginally greater increases in heart rate and blood pressure among those in the SET condition (although both conditions showed increases), which suggests that greater social pain translated into a stronger cardiovascular response. This finding is similar to findings of greater increases in cardiovascular reactivity under conditions in which the evaluative nature of the task is emphasized (T. W. Smith, Nealy, Kircher, & Limon, 1997) or when others act in nonsupportive ways (e.g., conveying boredom or disinterest, directly disagreeing, or undermining the participant; Gerin, Pieper, Levy, & Pickering, 1992; Lepore, Allen, & Evans, 1993; Sheffield & Carroll, 1994). In addition, when couples engage in a problem discussion task, the more hostile, socially painful interactions result in greater blood pressure reactivity (Kiecolt-Glaser et al., 1993), and hostile verbal exchanges have been linked with increases in blood pressure among female hypertension patients (Ewart, Taylor, Kraemer, & Agras, 1991).

Taken together, this research demonstrates that cardiovascular parameters such as heart rate and blood pressure often increase with experiences of social pain, and the severity or gravity of the experience may be related to the magnitude of these responses. Future research should continue to examine the specific psychophysiological processes responsible for these effects, and how these differ under social evaluative versus non-SET conditions. For example, increases in blood pressure and heart rate could result from two different processes: increased activation of the sympathetic nervous system (e.g., the fight-or-flight system) or decreased activation of the restorative parasympathetic nervous system (PNS), which is active during rest or restorative activities. Future studies that manipulate SET should examine how different social contexts may differentially influence SNS versus PNS activation.

IMMUNE RESPONSES TO SOCIALLY PAINFUL EXPERIENCES

Experiences of social pain can also lead to alterations in the functioning of the immune system. A meta-analysis found that stressors—including those with social evaluative components—reliably alter certain immune parameters (Segerstrom & Miller, 2004). In specific terms, acute stressors lead to increases in the number of natural killer (NK) cells and T-cytotoxic lymphocytes. In addition, there are functional changes in aspects of the immune system following acute stressors: NK cell cytotoxicity (e.g., ability of NK cells to lyse a target cell) increases, whereas lymphocytes' ability to proliferate (multiply and divide) upon stimulation decreases. These findings suggest an up-regulation or enhancement of natural immunity (associated with a quick, fast-acting response capable of attacking any pathogen), and a down-regulation or decline of specific immunity (associated with a more tailored response to specific pathogens); this pattern has been hypothesized to be adaptive in the face of an acute threat (Segerstrom & Miller, 2004). This meta-analysis examined all types of acute psychological stressors and found many tasks were capable of eliciting these changes; effects did not appear specific to those that were social evaluative or induced social pain (although the social stressors were indeed capable of eliciting these immunological changes as well). Very few studies have experimentally compared social evaluative and non–social evaluative tasks to examine whether those that induce social pain result in different patterns of immune changes compared with those that do not.

There is preliminary evidence that social threat may specifically induce one type of immune reaction: inflammation. In response to tissue injury or infection, the body can initiate inflammation; this process recruits blood cells to the scene of the injury or infection and promotes repair and healing. This process is orchestrated by specific proteins called proinflammatory cytokines. Given evidence that social threat in nonhuman animals can increase proinflammatory activity (e.g., increases in proinflammatory cytokines and other markers of inflammation; Avitsur, Stark, & Sheridan, 2001), my colleagues and I have been interested in whether SET leads to increases in these parameters as well. We (Dickerson, Gable, et al., 2009) recently tested whether social evaluative versus non–social evaluative tasks would increase proinflammatory cytokine production. We used a design similar to that used in the Gruenewald et al. (2004) study: Half of the participants delivered a speech and completed a computerized math task alone in a room (non-SET), and half did so in front of an evaluative audience (SET). Consistent with hypotheses, we found that only the social evaluative condition elicited increases in proinflammatory cytokine production (increases in tumor necrosis factor-alpha, or TNFα); those in the non-SET condition did not show increases in this parameter from pre- to posttask.

Furthermore, the increases in TNFα production were tied to perceptions of social evaluation; that is, those who felt more evaluated during the task showed greater increases in TNFα activity. This relationship did not emerge for other cognitive appraisals, such as task difficulty, controllability, or perceptions of how well they performed, and further, there were no differences between conditions along these dimensions. This finding suggests that increases in proinflammatory activity were specifically associated with appraisals of social evaluation rather than other factors assessed. This study provides evidence that experiences of social pain are capable of activating the production of proinflammatory cytokines.

In other work, we have examined how self-conscious emotions—a component of social pain—may specifically be tied to inflammatory markers. We randomly assigned participants to write about an experience in which they blamed themselves, or to write about a neutral, nonemotional topic (Dickerson, Kemeny, Aziz, Kim, & Fahey, 2004). We found that writing about an experience of self-blame led to increases in self-conscious emotions of shame and guilt, whereas writing about a neutral topic did not lead to changes in these emotions. In addition, those writing about experiences of self-blame showed increases in an inflammatory marker (the soluble receptor for TNFα) from pre- to postwriting; there were no changes as a result of writing about a neutral topic. Furthermore, those who showed the greatest increases in shame as a result of the procedures also showed the greatest increases in TNFα activity, which suggests that this emotion was specifically tied to this physiological response. This study, then, also provides evidence that emotions that can be experienced under conditions of social pain are also capable of increasing inflammatory activity.

Taken together, these findings suggest that experiences of social pain can lead to changes in components of the immune system and, in particular, may be specifically tied to inflammation. Future studies should continue to elucidate the wide variety of immune changes that may result from inducing social pain as well as to tease apart the potentially unique role that social pain and deleterious social relationships can have on immune parameters.

CHRONIC EXPERIENCES OF SOCIAL PAIN: PHYSIOLOGICAL AND HEALTH EFFECTS

The studies reviewed heretofore all examine the acute effects of social pain on the neuroendocrine, cardiovascular, and immune systems, and illustrate the ramifications that different stressors can have on physiological parameters up to approximately 90 min after they occur. Though these acute experiences can have relatively transient effects on physiological parameters, chronic experiences of social pain may have longer lasting consequences. Repeated or persistent experiences of social pain could occur in many contexts— when individuals are frequently exposed to social evaluative, rejecting experiences (e.g., constant criticism from employer or relationship partner), or if they are particularly sensitive to these experiences (e.g., those high on rejection sensitivity). Consequently, these individuals could experience social pain more often or for longer durations; this, in turn, could lead to more frequent or prolonged activation of the physiological systems, which could have negative consequences.

Research using longitudinal designs is needed to examine how the repeated acute elicitation of physiological systems that may accompany repeated experiences of social pain may, over time, contribute to negative health problems. However, there is theoretical—and preliminary empirical—evidence to suggest that experiences of social pain could lead to physiological dysregulation and, in turn, adverse health outcomes. McEwen and colleagues (e.g., McEwen, 1998; McEwen & Seeman, 2003) have proposed different pathways through which stressors may lead to negative effects on health; for example, the stress-responsive systems could be repeatedly activated because of frequent exposure to stressors, or these systems could fail to recover (i.e., fail to turn off the stress response) after the stressor has ended.

Under these conditions, the body could be overexposed to stress-relevant physiological hormones and other parameters. Consistent with this premise, several lines of evidence suggest that chronic experiences of social pain may lead to heightened levels of HPA activation. Miller, Chen, and Zhou (2007) conducted a meta-analysis that examined the effects of chronic stressors on cortisol activity. They found that chronic stressors that threatened the social self (and were therefore likely to induce social pain) were associated with higher levels of morning and afternoon–evening cortisol, compared with those stressors that lacked this social component. Furthermore, they found that chronic stressors that were likely to result in feelings of shame were also associated with higher afternoon–evening cortisol. These findings suggest that chronic social evaluative or shame-inducing events (i.e., chronic experiences of social pain) are associated with heightened cortisol activity throughout the day. These meta-analytic findings are consistent with research on loneliness, which often is experienced as social pain. Loneliness has also predicted higher levels of morning and night-time cortisol (Pressman et al., 2005) and greater cortisol responses to awakening (Adam, Hawkley, Kudielka, & Cacioppo, 2006; Steptoe, Owen, Kunz-Ebrecht, & Brydon, 2004). Taken together, these findings suggest that chronic experiences of social pain—including loneliness and certain chronic social threats—may be linked with elevations in HPA activity.

Over time, this overexposure to stress hormones could result in a cumulative toll on the body (e.g., allostatic load; McEwen, 1998). This could, in turn, lead to an increased risk of a variety of diseases, including diabetes, hypertension, and cardiovascular disease (for a review, see McEwen, 1998; McEwen & Seeman, 2003). Indeed, elevations in HPA or inflammatory markers have been linked with the incidence and progression of many disease states such as diabetes, metabolic syndrome, heart disease, depression, and autoimmune disease (Black, 2003; Danesh, Collins, Appleby, & Peto, 1998; Feldmann, Brennan, & Maini, 1996; Maes, 1999). In light of the fact that experiences of social pain can activate the stress-responsive cardiovascular, HPA, and inflammatory systems, these specific social threats and accompanying emotional states may be particularly likely to lead to allostatic load, with corresponding negative effects on health.

Research in the disease model of HIV has provided support for the linkages between social threat or social pain, increased physiological activation, and disease outcomes. Rejection sensitivity, an individual difference that may predispose one to experience social pain, has been associated with negative immunologic and health outcomes; HIV-positive men who were highly rejection-sensitive showed faster declines in disease-relevant immune parameters (CD4 cells) and faster times to AIDS diagnosis and death compared with those less rejection-sensitive (Cole, Kemeny, & Taylor, 1997). Furthermore, in another sample of HIV-positive gay men, rejection sensitivity was associated with higher levels of viral load (Cole, Kemeny, Fahey, Zach, & Naliboff, 2003). Additional analyses indicated that this effect was mediated by increased activation of the SNS. In other words, rejection sensitivity led to increased SNS activity, which in turn was linked with negative disease-related end points. This finding provides evidence that sensitivity to social pain could have negative health consequences partly as a result of increases in physiological activation.

Future research should continue to tease apart the causal pathways through which social pain may ultimately be associated with negative health outcomes. Research has demonstrated that acute experiences of social pain can elicit increases in cardiovascular, neuroendocrine, and immunological parameters. Further delineating these physiological responses may be one important factor for determining the mechanisms through which social pain could ultimately influence health and disease.

REFERENCES

Adam, E. K., Hawkley, L. C., Kudielka, B. M., & Cacioppo, J. T. (2006). Day-to-day dynamics of experience-cortisol associations in a population-based sample of older adults. *Proceedings of the National Academy of Sciences of the United States of America, 103,* 17058–17063. doi:10.1073/pnas.0605053103

Avitsur, R., Stark, J. L., & Sheridan, J. F. (2001). Social stress induces glucocorticoid resistance in subordinate animals. *Hormones and Behavior, 39,* 247–257. doi:10.1006/hbeh.2001.1653

Baumeister, R. F., & Leary, M. R. (1995). The need to belong: Desire for interpersonal attachments as a fundamental human motivation. *Psychological Bulletin, 117,* 497–529. doi:10.1037/0033-2909.117.3.497

Black, P. H. (2003). The inflammatory response is an integral part of the stress response: Implications for atherosclerosis, insulin resistance, type II diabetes, and metabolic syndrome X. *Brain, Behavior, and Immunity, 17,* 350–364. doi:10.1016/S0889-1591(03)00048-5

Blackhart, G. C., Eckel, L. A., & Tice, D. M. (2007). Salivary cortisol in response to acute social rejection and acceptance by peers. *Biological Psychology, 75,* 267–276. doi:10.1016/j.biopsycho.2007.03.005

Bowlby, J. (1969). *Attachment and loss: Vol. 1. Attachment.* New York, NY: Basic Books.

Cole, S. W., Kemeny, M. E., Fahey, J. L., Zach, J. A., & Naliboff, B. D. (2003). Psychological risk factors for HIV pathogenesis: Mediation by the autonomic nervous system. *Biological Psychiatry, 54,* 1444–1456. doi:10.1016/S0006-3223(02)01888-7

Cole, S. W., Kemeny, M. E., & Taylor, S. E. (1997). Social identity and physical health: Accelerated HIV progression in rejection-sensitive gay men. *Journal of Personality and Social Psychology, 72,* 320–335. doi:10.1037/0022-3514.72.2.320

Danesh, J., Collins, R., Appleby, P., & Peto, R. (1998). Association of fibrinogen, C-reactive protein, albumin, or leukocyte count with coronary heart disease: Meta-analysis of prospective studies. *JAMA, 279,* 1477–1482. doi:10.1001/jama.279.18.1477

Darwin, C. (1899). *The descent of man* (2nd ed.). London, England: Murray. (Original work published 1871)

Dickerson, S. S. (2008). Emotional and physiological responses to social-evaluative threat. *Social and Personality Psychology Compass, 2,* 1362–1378. doi:10.1111/j.1751-9004.2008.00095.x

Dickerson, S. S., Gable, S. L., Irwin, M. R., Aziz, N., & Kemeny, M. E. (2009). *Social-evaluative threat and proinflammatory cytokine regulation: An experimental laboratory investigation. Psychological Science, 20,* 1234–1244.

Dickerson, S. S., Gruenewald, T. L., & Kemeny, M. E. (2004). When the social self is threatened: Shame, physiology, and health. *Journal of Personality, 72,* 1191–1216. doi:10.1111/j.1467-6494.2004.00295.x

Dickerson, S. S., Gruenewald, T. L., & Kemeny, M. E. (2009). Psychobiological responses to social self threat: Functional or detrimental? *Self and Identity, 8*, 270–285.

Dickerson, S. S., & Kemeny, M. E. (2004). Acute stressors and cortisol responses: A theoretical integration and synthesis of laboratory research. *Psychological Bulletin, 130*, 355–391. doi:10.1037/0033-2909.130.3.355

Dickerson, S. S., Kemeny, M. E., Aziz, N., Kim, K. H., & Fahey, J. L. (2004). Immunological effects of induced shame and guilt. *Psychosomatic Medicine, 66*, 124–131. doi:10.1097/01.PSY.0000097338.75454.29

Dickerson, S. S., Mycek, P. J., & Zaldivar, F. (2008). Negative social evaluation—but not mere social presence—elicits cortisol responses in the laboratory. *Health Psychology, 27*, 116–121.

Eisenberger, N. I., & Lieberman, M. D. (2004). Why rejection hurts: A common neural alarm system for physical and social pain. *Trends in Cognitive Sciences, 8*, 294–300. doi:10.1016/j.tics.2004.05.010

Ewart, C. K., Taylor, C. B., Kraemer, H. C., & Agras, W. S. (1991). High blood pressure and marital discord: Not being nasty matters more than being nice. *Health Psychology, 10*, 155–163. doi:10.1037/0278-6133.10.3.155

Feldmann, M., Brennan, F. M., & Maini, R. N. (1996). Role of cytokines in rheumatoid arthritis. *Annual Review of Immunology, 14*, 397–440. doi:10.1146/annurev.immunol.14.1.397

Gerin, W., Pieper, C., Levy, R., & Pickering, T. G. (1992). Social support in social interaction: A moderator of cardiovascular reactivity. *Psychosomatic Medicine, 54*, 324–336.

Gilbert, P. (2000). Varieties of submissive behavior as forms of social defense: Their evolution and role in depression. In L. Sloman & P. Gilbert (Eds.), *Subordination and defeat: An evolutionary approach to mood disorders and their therapy* (pp. 3–45). Mahwah, NJ: Erlbaum.

Gruenewald, T. L., Dickerson, S. S., & Kemeny, M. E. (2007). A social function for the self-conscious emotions: Social-self-preservation theory. In J. Tracy, R. Robins, & J. Tangney (Eds.), *Self-conscious emotions* (2nd ed., pp. 68–87). New York, NY: Guilford Press.

Gruenewald, T. L., Kemeny, M. E., Aziz, N., & Fahey, J. L. (2004). Acute threat to the social self: Shame, social self-esteem, and cortisol activity. *Psychosomatic Medicine, 66*, 915–924. doi:10.1097/01.psy.0000143639.61693.ef

Gunnar, M. R., Sebanc, A. M., Tout, K., Donzella, B., & van Dulmen, M. M. H. (2003). Peer rejection, temperament, and cortisol activity in preschoolers. *Developmental Psychobiology, 43*, 346–368. doi:10.1002/dev.10144

James, W. J. (1950). *The principles of psychology* (Vol. 1). New York, NY: Dover. (Original work published 1890)

Keltner, D., & Buswell, B. N. (1996). Evidence for the distinctness of embarrassment, shame, and guilt: A study of recalled antecedents and facial expressions of emotion. *Cognition and Emotion, 10*, 155–172. doi:10.1080/026999396380312

Kiecolt-Glaser, J. K., Glaser, R., Cacioppo, J. T., MacCallum, R. C., Snydersmith, M., Kim, C., & Malarkey, W. B. (1997). Marital conflict in older adults: Endocrinological and immunological correlates. *Psychosomatic Medicine, 59,* 339–349.

Kiecolt-Glaser, J. K., Malarkey, W. B., Chee, M. A., Newton, T., Cacioppo, J. T., Mao, H. Y., & Glaser, R. (1993). Negative behavior during marital conflict is associated with immunological downregulation. *Psychosomatic Medicine, 55,* 395–409.

Kirschbaum, C., Pirke, K. M., & Hellhammer, D. H. (1993). The "Trier Social Stress Test": A tool for investigating psychobiological responses in a laboratory setting. *Neuropsychobiology, 28,* 76–81. doi:10.1159/000119004

Leary, M. R. (2007). Motivational and emotional aspects of the self. *Annual Review of Psychology, 58,* 317–344. doi:10.1146/annurev.psych.58.110405.085658

Lepore, S. J., Allen, K. A., & Evans, G. W. (1993). Social support lowers cardiovascular reactivity to an acute stressor. *Psychosomatic Medicine, 55,* 518–524.

Lewis, M., & Ramsay, R. (2002). Cortisol response to embarrassment and shame. *Child Development, 73,* 1034–1045. doi:10.1111/1467-8624.00455

Lovallo, W. R., & Thomas, T. L. (2000). Stress hormones in psychophysiological research: Emotional, behavioral, and cognitive implications. In J. Cacioppo, L. Tassinary, & G. Berntson (Eds.), *The handbook of psychophysiology* (pp. 342–367). Cambridge, England: Cambridge University Press.

MacDonald, G., & Leary, M. R. (2005). Why does social exclusion hurt? The relationship between social and physical pain. *Psychological Bulletin, 131,* 202–223. doi:10.1037/0033-2909.131.2.202

Maes, M. (1999). Major depression and activation of the inflammatory response system. *Advances in Experimental Medicine and Biology, 461,* 25–46. doi:10.1007/978-0-585-37970-8_2

Malarkey, W. B., Kiecolt-Glaser, J. K., Pearl, D., & Glaser, R. (1994). Hostile behavior during marital conflict alters pituitary and adrenal hormones. *Psychosomatic Medicine, 56,* 41–51.

Maslow, A. H. (1987). *Motivation and personality* (3rd ed.). New York, NY: Harper & Row.

McEwen, B. S. (1998). Protective and damaging effects of stress mediators. *The New England Journal of Medicine, 338,* 171–179. doi:10.1056/NEJM199801153380307

McEwen, B. S., & Seeman, T. E. (2003). Stress and affect: Applicability of the concepts of allostasis and allostatic load. In R. J. Davidson, K. R. Scherer, & H. H. Goldsmith (Eds.), *Handbook of affective sciences* (pp. 1117–1138). Oxford, England: Oxford University Press.

Miller, G. E., Chen, E., & Zhou, E. (2007). If it goes up, must it come down? Chronic stress and the hypothalamic-pituitary-adrenocortical axis in humans. *Psychological Bulletin, 133,* 25–45. doi:10.1037/0033-2909.133.1.25

Pressman, S. D., Cohen, S. D., Miller, G. E., Barkin, A., Rabin, B. S., & Treanor, J. J. (2005). Loneliness, social network size, and immune response to influenza vaccination in college freshmen. *Health Psychology, 24,* 297–306. doi:10.1037/0278-6133.24.3.297

Robbins, M. L., Dickerson, S. S., Epstein, E. B., & Zaldivar, F. (2009). *Cortisol responses to the potential for evaluation in the laboratory.* Unpublished manuscript.

Rohleder, N., Beulen, S. E., Chen, E., Wolf, J. M., & Kirschbaum, C. (2007). Stress on the dance floor: The cortisol stress response to social-evaluative threat in competitive ballroom dancers. *Personality and Social Psychology Bulletin, 33,* 69–84. doi:10.1177/0146167206293986

Sapolsky, R. M., Romero, L. M., & Munck, A. U. (2000). How do glucocorticoids influence stress responses? Integrating permissive, suppressive, stimulatory, and preparative actions. *Endocrine Reviews, 21,* 55–89. doi:10.1210/er.21.1.55

Segerstrom, S. C., & Miller, G. E. (2004). Psychological stress and the human immune system: A meta-analytic study of 30 years of inquiry. *Psychological Bulletin, 130,* 601–630. doi:10.1037/0033-2909.130.4.601

Sheffield, D., & Carroll, D. (1994). Social support and cardiovascular reactions to active laboratory stressors. *Psychology & Health, 9,* 305–316. doi:10.1080/08870449408407489

Smith, R. H., Webster, J. M., Parrott, W. G., & Eyre, H. L. (2002). The role of public exposure in moral and nonmoral shame and guilt. *Journal of Personality and Social Psychology, 83,* 138–159. doi:10.1037/0022-3514.83.1.138

Smith, T. W., Nealy, J. B., Kircher, J. C., & Limon, J. P. (1997). Social determinants of cardiovascular reactivity: Effects of incentive to exert influence and evaluative threat. *Psychophysiology, 34,* 65–73. doi:10.1111/j.1469-8986.1997.tb02417.x

Steptoe, A., Owen, N., Kunz-Ebrecht, S. R., & Brydon, L. (2004). Loneliness and neuroendocrine, cardiovascular, and inflammatory stress responses in middle-aged men and women. *Psychoneuroendocrinology, 29,* 593–611. doi:10.1016/S0306-4530(03)00086-6

Stroud, L. R., Salovey, P., & Epel, E. S. (2002). Sex differences in stress responses: Social rejection versus achievement stress. *Biological Psychiatry, 52,* 318–327. doi:10.1016/S0006-3223(02)01333-1

Stroud, L. R., Tanofsky-Kraff, M., Wilfley, D. E., & Salovey, P. (2000). The Yale Interpersonal Stressor (YIPS): Affective, physiological, and behavioral responses to a novel interpersonal rejection paradigm. *Annals of Behavioral Medicine, 22,* 204–213. doi:10.1007/BF02895115

4

GENETIC FACTORS IN SOCIAL PAIN

BALDWIN M. WAY AND SHELLEY E. TAYLOR

Social exclusion, rejection, and loss are among the most profoundly salient experiences that human beings undergo. This observation is consistent with the evolutionary perspective that underscores the significance of group living for human survival. In human prehistory, rejection or exclusion from the social group could have been tantamount to a death sentence. Complex systems for detecting, preventing, and responding to experiences of social pain would thus have had adaptive significance. As such, a number of genetically based biological regulatory systems are likely involved in the experience of social pain.

As yet, there is not a field devoted to the genetics of social pain, so the task of this chapter is to provide directions as to how such a field may be constructed. This chapter progresses in step-by-step fashion from the psychological level through the neurochemical to the genetic level. In the process, we underscore the usefulness and promise of the genetic approach for furthering the understanding of social pain at both the psychological and biological levels.

As is described in other chapters in this volume, social pain is a complex, multifaceted response to situations of real or potential relational devaluation (Leary, 2005; Williams, 2001). Therefore, identifying genetic contributions to social pain is likely to be facilitated by subdividing it into component processes, as there is unlikely to be a single gene influencing all the different forms and components of social pain (Kendler, 2005). For the sake of this discussion, we have chosen to restrict our focus to the areas of research on social pain that have received the most study with genetic methods, specifically the experience of social pain as well as processes associated with its counterpart, social support. Interwoven with this discussion is a consideration of personality factors that are known to influence perceptions of both social pain and support. Finally, we conclude with a discussion of how the early childhood environment interacts with genetic makeup to influence responses to social pain.

GENETIC CONTRIBUTIONS TO SOCIAL PAIN

Twin Studies

The foundational assumption of this chapter is that there is a genetic contribution to social pain. The traditional first step for verifying this assumption has been the twin study. Using loneliness as a measure of social pain, researchers estimated that as much as 50% of the variance in the experience of loneliness may have genetic bases (Boomsma, Willemsen, Dolan, Hawkley, & Cacioppo, 2005). Similarly, other researchers estimated that as much as 30% of the variance in the experience of social support stems from genetic factors, possibly involving the ability to construe one's social environment as supportive or the ability to attract a socially supportive network through social competence skills (Kessler, Kendler, Heath, Neale, & Eaves, 1992). Conversely, people high in neuroticism, prone to experiencing negative affect, or low in extraversion are less likely to construe their environments as socially supportive. These personality traits have a strong genetic basis, with estimates of the variance explained by genetic factors ranging from 30% to 60% (Fanous, Gardner, Prescott, Cancro, & Kendler, 2002). Although the evidence from these twin studies is not comprehensive, it is certainly suggestive that there is a genetic component to different facets of social pain. Hence, the next question becomes, How does one identify specific genes associated with social pain processes?

One approach to solving this needle-in-the-haystack problem is to propose genetic hypotheses based on pharmacological and neurochemical studies of social pain that have been conducted over the past several decades. These studies have implicated the opioid, dopamine, serotonin, and oxytocin systems in social pain–related processes, and hence it is likely that variation in the genes controlling signaling within these systems is involved in social pain. Therefore, the following discussion centers on how variation in genes belonging to each of these systems is related to social pain and addresses each of these systems in succession.

Before beginning that discussion, however, we note that we have deliberately avoided technical genetic jargon to make the article more comprehensible for psychologists not trained in the physiological sciences. Nonetheless, several key terms need to be defined. When a portion of the DNA sequence is variable, it is referred to as a *polymorphism,* and the different forms of variation at this position in the DNA are referred to with the interchangeable terms *variant* or *allele.* Each person has two alleles, and the combination of the two alleles is referred to as a *genotype,* which is denoted with a slash (e.g., allele A/allele B). For a more detailed primer on genetic variation and its applications to psychology, readers are referred to other sources (Robinson, 2005; Way & Gurbaxani, 2008).

Physical Pain and Social Pain Overlap: The Opioids

The hypothesis that social pain and physical pain share overlapping physiological substrates provides a useful foundation for identifying potential genes influencing the experience of social pain. Support for this hypothesis comes from multiple sources. At the neuroanatomical level, brain regions that are involved in the unpleasant, affective component of pain (e.g., dorsal anterior cingulated [dACC]) are also critically involved in the subjective distress of being excluded by peers (Eisenberger et al., 2003). Similarly, at the neurochemical level, drugs used to blunt physical pain (e.g., morphine) also appear to blunt the social pain of being separated from loved ones and attachment figures (Herman & Panksepp, 1978). Because morphine acts on the opioid system, particularly the mu-opioid receptor, Panksepp (1998) hypothesized that the tonic level of endogenous opioid activity is a barometer of the quality of the social environment. Consistent with this notion, monkeys being groomed exhibit increased brain levels of endogenous opioids that act on the mu-opioid receptor (Keverne, Martensz, & Tuite, 1989). In addition, inhibiting opioid transmission by blocking the mu-opioid receptor leads to increased need for affiliation (Martel, Nevison, Simpson, & Keverne, 1995).

Although there are still missing pieces to the puzzle, evidence in humans indicates that tonic levels of endogenous opioid signaling may also be related to social connectedness. According to one line of work, when participants recalled a time of separation distress (e.g., the ending of a romantic relationship), endogenous opioid transmission decreased (Zubieta, Ketter, et al., 2003). Thus, imagined social pain decreases mu-opioid dependent signaling in humans, as in animal studies.

On the basis of the centrality of the mu-opioid receptor to social pain, the gene coding for this receptor is a logical starting place for identifying genetic contributors to social pain. Within the mu-opioid receptor gene (*OPRM1*) is a polymorphism (A118G) that influences the amount of receptor produced

(Zhang, Wang, Johnson, Papp, & Sadee, 2005). The less frequent G allele is associated with reduced receptor expression, relative to the A allele.

Preliminary analyses from our laboratory indicate that the G allele is associated with higher levels of self-reported rejection sensitivity (Mehrabian, 1994). At the physiological level, the G allele carriers also had greater increases in salivary cortisol responses during the Trier Social Stress Test, a laboratory procedure in which subjects perform mental arithmetic and give a speech in front of an unreceptive audience. These associations of the G allele with greater response to social threat were primarily limited to female subjects.

We have also recently assessed the relationship between the A118G polymorphism and social pain responses during a different laboratory measure of social pain. To study social exclusion within the confines of a magnetic resonance imaging scanner, researchers had participants play an online, virtual ball-tossing game in which the other players gradually exclude the participant (Williams & Jarvis, 2006). Previous research has found that this task induces feelings of rejection and invisibility, self-assessments that are positively correlated with neural activity in the dACC (Eisenberger, Lieberman, & Williams, 2003). Carriers of the G allele, relative to individuals with two copies of the A allele, exhibited greater anterior cingulate cortex (ACC) responses during social exclusion. Thus, across multiple measures of social pain, the G allele is associated with greater distress.

Further support for a role of the G allele in social-related distress comes from studies in the rhesus monkey. Fortunately, this species has a polymorphism (C177G) very similar to that of humans in the mu-opioid receptor (Miller et al., 2004). Infants with the rare G allele exhibit greater distress vocalization upon repeated separation from their mothers and also spend more time clinging to their mothers upon reunification (Barr et al., 2008). In addition, the G allele has also been associated with alterations in basal plasma cortisol concentrations (Miller et al., 2004). This commonality of effects across species strongly indicates that this polymorphism is indeed functional and has broad effects on social pain.

With respect to the physiological overlap between social pain and physical pain, the A118G polymorphism has also been linked to differences in responses to physical pain in laboratory paradigms (Fillingim et al., 2005), as well as to dosage of analgesic required in clinical patients (Lötsch & Geisslinger, 2006). Thus, in addition to evidence provided at the neurochemical and neuroanatomical levels, there is now genetic evidence supporting the overlap between physical pain and social pain. This multimethod convergence strongly indicates that physical pain and social pain share common foundations and that each field can serve as a source of hypotheses for the other.

In methodological terms, the genotyping approach for the study of social pain experience has several advantages over traditional neurochemical methods. For example, the required use of a positron emission tomography scanner to measure opioid levels has obvious methodological limitations, and the less invasive genotyping approach (only a saliva sample is required) creates the opportunity to study opioid involvement in a greater diversity of contexts and paradigms. Hence, genotyping methods can be a useful complement to traditional research methods and thereby facilitate a better understanding of which components of social pain are governed by the opioid system.

Monoamine Oxidase A and the Social Pain Experience

In addition to the opioids, other neural systems are also likely to influence the experience of social pain. To identify one of these additional systems, we used a slightly different theoretical approach than in the previous example that built on the overlap between physical pain and social pain. We hypothesized that chronic social pain and clinical depression are likely to share some common physiological underpinnings, and accordingly, the endogenous targets of antidepressant drugs may influence sensitivity to social pain. One such target is monoamine oxidase A (MAOA), an enzyme that breaks down neurochemicals such as serotonin and dopamine (Shih, Chen, & Ridd, 1999) and that is present in high concentrations within the anterior cingulate (Ginovart et al., 2006), a brain region closely associated with the distress of social pain (Eisenberger, Lieberman, & Williams, 2003).

Within the gene coding for MAOA, there is a particular form of variation (referred to as the MAOA-uVNTR) that is associated with differences in the production of MAOA (Sabol, Hu, & Hamer, 1998). Using the previously described social exclusion task in the scanner, our group found that the MAOA-uVNTR was associated with degree of exclusion-related neural activation, such that the individuals with the low expressing alleles had the greatest response within the portion of the dACC associated with self-reported distress (Eisenberger, Way, Taylor, Welch, & Lieberman, 2007). Thus, it appears that the MAOA gene also influences the degree of distress experienced in response to social exclusion.

In addition to providing a marker for individual differences in social pain, these data also provide an example of how genetics can help to clarify basic psychological processes. In epidemiological studies, men with the low expressing alleles of the MAOA-uVNTR are more likely to engage in aggressive and antisocial behavior than are men with the high expressing alleles, particularly when they had been exposed to maltreatment as a child (Caspi et al., 2002; Kim-Cohen et al., 2006). However, what is difficult to ascertain from epidemiological studies is the psychological pathways by which this polymorphism influences aggressive behavior. According to theories of aggression (e.g., Buss, 1961), men with low expressing alleles may be more aggressive either because of a callous indifference to the suffering of others or because of a proclivity to overreact to social slights. In support of the latter social hypersensitivity hypothesis, our group found that both men and women with the low expressing alleles reported higher trait aggression and higher levels of trait interpersonal hypersensitivity (e.g., "How bothered do you feel about your feelings being easily hurt?"). It is important to note that the relationship between genotype and trait aggression was mediated by the dACC response (Eisenberger, Way, Taylor, Welch, & Lieberman, 2007). Thus, in light of the well-documented link between rejection and aggression (Leary, Twenge, & Quinlivan, 2006), it appears that those with a genotype predisposing them to feel greater social pain are also more likely to behave aggressively, and this proclivity to reactive aggression appears to be due to hypersensitivity to social slights. The ability to study correlates of the same biological marker in both laboratory and epidemiological investigations is another benefit of the genetic approach, and it is hoped that this integration will lead to improved understanding of the relationship between laboratory experiences of social pain and responses to real-world events.

Dopamine, Catechol-O-methyltransferase, and Social Pain

One of the neurochemical systems influenced by the MAOA-uVNTR is the dopamine system (Ducci et al., 2006), and unlike most of the other neurochemical systems discussed in this chapter, it is possible to measure dopamine signaling in the human brain during social pain. Therefore, rather than using pharmacological evidence to derive hypotheses concerning candidate genes in the dopamine system involved in social pain, one can use neurochemical evidence. Using a modified Trier Social Stress Test, researchers have found that the magnitude of the cortisol response to social threat is positively correlated with the magnitude of dopamine released in the striatum, as measured either during the actual stressor (Pruessner, Champagne, Meaney, & Dagher, 2004) or on a separate occasion using a pharmacological probe (Wand et al., 2007).

In light of this relationship between dopamine signaling and pain in a socially evaluative context, it is logical to ask if variation in genes regulating dopamine signaling also affects these pain processes. One gene with potential for such a role is the COMT (catechol-O-methyltransferase) gene, which codes for an enzyme that regulates levels of dopamine in the synapse. A particular polymorphism in the COMT gene (val[158]met) leads to two different alleles that appear to affect activity of the COMT enzyme (Lotta et al., 1995). The reduced activity of the met allele is thought to lead to higher synaptic levels of dopamine, because the enzyme is less able to metabolize the neurotransmitter. Consistent with the evidence found for dopamine signaling during social stress, individuals with two copies of the met allele (met/met) have been found to have greater subjective and hormonal responses to social evaluative threat than do individuals with other allele combinations (Jabbi et al., 2007).

In terms of other situations eliciting social pain, our group did not find a relationship between COMT val^{158}met and the magnitude of dACC response to social exclusion. Thus, it is possible that COMT is associated only with particular types of social pain experiences. On the other hand, the lack of an effect could be due to recently identified complexity in the COMT gene. Polymorphisms in the vicinity of COMT val^{158}met also influence COMT activity (Nackley et al., 2006). Accounting for the effects of these additional polymorphisms has helped to clarify the relationship between COMT and physical pain (Diatchenko et al., 2006), so it may also prove useful to incorporate these additional markers into future social pain studies.

Although clarifying the role of COMT in pain processes requires more work at the genetic level, a psychological perspective may also help to clarify this relationship. There is an extensive overlap between anxiety levels and the experience of physical pain (Tsao, Lu, Kim, & Zeltzer, 2006). The COMT val^{158}met polymorphism has been linked to various anxiety-related constructs, with the bulk of the studies associating the met allele with heightened anxiety, particularly in women (Enoch, Xu, Ferro, Harris, & Goldman, 2003; Olsson et al., 2005). These studies have also been supported by functional neuroimaging studies, which show that met allele carriers have stronger responses to anxiety-eliciting stimuli within limbic brain areas than do individuals with two copies of the val allele (Drabant et al., 2006; Smolka et al., 2005). This influence of the met allele on anxiety suggests that social and physical pain studies of COMT should incorporate anxiety-related measures because at least part of the effect of COMT on physical and social pain may be attributable to the propensity of anxious people to construe their circumstances as painful. Thus, these data underscore the valuable contributions that psychological perspectives can make to genetic studies.

It is worth noting that although we have discussed each gene and its corresponding neurochemical system separately for the purpose of conceptual clarity, extensive interaction among them is likely. This has been best demonstrated with respect to COMT and the opioid system. For example, the COMT val^{158}met genotype is correlated with the degree of mu-opioid-related peptide release in response to sustained pain. Not only did met/met individuals have the highest negative affect in response to pain induction, but they also had the least endogenous activation of mu-opioid signaling (Zubieta, Heitzeg, et al., 2003). In addition, met/met individuals exhibited the greatest cortisol release in response to blockade of the mu-opioid receptor (Oswald, McCaul, Choi, Yang, & Wand, 2004). Similarly, COMT val^{158}met genotype also affects morphine dosage requirements (Rakvåg et al., 2005; Reyes-Gibby et al., 2007). Thus, there are multiple psychological and neurochemical routes by which opioids in conjunction with COMT affect social pain. The ability to assess such interactions between multiple neurochemical systems has been greatly facilitated by genotyping methodologies because multiple systems can be probed more readily than has been possible with traditional neurochemical or pharmacological methodologies.

The COMT and OPRM1 genes also point to an additional consideration that is likely to be of importance in genetic studies of social pain: sex differences. On the basis of findings in the physical pain literature (Craft, Mogil, & Aloisi, 2004), it has been hypothesized that sex differences in pain sensitivity may not be just the result of different levels of activity in a common pain system, but rather may reflect different genetic organizations of the pain system in the two sexes. Thus, different sets of genes may be involved in social pain for women than for men. For example, most of the associations of COMT val[158]met with physical pain and anxiety are limited to women (Diatchenko et al., 2005; Enoch, Xu, Ferro, Harris, & Goldman, 2003; Hagen, Pettersen, Stovner, Skorpen, & Zwart, 2006; Kim, Mittal, Iadarola, & Dionne, 2006; Olsson et al., 2005). In addition, although evidence is still preliminary, there may be opposite effects of the OPRM1 A118G polymorphism in males and females, with the presence of the G allele being associated with reduced pain sensitivity in males and heightened sensitivity in females (Fillingim et al., 2005). Consistent with this latter finding, our preliminary data discussed earlier indicate that women, but not men, with the G allele exhibit greater increases in cortisol during social evaluative threat. Moreover, Chong et al. (2006) found in a primarily male sample that the G allele was associated with blunted cortisol responses during the same social stressor. Thus, the genetic approach may reveal that the pain system in the two sexes is constructed differently, which is an observation that would have been unlikely to have been made on the basis of behavioral data alone.

Social Support

One of the most critical influences on the social pain experience is likely to be social support. High levels of daily social support are correlated with lower levels of dACC activation during a social exclusion experience and lower cortisol release during an experience of social evaluative threat, indicating a blunting effect of social support on social pain (Eisenberger, Taylor, Gable, Hilmert, & Lieberman, 2007). Consistent with the overlap between social and physical pain, social support also blunts the experience of physical pain in clinical conditions (Zaza & Baine, 2002) as well as in experimental studies (Brown, Sheffield, Leary, & Robinson, 2003).

A neurochemical system likely to affect social support is the serotonin system. For example, free-ranging rhesus monkeys with higher levels of central serotonin, as measured by metabolites in the cerebrospinal fluid, are more "popular." They spend more time grooming and in the vicinity of other monkeys and have more monkeys sitting close to them than do monkeys with low central serotonin levels (Mehlman et al., 1995). Similarly, in humans, pharmacological facilitation of serotonin signaling can increase affiliative behavior (Knutson et al., 1998; Tse & Bond, 2002) and agreeableness (aan het Rot, Moskowitz, Pinard, & Young, 2006). As these studies require rather invasive methodologies (spinal tap or drug administration, respectively), progress in understanding the physiology of social support processes is likely to be aided by the less invasive genotyping approach. With this methodology, genetic variation in the serotonin system has been associated with social popularity in humans. In specific terms, variation in the serotonin 2A receptor gene (HTR2A G-1438A) has been linked to sociometric ratings after participants work together on cooperative tasks (Burt, 2008). Participants were liked better if they were homozygous for the G allele. Thus, these individuals may be better able to recruit social support, which may diminish both their vulnerability to and their subjective experience of social pain.

Another gene that may be related to the ability to develop social networks is the dopamine 4 receptor gene (DRD4). In a recent meta-analysis (Munafò, Yalcin, Willis-Owen, & Flint, 2008), allelic variation in DRD4 was associated with novelty seeking, a psychological construct closely related to extraversion. Thus, DRD4 variation may influence the establishment of social networks by affecting behavioral and social approach in novel situations. The relationship between this polymorphism and approach-related traits appears to be fairly robust, as the association has been made across multiple species, including monkeys, horses, dogs, and birds (Bailey, Breidenthal, Jorgensen, McCracken, & Fairbanks, 2007; Fidler et al., 2007; Hejjas et al., 2007; Ito et al., 2004; Momozawa, Takeuchi, Kusunose, Kikusui, & Mori, 2005).

Neuroticism, characterized by chronic negative affect, also appears to influence the construal of social circumstances as painful or supportive. Higher levels of neuroticism are associated with a propensity to experience multiple forms of social pain (MacDonald & Leary, 2005) as well as physical pain (Wade, Dougherty, Hart, Rafii, & Price, 1992). A meta-analysis revealed a small effect of the short allele of a polymorphism in the serotonin transporter gene (5-HTTLPR) on higher levels of neuroticism (Schinka, Busch, & Robichaux-Keene, 2004). However, attempts to identify other reliable genetic correlates of neuroticism with larger effect sizes have been unsuccessful (Shifman et al., 2008).

Oxytocin and Vasopressin

In addition to genes related to the serotonin, dopamine, and opioid systems, polymorphisms in the oxytocin (OT) and vasopressin (AVP) systems may be associated with both social affiliation and pain experiences. At present, the specific roles of oxytocin and vasopressin in social pain and support have not been clearly elucidated in humans, and little is known about which genes within these systems are associated with social processes. Thus, our discussion of the genetic bases of these systems has a greater focus on animal models and is more conjectural than has been true for the discussions in other sections.

Elevated plasma OT may be a signal of social pain, as both human (Taylor, Gonzaga, et al., 2006; Turner, Altemus, Enos, Cooper, & McGuinness, 1999) and animal (Grippo et al., 2007) studies have found that elevations in OT accompany social isolation or deficits in social contacts. This elevation may act as a biological signal that prompts affiliative activity. Both exogenous administration of OT and endogenous OT have also been tied to a broad array of affiliative activities. For example, OT has been related to increases in physical proximity, maternal behavior, grooming, and preferences for familiar conspecifics in multiple animal studies (e.g., Carter, 1998; Carter, Lederhendler, & Kirkpatrick, 1997). Thus, paradoxically, increases in OT have been found in conjunction with both social pain–isolation and affiliation–support experiences. Further research is needed to clarify these effects, and the use of genetic methodologies is likely to be a valuable approach toward this end.

Consistent with a role for OT genes in social processes, deletion of the gene responsible for making OT prevents mice from developing social memory (Ferguson et al., 2000). Infant OT knockout mice are deficient in vocalization following separation from their mother and, as adults, show more aggression in isolation-induced and resident-intruder tests of aggression (Winslow et al., 2000). Thus, the absence of exposure to oxytocin during development appears to lead to abnormalities in socioemotional behavior (Winslow et al., 2000). In humans, variation in the OT receptor gene (OXTR) has been tied to social behavior. Carriers of the A allele of a single nucleotide polymorphism (rs 53576) are at heightened risk of autism (Wu et al., 2005) as well as insensitive parenting (Bakermans-Kranenburg & Van IJzendoorn, 2008).

The vasopressin system may also be involved in social affiliation. For example, transfer of the vasopressin 1A receptor gene has been found to enhance male social affiliation in animal studies (Keverne & Curley, 2004). In humans, a polymorphism within the vasopressin 1A receptor gene (AVPR1A) has recently been identified and appears to be related to empathy and altruistic behavior (Bachner-Melman et al., 2005; Knafo et al., 2008). Hence, this polymorphism provides an opportunity to examine the role of the human vasopressin system in social pain and support and determine if findings in animal models translate to humans.

MODERATION OF GENETIC ASSOCIATIONS WITH
SOCIAL PAIN BY THE ENVIRONMENT

Up to this point, we have largely been discussing unidirectional effects of genetic variation on the dependent measures. However, one of the key advances made possible by the genotyping approach is the ability to study the interaction of life experience and markers of neurochemical function. One of the most salient environmental influences on emotionality and social behavior across the life span is the harshness or nurturance of the early environment (e.g., Liu et al., 1997; Repetti, Taylor, & Seeman, 2002). These social effects are moderated by many of the same polymorphisms already discussed.

One such polymorphism is in the regulatory region of the serotonin transporter gene (5-HTTLPR). People with two copies of the 5-HTTLPR short allele (short/short) who have experienced childhood maltreatment are more likely to be diagnosed with major depressive disorder than are individuals with one or two copies of the long allele who have experienced similar environments (Caspi et al., 2003; Kaufman et al., 2004). A study from our laboratory (Taylor, Way, et al., 2006) suggests that the short allele may function not only as a risk allele for depression in the face of an adverse environment but also as a general sensitivity allele, providing protection from symptoms of depression when the environment is nurturant. Using a non-clinical sample of 118 adult men and women, we assessed nurturance of the early family environment, depressive symptomatology, and 5-HTTLPR genotype. As expected, a stressful early family environment by itself was significantly related to depressive symptomatology. However, we also found that a significant gene-by-environment interaction between 5-HTTLPR and the nurturance of the early family environment qualified the risk of depression. In specific terms, individuals with two copies of the short allele had greater depressive symptomatology if they had experienced early familial adversity compared with participants with the short/long or long/long genotypes, but significantly less depressive symptomatology if they reported a supportive early environment. It is notable that the adverse early family environments studied were ones in which the degree of social pain was fairly mild, consisting of some conflict, moderate household chaos, or cold, unaffectionate, and distant behaviors, rather than explicit maltreatment in the form of physical or sexual abuse.

Of interest, this differential sensitivity to the environment does not appear to be limited to childhood; it is present in adulthood as well. Thus, people with the short/short genotype who reported being in a currently highly stressful environment had higher levels of depressive symptomatology relative to those with short/long or long/long variants, whereas those who reported currently being in a low-stress environment had significantly lower levels of depressive symptomatology. Reports of the early and current environment were only modestly correlated with each other, and so these results are fairly independent of each other. Thus, with respect to depressive symptoms, the short/short genotype appears to be risky in harsh environments but protective in nurturant environments. Consistent with this latter point, short/short individuals have been found to be more responsive to the protective effects of social support as well (Kaufman et al., 2004; Kilpatrick et al., 2007).

Thus, it appears that genetic variation affecting social pain may also affect responses to social support and nurturance, reflecting a sensitivity to the social environment in general, rather than just its negative aspects. Whether such influences on social sensitivity apply to all genes affecting social pain is not clear; however, a similar effect has been documented for the *DRD4* receptor gene (exon 3 VNTR) and externalizing behavior, as we discuss next.

As with early studies of environmental moderation of the effects of 5-HTTLPR, the initial focus of the *DRD4* studies was on interaction of variation in this gene with negative outcomes resulting from emotionally distant and insensitive parenting. Multiple research laboratories found that when exposed to nonnurturant parenting, people with a particular allele at this polymorphism (though not always the same allele) were at higher risk of either externalizing behaviors (Bakermans-Kranenburg & van IJzendoorn, 2006; Propper, Willoughby, Halpern, Carbone, & Cox, 2007) or high levels of novelty seeking (Keltikangas-Järvinen, Räikkönen, Ekelund, & Peltonen, 2004; Sheese, Voelker, Rothbart, & Posner, 2007) than were individuals with the other alleles. However, recent evidence indicates that the long allele may increase sensitivity to positive as well as negative parental influences. Thus, when the environment is nurturant, individuals with the long DRD4 allele had low levels of externalizing behavior, but when the environment was one of frequent social pain, individuals with the same allele had high levels of externalizing behavior. The behavior of individuals with the other alleles was less responsive to parenting quality (Bakermans-Kranenburg & van IJzendoorn, 2007).

Providing experimental support for the differential sensitivity hypothesis, Bakermans-Kranenburg and colleagues (2008) found that toddlers with the long allele were the most responsive to a parental educational program designed to reduce externalizing behavior through increasing the attentiveness of parenting. This finding is especially interesting for clinical researchers because it indicates that particular therapies may be more effective with people who have particular genotypes. Furthermore, it may even be worthwhile to specifically design and target therapies according to individual genotypes.

Findings such as these offer significant evidence that the social environment can powerfully shape genetic effects. For researchers, these data raise intriguing questions concerning the mechanisms by which social pain and the *DRD4* and 5-HTTLPR variants affect lasting changes in behavior. There are multiple possibilities. One is that because the 5-HTTLPR polymorphism lies within the upstream regulatory region of the serotonin transporter gene, it is poised to modulate transporter expression in response to environmental factors, including social ones. Over time, such changes could lead to alterations in the structure of the brain, particularly in areas such as the anterior cingulate cortex, are integral to social pain processes. Stressful early-life experiences, most of which involve social pain, appear to reduce the volume of the ACC in adulthood (Cohen et al., 2006). Although such sequelae of social pain have never been analyzed in combination with genetics, the ACC is likely to be a neural site of gene-by-environment interaction because the 5-HTTLPR (Pezawas et al., 2005), DRD4 exon 3 VNTR (Shaw et al., 2007), and MAOA-uVNTR (Meyer-Lindenberg, Buckholtz, et al., 2006) have all been shown to relate to ACC volume.

Thus, variation in these genes may affect sensitivity to the social environment by setting the degree to which neural networks are under environmental control. In a nurturant family environment, synaptic connectivity would flourish, leading to a richly connected neural network that might, for example, yield better emotion regulation capabilities. Conversely, in an environment of social pain, there would be less synaptic integration, which would presumably lead to diminished emotion regulation capabilities.

In addition to environmental moderation of genetic influences, the maternal environment can also induce lasting changes in the function of genes, which is an additional mechanism by which experiences of social pain can induce long-term behavioral alterations. In animal studies, Meaney and colleagues have shown that rat pups exposed to highly nurturant mothering show less emotionality to novel circumstances and more normative social behavior including mothering in adulthood, compared with recipients of normal mothering (Francis, Diorio, Liu, & Meaney, 1999; Weaver et al., 2004). Studies with monkeys have shown similar effects. For example, Suomi (1987) reported that highly reactive monkeys cross-fostered to nurturant mothers develop good socioemotional skills and achieve high status in the dominance hierarchy, whereas monkeys with reactive temperaments who are peer-raised develop poor socioemotional skills and end up at the bottom of the dominance hierarchy.

Such long-term effects of maternal care appear to be a result of epigenetic structural alterations (methylation) to the glucocorticoid receptor gene that occur in the first week after birth and affect its expression throughout the life span (Meaney & Szyf, 2005). This process is affected by each of the neurochemical systems discussed in this chapter, and thus polymorphisms in these systems that affect signaling are likely to have downstream effects on this process. Mothers showing high levels of nurturant behavior exhibit greater increases in oxytocin receptors during pregnancy, which is thought to trigger maternal responsivity (Meaney, 2001), and have higher levels of dopamine release when caring for their pups (Champagne et al., 2004). This more nurturant mothering triggers greater increases in serotonin turnover in the pup, which initiates the cascade leading to the altered glucocorticoid receptor expression that affects adulthood reactivity to stress (Meaney & Szyf, 2005). Identifying the specific manner in which the genetic variants discussed in this chapter affect such processes will be a productive area for future research.

CONCLUSIONS

The study of genetic factors in the experience of social pain is in its infancy, yet several variants have been identified that are likely to influence individual differences in response to social pain. Each of the discussed variants appears to be involved in physical pain as well, supporting the hypothesis that the distressing aspects of physical and social pain share similar physiological underpinnings. The identification of these variants was a result of hypotheses developed from prior neurochemical studies, which we believe are likely to be a useful means of identifying future variants affecting social pain.

A key advantage of the genetic approach is that its easy-to-use methodology provides the opportunity to examine how genes affect responses to life experiences outside the laboratory. In particular, variation within each of the genes described in this chapter influences individual sensitivity to the environment, either amplifying or dampening the effects of experience. Far from being a deterministic process, genetic influences on psychological end points reflect an interaction with environment variables.

As should be clear from this discussion, not all genes implicated in social pain may be specific for the experience of social pain; rather, genes that more generally predispose to psychological and social distress, such as those implicated in anxiety, neuroticism, and depression, may be involved as well. As such, these genes may exert their effects on the experience of social pain by affecting the ability to develop social skills, extract social support from others, and construe the social environment as a beneficent one.

Although we have advocated for the merits of the genetic approach in this chapter, there are methodological problems involved in linking genetic variation directly to the experiences of social pain or social support. A principal one concerns insufficient understanding of the molecular mechanisms by which polymorphisms, particularly the interacting effects of adjacent polymorphisms, affect the function of proteins and thus the function of neurons and neural circuits. In addition, the small effect sizes involved with any one particular variant, as well as heterogeneity in the methods used to evaluate the relations of genetic and psychological factors, are also problems with studies conducted to date. Complex phenotypes typically show small relations to specific genes, and so methodological differences between studies can obscure the relations between polymorphisms and psychological characteristics. Moreover, complex phenotypes are likely to be influenced by several, perhaps many, genes, and efforts to tie a phenotype to a particular gene may thus be hampered by not knowing about and controlling for the other genes involved. Genetic heterogeneity within a population also represents a difficulty because many of the samples that researchers recruit are multiethnic, and even efforts to explore relations within ethnically homogeneous samples may nonetheless include substantial heterogeneity. In light of these factors, it is prudent to treat results of the genetic association studies reported here cautiously until multiple replications have been performed.

Several factors, however, provide bases for optimism, particularly with respect to the phenotype of social pain. First, experiences of social pain can be reliably induced in the laboratory and in neuroimaging studies, rendering the phenomenon highly tractable to controlled experimentation. Second, social pain is continuously distributed (unlike most disease processes that are defined categorically; e.g., affected or unaffected). This makes the social pain experience sensitive to detecting genetic effects because normal allelic variation most likely influences position of the phenotype within a continuous distribution (Plomin, 2003). Although studying extremes of phenotypes (e.g., people diagnosed with depression or anxiety disorders) has been used as a method to try to address genetic bases of social pain, in so doing, investigators may inadvertently restrict the range of psychological characteristics. In such a case, true effects or interactions with environmental factors can be obscured (for a discussion of this issue, see Taylor, Way, et al., 2006).

For the genetic approach to work to full advantage, it will be necessary to have a narrowly defined phenotype. Because of the infancy of the field, we have deliberately used a broad definition of social pain and focused on genetic variation that is likely to be common to different subtypes of social pain. However, in the future, genes that are involved in different subtypes of social pain may be identified. For example, social evaluative threat may involve genetic mediators that are somewhat different from those involved in separation distress.

In the future, incorporating a genetic approach into the study of social pain not only will improve understanding of the neurochemical systems influencing social pain but is also likely to generate new conceptual insights into the process of social pain. Thus, as each additional gene becomes linked to social pain, social pain then becomes associated with other traits or psychological processes associated with this gene. Just as associating social pain with physical pain has been a rich source of hypotheses, associating social pain with these as yet unknown processes could function like a psychological Rosetta stone, providing new theories about social pain.

Although this chapter has centered on deriving genetic hypotheses from neurochemical data, one of the great advantages of the new genetic technologies is the opportunity to go beyond previous neurochemically derived hypotheses to discover new genes and pathways involved in social pain. One approach to doing so is by studying rare disorders related to physical and social pain, such as Williams syndrome, congenital indifference to pain, and autism. For example, Williams syndrome is characterized by excessively friendly behavior and an apparently reduced capacity to experience social pain (Meyer-Lindenberg, Mervis, & Berman, 2006). Identifying the particular deleted genes that cause excessive gregariousness will help determine if these genes are related to normal variation in social pain processes.

An additional way to identify novel genes involved in social pain is through large-scale studies that sample the entire genome in a non-hypothesis-driven manner. Such whole-genome association studies have recently successfully identified many disease genes and are likely to be influential in studying normal variation in physiological processes as well (McCarthy et al., 2008).

It is clear that the next decades will greatly advance the understanding of the genetic contributions to social pain. As the field unfolds, some of the suggestions and concerns offered here may prove to be misplaced. That is an inherent risk of reviewing a field that is in its early stages. Nonetheless, the effort to bring coherence to these diverse investigations is a first step to pointing researchers in useful directions for future discoveries.

REFERENCES

aan het Rot, M., Moskowitz, D. S., Pinard, G., & Young, S. N. (2006). Social behaviour and mood in everyday life: The effects of tryptophan in quarrelsome individuals. *Journal of Psychiatry and Neuroscience, 31,* 253–262.

Bachner-Melman, R., Dina, C., Zohar, A. H., Constantini, N., Lerer, E., Hoch, S., . . . Ebstein, R. (2005). AVPR1a and SLC6A4 gene polymorphisms are associated with creative dance performance. *Public Library of Science: Genetics, 1,* e42.

Bailey, J. N., Breidenthal, S. E., Jorgensen, M. J., McCracken, J. T., & Fairbanks, L. A. (2007). The association of DRD4 and novelty seeking is found in a nonhuman primate model. *Psychiatric Genetics, 17,* 23–27. doi:10.1097/YPG.0b013e32801140f2

Bakermans-Kranenburg, M. J., & van IJzendoorn, M. H. (2006). Gene-environment interaction of the dopamine D4 receptor (DRD4) and observed maternal insensitivity predicting externalizing behavior in preschoolers. *Developmental Psychobiology, 48,* 406–409. doi:10.1002/dev.20152

Bakermans-Kranenburg, M. J., & van IJzendoorn, M. H. (2007). Research review: Genetic vulnerability or differential susceptibility in child development: The case of attachment. *Journal of Child Psychology and Psychiatry, and Allied Disciplines, 48,* 1160–1173. doi:10.1111/j.1469-7610.2007.01801.x

Bakermans-Kranenburg, M. J., van IJzendoorn, M. H., Pijlman, F. T., Mesman, J., & Juffer, F. (2008). Experimental evidence for differential susceptibility: Dopamine D4 receptor polymorphism (DRD4 VNTR) moderates intervention effects on toddlers' externalizing behavior in a randomized controlled trial. *Developmental Psychology, 44*, 293–300. doi:10.1037/0012-1649.44.1.293

Bakermans-Kranenburg, M. J., & van IJzendoorn, M. H. (2008). Oxytocin receptor (OXTR) and serotonin transporter (5-HTT) genes associated with observed parenting. *Social Cognitive and Affective Neuroscience, 3*, 128–134.

Barr, C. S., Schwandt, M. L., Lindell, S. G., Higley, J. D., Maestripieri, D., Goldman, D., . . . Heilig, M. (2008). Variation at the mu-opioid receptor gene (OPRM1) influences attachment behavior in infant primates. *Proceedings of the National Academy of Sciences of the United States of America, 105*, 5277–5281. doi:10.1073/pnas.0710225105

Boomsma, D. I., Willemsen, G., Dolan, C. V., Hawkley, L. C., & Cacioppo, J. T. (2005). Genetic and environmental contributions to loneliness in adults: The Netherlands twin register study. *Behavior Genetics, 35*, 745–752. doi:10.1007/s10519-005-6040-8

Brown, J. L., Sheffield, D., Leary, M. R., & Robinson, M. E. (2003). Social support and experimental pain. *Psychosomatic Medicine, 65*, 276–283. doi:10.1097/01.PSY.0000030388.62434.46

Burt, S. A. (2008). Genes and popularity: Evidence of an evocative gene-environment correlation. *Psychological Science, 19*, 112–113. doi:10.1111/j.1467-9280.2008.02055.x

Buss, A. H. (1961). *The psychology of aggression*. New York, NY: Wiley. doi:10.1037/11160-000

Carter, C. S. (1998). Neuroendocrine perspectives on social attachment and love. *Psychoneuroendocrinology, 23*, 779–818. doi:10.1016/S0306-4530(98)00055-9

Carter, C. S., Lederhendler, I., & Kirkpatrick, B. (1997). The integrative neurobiology of affiliation. Introduction. *Annals of the New York Academy of Sciences, 807*, xiii–xviii. doi:10.1111/j.1749-6632.1997.tb51909.x

Caspi, A., McClay, J., Moffitt, T. E., Mill, J., Martin, J., Craig, I. W., . . . Poulton, R. (2002, August 2). Role of genotype in the cycle of violence in maltreated children. *Science, 297*, 851–854. doi:10.1126/science.1072290

Caspi, A., Sugden, K., Moffitt, T. E., Taylor, A., Craig, I. W., Harrington, H., . . . Poulton, R. (2003, July 18). Influence of life stress on depression: Moderation by a polymorphism in the 5-HTT gene. *Science, 301*, 386–389. doi:10.1126/science.1083968

Champagne, F. A., Chretien, P., Stevenson, C. W., Zhang, T. Y., Gratton, A., & Meaney, M. J. (2004). Variations in nucleus accumbens dopamine associated with individual differences in maternal behavior in the rat. *The Journal of Neuroscience, 24*, 4113–4123. doi:10.1523/JNEUROSCI.5322-03.2004

Chong, R. Y., Oswald, L., Yang, X., Uhart, M., Lin, P. I., & Wand, G. S. (2006). The micro-opioid receptor polymorphism A118G predicts cortisol responses to naloxone and stress. *Neuropsychopharmacology, 31,* 204–211.

Cohen, R. A., Grieve, S., Hoth, K. F., Paul, R. H., Sweet, L., Tate, D., . . . Williams, L. M. (2006). Early life stress and morphometry of the adult anterior cingulate cortex and caudate nuclei. *Biological Psychiatry, 59,* 975–982. doi:10.1016/j.biopsych.2005.12.016

Craft, R. M., Mogil, J. S., & Aloisi, A. M. (2004). Sex differences in pain and analgesia: The role of gonadal hormones. *European Journal of Pain, 8,* 397–411. doi:10.1016/j.ejpain.2004.01.003

Diatchenko, L., Nackley, A. G., Slade, G. D., Bhalang, K., Belfer, I., Max, M. B., . . . Maixner, W. (2006). Catechol-O-methyltransferase gene polymorphisms are associated with multiple pain-evoking stimuli. *Pain, 125,* 216–224. doi:10.1016/j.pain.2006.05.024

Diatchenko, L., Slade, G. D., Nackley, A. G., Bhalang, K., Sigurdsson, A., Belfer, I., . . . Maixner, W. (2005). Genetic basis for individual variations in pain perception and the development of a chronic pain condition. *Human Molecular Genetics, 14,* 135–143. doi:10.1093/hmg/ddi013

Drabant, E. M., Hariri, A. R., Meyer-Lindenberg, A., Munoz, K. E., Mattay, V. S., Kolachana, B. S., . . . Weinberger, D. R. (2006). Catechol O-methyltransferase val158met genotype and neural mechanisms related to affective arousal and regulation. *Archives of General Psychiatry, 63,* 1396–1406. doi:10.1001/archpsyc.63.12.1396

Ducci, F., Newman, T. K., Funt, S., Brown, G. L., Virkkunen, M., & Goldman, D. (2006). A functional polymorphism in the MAOA gene promoter (MAOA-LPR) predicts central dopamine function and body mass index. *Molecular Psychiatry, 11,* 858–866. doi:10.1038/sj.mp.4001856

Eisenberger, N. I., Lieberman, M. D., & Williams, K. D. (2003, October 10). Does rejection hurt? An FMRI study of social exclusion. *Science, 302,* 290–292. doi:10.1126/science.1089134

Eisenberger, N. I., Taylor, S. E., Gable, S. L., Hilmert, C. J., & Lieberman, M. D. (2007). Neural pathways link social support to attenuated neuroendocrine stress responses. *NeuroImage, 35,* 1601–1612. doi:10.1016/j.neuroimage.2007.01.038

Eisenberger, N. I., Way, B. M., Taylor, S. E., Welch, W. T., & Lieberman, M. D. (2007). Understanding genetic risk for aggression: Clues from the brain's response to social exclusion. *Biological Psychiatry, 61,* 1100–1108. doi:10.1016/j.biopsych.2006.08.007

Enoch, M. A., Xu, K., Ferro, E., Harris, C. R., & Goldman, D. (2003). Genetic origins of anxiety in women: A role for a functional catechol-O-methyltransferase polymorphism. *Psychiatric Genetics, 13,* 33–41. doi:10.1097/00041444-200303000-00006

Fanous, A., Gardner, C. O., Prescott, C. A., Cancro, R., & Kendler, K. S. (2002). Neuroticism, major depression and gender: A population-based twin study. *Psychological Medicine*, *32*, 719–728. doi:10.1017/S003329170200541X

Ferguson, J. N., Young, L. J., Hearn, E. F., Matzuk, M. M., Insel, T. R., & Winslow, J. T. (2000). Social amnesia in mice lacking the oxytocin gene. *Nature Genetics*, *25*, 284–288. doi:10.1038/77040

Fidler, A. E., van Oers, K., Drent, P. J., Kuhn, S., Mueller, J. C., & Kempenaers, B. (2007). DRD4 gene polymorphisms are associated with personality variation in a passerine bird. *Proceedings of the Royal Society B. Biological Sciences*, *274*, 1685–1691.

Fillingim, R. B., Kaplan, L., Staud, R., Ness, T. J., Glover, T. L., Campbell, C. M., . . . Wallace, M. R. (2005). The A118G single nucleotide polymorphism of the mu-opioid receptor gene (OPRM1) is associated with pressure pain sensitivity in humans. *The Journal of Pain*, *6*, 159–167. doi:10.1016/j.jpain.2004.11.008

Francis, D., Diorio, J., Liu, D., & Meaney, M. J. (1999, November 5). Nongenomic transmission across generations of maternal behavior and stress responses in the rat. *Science*, *286*, 1155–1158. doi:10.1126/science.286.5442.1155

Ginovart, N., Meyer, J. H., Boovariwala, A., Hussey, D., Rabiner, E. A., Houle, S., & Wilson, A. A. (2006). Positron emission tomography quantification of [11C]-harmine binding to monoamine oxidase-A in the human brain. *Journal of Cerebral Blood Flow and Metabolism*, *26*, 330–344. doi:10.1038/sj.jcbfm.9600197

Grippo, A. J., Gerena, D., Huang, J., Kumar, N., Shah, M., Ughreja, R., & Carter, C. S. (2007). Social isolation induces behavioral and neuroendocrine disturbances relevant to depression in female and male prairie voles. *Psychoneuroendocrinology*, *32*, 966–980. doi:10.1016/j.psyneuen.2007.07.004

Hagen, K., Pettersen, E., Stovner, L. J., Skorpen, F., & Zwart, J. A. (2006). The association between headache and Val158Met polymorphism in the catechol-O-methyltransferase gene: The HUNT Study. *The Journal of Headache and Pain*, *7*, 70–74. doi:10.1007/s10194-006-0281-7

Hejjas, K., Vas, J., Topal, J., Szantai, E., Ronai, Z., Szekely, A., . . . Miklosi, A. (2007). Association of polymorphisms in the dopamine D4 receptor gene and the activity-impulsivity endophenotype in dogs. *Animal Genetics*, *38*, 629–633.

Herman, B. H., & Panksepp, J. (1978). Effects of morphine and naloxone on separation distress and approach attachment: Evidence for opiate mediation of social affect. *Pharmacology, Biochemistry, and Behavior*, *9*, 213–220. doi:10.1016/0091-3057(78)90167-3

Ito, H., Nara, H., Inoue-Murayama, M., Shimada, M. K., Koshimura, A., Ueda, Y., . . . Ito, S. (2004). Allele frequency distribution of the canine dopamine receptor D4 gene exon III and I in 23 breeds. *Journal of Veterinary Medical Science*, *66*, 815–820. doi:10.1292/jvms.66.815

Jabbi, M., Kema, I. P., van der Pompe, G., te Meerman, G. J., Ormel, J., & den Boer, J. A. (2007). Catechol-o-methyltransferase polymorphism and susceptibility to major depressive disorder modulates psychological stress response. *Psychiatric Genetics*, *17*, 183–193. doi:10.1097/YPG.0b013e32808374df

Kaufman, J., Yang, B. Z., Douglas-Palumberi, H., Houshyar, S., Lipschitz, D., Krystal, J. H., & Gelernter, J. (2004). Social supports and serotonin transporter gene moderate depression in maltreated children. *Proceedings of the National Academy of Sciences of the United States of America, 101,* 17316–17321. doi:10.1073/pnas.0404376101

Keltikangas-Järvinen, L., Räikkönen, K., Ekelund, J., & Peltonen, L. (2004). Nature and nurture in novelty seeking. *Molecular Psychiatry, 9,* 308–311. doi:10.1038/sj.mp.4001433

Kendler, K. S. (2005). "A gene for . . .": the nature of gene action in psychiatric disorders. *The American Journal of Psychiatry, 162,* 1243–1252. doi:10.1176/appi.ajp.162.7.1243

Kessler, R. C., Kendler, K. S., Heath, A., Neale, M. C., & Eaves, L. J. (1992). Social support, depressed mood, and adjustment to stress: A genetic epidemiologic investigation. *Journal of Personality and Social Psychology, 62,* 257–272. doi:10.1037/0022-3514.62.2.257

Keverne, E. B., & Curley, J. P. (2004). Vasopressin, oxytocin and social behaviour. *Current Opinion in Neurobiology, 14,* 777–783. doi:10.1016/j.conb.2004.10.006

Keverne, E. B., Martensz, N. D., & Tuite, B. (1989). Beta-endorphin concentrations in cerebrospinal fluid of monkeys are influenced by grooming relationships. *Psychoneuroendocrinology, 14,* 155–161. doi:10.1016/0306-4530(89)90065-6

Kilpatrick, D. G., Koenen, K. C., Ruggiero, K. J., Acierno, R., Galea, S., Resnick, H. S., . . . Gelernter, J. (2007). The serotonin transporter genotype and social support and moderation of posttraumatic stress disorder and depression in hurricane-exposed adults. *The American Journal of Psychiatry, 164,* 1693–1699. doi:10.1176/appi.ajp.2007.06122007

Kim, H., Mittal, D. P., Iadarola, M. J., & Dionne, R. A. (2006). Genetic predictors for acute experimental cold and heat pain sensitivity in humans. *Journal of Medical Genetics, 43,* e40. doi:10.1136/jmg.2005.036079

Kim-Cohen, J., Caspi, A., Taylor, A., Williams, B., Newcombe, R., Craig, I. W., & Moffitt, T. E. (2006). MAOA, maltreatment, and gene-environment interaction predicting children's mental health: New evidence and a meta-analysis. *Molecular Psychiatry, 11,* 903–913. doi:10.1038/sj.mp.4001851

Knafo, A., Israel, S., Darvasi, A., Bachner-Melman, R., Uzefovsky, F., Cohen, L., . . . Ebstein, R. P. (2008). Individual differences in allocation of funds in the dictator game associated with length of the arginine vasopressin 1a receptor RS3 promoter region and correlation between RS3 length and hippocampal mRNA. *Genes, Brain & Behavior, 7,* 266–275. doi:10.1111/j.1601-183X.2007.00341.x

Knutson, B., Wolkowitz, O. M., Cole, S. W., Chan, T., Moore, E. A., Johnson, R. C., . . . Reus, V. I. (1998). Selective alteration of personality and social behavior by serotonergic intervention. *The American Journal of Psychiatry, 155,* 373–379.

Leary, M. R. (Ed.). (2005). Varieties of interpersonal rejection. In K. D. Williams, J. P. Forgas, & W. von Hippel (Eds.), *The social outcast: Ostracism, social exclusion, rejection, and bullying* (pp. 35–52). New York, NY: Psychology Press.

Leary, M. R., Twenge, J. M., & Quinlivan, E. (2006). Interpersonal rejection as a determinant of anger and aggression. *Personality and Social Psychology Review, 10*, 111–132. doi:10.1207/s15327957pspr1002_2

Liu, D., Diorio, J., Tannenbaum, B., Caldji, C., Francis, D., Freedman, A., . . . Meaney, M. J. (1997, September 12). Maternal care, hippocampal glucocorticoid receptors, and hypothalamic-pituitary-adrenal responses to stress. *Science, 277*, 1659–1662. doi:10.1126/science.277.5332.1659

Lötsch, J., & Geisslinger, G. (2006). Current evidence for a genetic modulation of the response to analgesics. *Pain, 121*, 1–5. doi:10.1016/j.pain.2006.01.010

Lotta, T., Vidgren, J., Tilgmann, C., Ulmanen, I., Melen, K., Julkunen, I., & Taskinen, J. (1995). Kinetics of human soluble and membrane-bound catechol O-methyltransferase: A revised mechanism and description of the thermolabile variant of the enzyme. *Biochemistry, 34*, 4202–4210. doi:10.1021/bi00013a008

MacDonald, G., & Leary, M. R. (2005). Why does social exclusion hurt? The relationship between social and physical pain. *Psychological Bulletin, 131*, 202–223. doi:10.1037/0033-2909.131.2.202

Martel, F. L., Nevison, C. M., Simpson, M. J., & Keverne, E. B. (1995). Effects of opioid receptor blockade on the social behavior of rhesus monkeys living in large family groups. *Developmental Psychobiology, 28*, 71–84. doi:10.1002/dev.420280202

McCarthy, M. I., Abecasis, G. R., Cardon, L. R., Goldstein, D. B., Little, J., Ioannidis, J. P., & Hirschhorn, J. N. (2008). Genome-wide association studies for complex traits: Consensus, uncertainty and challenges. *Nature Reviews. Genetics, 9*, 356–369. doi:10.1038/nrg2344

Meaney, M. J. (2001). Maternal care, gene expression, and the transmission of individual differences in stress reactivity across generations. *Annual Review of Neuroscience, 24*, 1161–1192. doi:10.1146/annurev.neuro.24.1.1161

Meaney, M. J., & Szyf, M. (2005). Environmental programming of stress responses through DNA methylation: Life at the interface between a dynamic environment and a fixed genome. *Dialogues in Clinical Neuroscience, 7*, 103–123.

Mehlman, P. T., Higley, J. D., Faucher, I., Lilly, A. A., Taub, D. M., Vickers, J., . . . Linnoila, M. (1995). Correlation of CSF 5-HIAA concentration with sociality and the timing of emigration in free-ranging primates. *The American Journal of Psychiatry, 152*, 907–913.

Mehrabian, A. (1994). Evidence bearing on the Affiliative Tendency (MAFF) and Sensitivity to Rejection (MSR) scales. *Current Psychology, 13*, 97–116. doi:10.1007/BF02686794

Meyer-Lindenberg, A., Buckholtz, J. W., Kolachana, B., Hariri, A. R., Pezawas, L., Blasi, G., . . . Weinberger, D. R. (2006). Neural mechanisms of genetic risk for impulsivity and violence in humans. *Proceedings of the National Academy of Sciences of the United States of America, 103*, 6269–6274. doi:10.1073/pnas.0511311103

Meyer-Lindenberg, A., Mervis, C. B., & Berman, K. F. (2006). Neural mechanisms in Williams syndrome: A unique window to genetic influences on cognition and behaviour. *Nature Reviews. Neuroscience, 7*, 380–393. doi:10.1038/nrn1906

Miller, G. M., Bendor, J., Tiefenbacher, S., Yang, H., Novak, M. A., & Madras, B. K. (2004). A mu-opioid receptor single nucleotide polymorphism in rhesus monkey: Association with stress response and aggression. *Molecular Psychiatry, 9,* 99–108. doi:10.1038/sj.mp.4001378

Momozawa, Y., Takeuchi, Y., Kusunose, R., Kikusui, T., & Mori, Y. (2005). Association between equine temperament and polymorphisms in dopamine D4 receptor gene. *Mammalian Genome, 16,* 538–544. doi:10.1007/s00335-005-0021-3

Munafò, M. R., Yalcin, B., Willis-Owen, S. A., & Flint, J. (2008). Association of the dopamine D4 receptor (DRD4) gene and approach-related personality traits: Meta-analysis and new data. *Biological Psychiatry, 63,* 197–206. doi:10.1016/j.biopsych.2007.04.006

Nackley, A. G., Shabalina, S. A., Tchivileva, I. E., Satterfield, K., Korchynskyi, O., Makarov, S. S., . . . Diatchenko, L. (2006, December 22). Human catechol-O-methyltransferase haplotypes modulate protein expression by altering mRNA secondary structure. *Science, 314,* 1930–1933. doi:10.1126/science.1131262

Olsson, C. A., Anney, R. J., Lotfi-Miri, M., Byrnes, G. B., Williamson, R., & Patton, G. C. (2005). Association between the COMT Val158Met polymorphism and propensity to anxiety in an Australian population-based longitudinal study of adolescent health. *Psychiatric Genetics, 15,* 109–115. doi:10.1097/00041444-200506000-00007

Oswald, L. M., McCaul, M., Choi, L., Yang, X., & Wand, G. S. (2004). Catechol-O-methyltransferase polymorphism alters hypothalamic-pituitary-adrenal axis responses to naloxone: A preliminary report. *Biological Psychiatry, 55,* 102–105. doi:10.1016/j.biopsych.2003.07.003

Panksepp, J. (1998). *Affective neuroscience.* New York, NY: Oxford University Press.

Pezawas, L., Meyer-Lindenberg, A., Drabant, E. M., Verchinski, B. A., Munoz, K. E., Kolachana, B. S., . . . Weinberger, D. R. (2005). 5-HTTLPR polymorphism impacts human cingulate-amygdala interactions: A genetic susceptibility mechanism for depression. *Nature Neuroscience, 8,* 828–834. doi:10.1038/nn1463

Plomin, R. (2003). *Genes and behaviour: Cognitive abilities and disabilities in normal populations.* New York, NY: Cambridge University Press.

Propper, C., Willoughby, M., Halpern, C. T., Carbone, M. A., & Cox, M. (2007). Parenting quality, DRD4, and the prediction of externalizing and internalizing behaviors in early childhood. *Developmental Psychobiology, 49,* 619–632. doi:10.1002/dev.20249

Pruessner, J. C., Champagne, F., Meaney, M. J., & Dagher, A. (2004). Dopamine release in response to a psychological stress in humans and its relationship to early life maternal care: A positron emission tomography study using [11C]raclopride. *The Journal of Neuroscience, 24,* 2825–2831. doi:10.1523/JNEUROSCI.3422-03.2004

Rakvåg, T. T., Klepstad, P., Baar, C., Kvam, T. M., Dale, O., Kaasa, S., . . . Skorpen, F. (2005). The Val158Met polymorphism of the human catechol-O-methyltransferase (COMT) gene may influence morphine requirements in cancer pain patients. *Pain, 116,* 73–78. doi:10.1016/j.pain.2005.03.032

Repetti, R. L., Taylor, S. E., & Seeman, T. E. (2002). Risky families: Family social environments and the mental and physical health of offspring. *Psychological Bulletin, 128,* 330–366. doi:10.1037/0033-2909.128.2.330

Reyes-Gibby, C. C., Shete, S., Rakvåg, T., Bhat, S. V., Skorpen, F., Bruera, E., . . . Klepstad, P. (2007). Exploring joint effects of genes and the clinical efficacy of morphine for cancer pain: OPRM1 and COMT gene. *Pain, 130,* 25–30. doi:10.1016/j.pain.2006.10.023

Robinson, T. R. (2005). *Genetics for dummies.* Hoboken, NJ: Wiley.

Sabol, S. Z., Hu, S., & Hamer, D. (1998). A functional polymorphism in the monoamine oxidase A gene promoter. *Human Genetics, 103,* 273–279. doi:10.1007/s004390050816

Schinka, J. A., Busch, R. M., & Robichaux-Keene, N. (2004). A meta-analysis of the association between the serotonin transporter gene polymorphism (5-HTTLPR) and trait anxiety. *Molecular Psychiatry, 9,* 197–202. doi:10.1038/sj.mp.4001405

Shaw, P., Gornick, M., Lerch, J., Addington, A., Seal, J., Greenstein, D., . . . Rapoport, J. L. (2007). Polymorphisms of the dopamine D4 receptor, clinical outcome, and cortical structure in attention-deficit/hyperactivity disorder. *Archives of General Psychiatry, 64,* 921–931. doi:10.1001/archpsyc.64.8.921

Sheese, B. E., Voelker, P. M., Rothbart, M. K., & Posner, M. I. (2007). Parenting quality interacts with genetic variation in dopamine receptor D4 to influence temperament in early childhood. *Development and Psychopathology, 19,* 1039–1046. doi:10.1017/S0954579407000521

Shifman, S., Bhomra, A., Smiley, S., Wray, N. R., James, M. R., Martin, N. G., . . . Flint, J. (2008). A whole genome association study of neuroticism using DNA pooling. *Molecular Psychiatry, 13,* 302–312. doi:10.1038/sj.mp.4002048

Shih, J. C., Chen, K., & Ridd, M. J. (1999). Monoamine oxidase: From genes to behavior. *Annual Review of Neuroscience, 22,* 197–217. doi:10.1146/annurev.neuro.22.1.197

Smolka, M. N., Schumann, G., Wrase, J., Grusser, S. M., Flor, H., Mann, K., . . . Heinz, A. (2005). Catechol-O-methyltransferase val158met genotype affects processing of emotional stimuli in the amygdala and prefrontal cortex. *The Journal of Neuroscience, 25,* 836–842. doi:10.1523/JNEUROSCI.1792-04.2005

Suomi, S. J. (1987). Genetic and maternal contributions to individual differences in rhesus monkey biobehavioral development. In N. A. Krasnagor, E. M. Blass, M. A. Hofer, & W. P. Smotherman (Eds.), *Perinatal development: A psychobiological perspective* (pp. 397–419). New York, NY: Academic Press.

Taylor, S. E., Gonzaga, G. C., Klein, L. C., Hu, P., Greendale, G. A., & Seeman, T. E. (2006). Relation of oxytocin to psychological stress responses and hypothalamic-pituitary-adrenocortical axis activity in older women. *Psychosomatic Medicine, 68,* 238–245. doi:10.1097/01.psy.0000203242.95990.74

Taylor, S. E., Way, B. M., Welch, W. T., Hilmert, C. J., Lehman, B. J., & Eisenberger, N. I. (2006). Early family environment, current adversity, the serotonin transporter promoter polymorphism, and depressive symptomatology. *Biological Psychiatry, 60,* 671–676. doi:10.1016/j.biopsych.2006.04.019

Tsao, J. C., Lu, Q., Kim, S. C., & Zeltzer, L. K. (2006). Relationships among anxious symptomatology, anxiety sensitivity and laboratory pain responsivity in children. *Cognitive Behaviour Therapy, 35,* 207–215. doi:10.1080/16506070600898272

Tse, W. S., & Bond, A. J. (2002). Serotonergic intervention affects both social dominance and affiliative behaviour. *Psychopharmacology, 161,* 324–330. doi:10.1007/s00213-002-1049-7

Turner, R. A., Altemus, M., Enos, T., Cooper, B., & McGuinness, T. (1999). Preliminary research on plasma oxytocin in normal cycling women: Investigating emotion and interpersonal distress. *Psychiatry: Interpersonal and Biological Processes, 62,* 97–113.

Wade, J. B., Dougherty, L. M., Hart, R. P., Rafii, A., & Price, D. D. (1992). A canonical correlation analysis of the influence of neuroticism and extraversion on chronic pain, suffering, and pain behavior. *Pain, 51,* 67–73. doi:10.1016/0304-3959(92)90010-9

Wand, G. S., Oswald, L. M., McCaul, M. E., Wong, D. F., Johnson, E., Zhou, Y., . . . Kumar, A. (2007). Association of amphetamine-induced striatal dopamine release and cortisol responses to psychological stress. *Neuropsychopharmacology, 32,* 2310–2320. doi:10.1038/sj.npp.1301373

Way, B. M., & Gurbaxani, B. M. (2008). A genetics primer for social health research. *Social and Personality Psychology Compass, 2,* 785–816. doi:10.1111/j.1751-9004.2008.00084.x

Weaver, I. C., Cervoni, N., Champagne, F. A., D'Alessio, A. C., Sharma, S., Seckl, J. R., . . . Meaney, M. J. (2004). Epigenetic programming by maternal behavior. *Nature Neuroscience, 7,* 847–854. doi:10.1038/nn1276

Williams, K. D. (2001). *Ostracism: The power of silence.* New York, NY: Guilford Press.

Williams, K. D., & Jarvis, B. (2006). Cyberball: A program for use in research on interpersonal ostracism and acceptance. *Behavior Research Methods, 38,* 174–180.

Winslow, J. T., Hearn, E. F., Ferguson, J., Young, L. J., Matzuk, M. M., & Insel, T. R. (2000). Infant vocalization, adult aggression, and fear behavior of an oxytocin null mutant mouse. *Hormones and Behavior, 37,* 145–155. doi:10.1006/hbeh.1999.1566

Wu, S., Jia, M., Ruan, Y., Liu, J., Guo, Y., Shuang, M., . . . Zhang, D. (2005). Positive association of the oxytocin receptor gene (OXTR) with autism in the Chinese Han population. *Biological Psychiatry, 58,* 74–77. doi:10.1016/j.biopsych.2005.03.013

Zaza, C., & Baine, N. (2002). Cancer pain and psychosocial factors: A critical review of the literature. *Journal of Pain and Symptom Management, 24,* 526–542. doi:10.1016/S0885-3924(02)00497-9

Zhang, Y., Wang, D., Johnson, A. D., Papp, A. C., & Sadee, W. (2005). Allelic expression imbalance of human mu opioid receptor (OPRM1) caused by variant A118G. *The Journal of Biological Chemistry, 280,* 32618–32624. doi:10.1074/jbc.M504942200

Zubieta, J. K., Heitzeg, M. M., Smith, Y. R., Bueller, J. A., Xu, K., Xu, Y., . . . Goldman, D. (2003, February 21). *COMT* val158met genotype affects mu-opioid neurotransmitter responses to a pain stressor. *Science, 299,* 1240–1243. doi:10.1126/science.1078546

Zubieta, J. K., Ketter, T. A., Bueller, J. A., Xu, Y., Kilbourn, M. R., Young, E. A., & Koeppe, R. A. (2003, February 21). Regulation of human affective responses by anterior cingulate and limbic mu-opioid neurotransmission. *Archives of General Psychiatry, 60,* 1145–1153. doi:10.1001/archpsyc.60.11.1145

II

SOCIAL PAIN IN INTERPERSONAL RELATIONSHIPS

5

ACETAMINOPHEN DULLS PSYCHOLOGICAL PAIN

C. NATHAN DeWALL, RICHARD S. POND JR.,
AND TIMOTHY DECKMAN

Imagine taking a leisurely walk that ends with severe physical injury. If you are asked to describe how you felt at the end of the walk, words such as *pained* and *hurt* might come to mind. People use similar words to describe socially painful events such as social exclusion, rejection, and ostracism. Emerging evidence suggests that this linguistic similarity extends beyond mere metaphor. In this chapter, we review evidence that people show similar responses to socially and physically painful events. Moreover, we discuss how, by the use of an over-the-counter painkiller, the emotional pain that is often linked with belongingness threats is reduced. These findings demonstrate that social exclusion is painful and how dulling physical pain provides an effective means of reducing the sting of social disconnection.

THE NEED TO BELONG

Humans are social animals. People have a fundamental motivation to seek out positive relationships with others (Baumeister & Leary, 1995). This need to belong is pervasive across time and cultures. When people are deprived of belongingness, they suffer various negative mental and physical health effects. For example, loneliness is associated with high blood pressure, high levels of daily total peripheral resistance, and low cardiac output (Cacioppo et al., 2002; Hawkley, Burleson, Berntson, & Cacioppo, 2003). Mere social contact without the intimacy needed to fulfill belongingness leads to a state of "emotional isolation" (Shaver & Buhrmester, 1983). Social exclusion is particularly detrimental because it often elicits responses that preclude the possibility of gaining future social acceptance in a self-reinforcing fashion.

THE EFFECTS OF SOCIAL EXCLUSION

Social exclusion influences a variety of processes. To illustrate the widespread effects of social exclusion, in this section we review research investigating the effects of social exclusion on cognitive, behavioral, and emotional processes.

Cognitive Effects

Social exclusion affects cognition in at least two ways. First, exclusion produces a mental state that is similar to what is found among people who are in a presuicidal mind-set, a state referred to as one of defensive, *cognitive deconstruction* (Baumeister, 1990). Cognitive deconstruction is characterized by the rejection of meaningful thought and self-awareness. When people suffer a personal failure, they enter cognitive deconstruction as a means of escaping a negative affective response. Social exclusion produces known symptoms of cognitive deconstruction, including lethargy, emotional numbness, passivity, and an inability to delay gratification (Twenge, Catanese, & Baumeister, 2003). The second way exclusion affects cognition is by reducing intellectual performance on various tasks. Compared with nonexcluded people, those who experience social exclusion perform poorly on tasks that require logical reasoning, such as IQ tests and reading comprehension (Baumeister, Twenge, & Nuss, 2002). Tasks that require little effort, such as rote memory recall, are unaffected by exclusion. Because responses become passive and lethargic, the deconstructed state that excluded people show may help explain their low intellectual performance on tasks that require active volition and effort.

Behavioral Effects

When in a state of cognitive deconstruction, people are prone to act irrationally (Baumeister, 1990). Therefore, the deconstructed state may also help explain some of the behavioral consequences of social exclusion. For example, exclusion increases self-defeating behaviors (Twenge, Catanese, &

Baumeister, 2002). When given time to study for a test, excluded people procrastinate more than do accepted people. Exclusion also decreases willingness to self-regulate (Baumeister, DeWall, Ciarocco, & Twenge, 2005). In one study, excluded participants were less willing to make themselves drink a bad-tasting, but healthy, drink compared with nonexcluded participants. In addition, compared with accepted and control participants, excluded participants ate more fattening cookies, spent less time trying to solve an unsolvable puzzle, and were less willing to control their attention on a dichotic listening task (Baumeister et al., 2005). Yet, a monetary incentive was enough to eliminate the negative effects of social exclusion on self-regulation (Baumeister et al., 2005). The results indicate that excluded individuals are unwilling to exert effort to self-regulate effectively unless they are presented with a self-serving incentive to do so.

A common finding among several labs is that exclusion increases aggression and decreases prosocial behavior (Buckley, Winkel, & Leary, 2004; Kirkpatrick, Waugh, Valencia, & Webster, 2002; Twenge, Baumeister, DeWall, Ciarocco, & Bartels, 2007; Twenge, Baumeister, Tice, & Stucke, 2001; Warburton, Williams, & Cairns, 2006). Excluded individuals are less likely than accepted individuals to donate money to a student emergency fund, to help an experimenter after a mishap, or to cooperate in a prisoner's dilemma game (Twenge, Baumeister, et al., 2007). One study examined the effect of social exclusion on aggression using a blast of noise as its aggression measure (Twenge et al., 2001). Participants were able to adjust the intensity and duration of aversive sound that another participant would hear. The results indicated that excluded participants blasted strangers with more intense and prolonged aversive noise compared with nonexcluded individuals (Twenge et al., 2001).

Exclusion does not cause invariable shifts toward irrational, self-defeating, and antisocial behavior. Indeed, there is some evidence that exclusion can produce prosocial behaviors (Maner, DeWall, Baumeister, & Schaller, 2007; Williams, Cheung, & Choi, 2000; Williams & Sommer, 1997). One study found that excluded people desired participation in student services for making friends more than did accepted people (Maner et al., 2007). Excluded participants also desired group work more than did accepted participants, and they were even more likely to perceive others as nicer and friendlier (Maner et al., 2007). What promotes this prosocial behavior is the anticipation of future social contact with a potential source of social acceptance (Maner et al., 2007). Because the need to belong is a fundamental motivation, people deprived of belongingness will want to replenish it, thereby alleviating the effects of exclusion. A brief, friendly social interaction is enough to reduce the effect of exclusion on aggression (Twenge, Zhang, et al., 2007).

Emotional Effects

Because the need to belong is a basic and fundamental motive (Baumeister & Leary, 1995), it would follow that threats to belongingness would lead to intense emotional reactions. The emotional distress might then mediate the negative effects associated with exclusion. Yet those researchers who found that rejection negatively impacts mood (Williams et al., 2000) and increases feelings of anger and sadness (Buckley et al., 2004) failed to show that the emotional distress mediates the behavioral effects of rejection. Some laboratory investigations show that excluded individuals report neutral emotional states or an emotional "numbness" (Baumeister et al., 2005; DeWall & Baumeister, 2006; Twenge et al., 2001, 2002, 2003). Hence social exclusion is perceived as a severe threat. Sometimes excluded people reported high levels of emotional distress, whereas other times people go numb as a means of coping with the threat of social exclusion.

WHY IS THERE SOCIAL PAIN?

Living in supportive groups was a necessity during human evolutionary history, and social exclusion was tantamount to death. Those early humans who were able to live in cohesive groups were better equipped for surviving and passing on their genes to subsequent generations compared with those who faced the wilderness alone (Leary & Springer, 2001). Because of the survival value of group living for early hunter-gatherers, enduring a socially painful event, such as social rejection, was as traumatic to the individual as experiencing physical tissue damage. Therefore, psychological mechanisms for motivating a social life and protecting against social threats co-evolved (Leary & Springer, 2001). Just as people experience physical pain when they break an arm or a leg, people experience social pain when they perceive that they are being excluded, rejected, or otherwise made to feel devalued by one or more people (MacDonald & Leary, 2005).

Pain, whether it is social or physical, serves as an alarm to the organism that it is in danger (Price, 1988). Panksepp and colleagues first suggested that evolution coopted the body's existing physical pain system for responding to social threats (Herman & Panksepp, 1978; Panksepp, Herman, Conner, Bishop, & Scott, 1978; Panksepp, Vilberg, Bean, Coy, & Kastin, 1978). Because responding to social threats was as important to survival as was responding to physical threats, one system that monitors physical and social pain is more efficient and economical than are two systems that regulate both separately. One shared pain system would also imply that physical and social pain are encoded and responded to in the same way. MacDonald and Leary (2005) pointed to several neural mechanisms that respond to physical and social pain in similar ways, including the anterior cingulate cortex (ACC) and the periaqueductal gray (PAG).

The ACC is a neural structure that functions as an alarm signaling threats in the environment (Bush, Luu, & Posner, 2000; Nelson & Panksepp, 1998; Panksepp, 1998). Recent functional magnetic resonance imaging (fMRI) research has indicated that the ACC plays a role in detecting threats to belongingness as well. Eisenberger, Lieberman, and Williams (2003) conducted an experiment to see which regions of the brain were activated by instances of ostracism. fMRI scans were taken of participants while they played Cyberball, an online ball-tossing game used to elicit ostracism (Williams et al., 2000). Participants believed that they were playing the ball-tossing game with two other participants in fMRI scanners. In reality, the other participants were part of the computer program. The virtual players were programmed to include the participant in the ball toss part of the time, and at other times the virtual players excluded the participant. As predicted, the fMRI data indicated that the dorsal ACC (dACC) was more active during times of exclusion than inclusion. Results also revealed increased activity in the right ventral prefrontal cortex (RVPFC) during exclusion relative to inclusion. This finding suggests that the RVPFC may play a role in regulating the distress of social exclusion (Eisenberger et al., 2003). Further studies continue to strengthen the association between dACC activation and social pain. Individuals who report interacting with close and supportive others on a daily basis show less dACC activity during a social rejection task when compared with those who experience little meaningful social interactions daily (Eisenberger, Taylor, Gable, Hilmert, & Lieberman, 2007).

The PAG is another brain structure tied to physical and social pain responses. The PAG is a neural structure associated with detecting injury and reducing pain (i.e., analgesia), and it is important for animal bonding behavior (Craig & Dostrovsky, 1999; Price, 1988). Research shows that activation of the PAG reduces normal pain responses (e.g., to electrical shock, pinching, and heating of skin) in rats (Price, 1988). PAG stimulation is also associated with increased separation distress cries in rats (Panksepp, 1998), whereas lesioning the PAG leads to a reduction of these cries (Wiedenmayer, Goodwin, & Barr, 2000). In a related vein, distress created by social isolation seems to elicit analgesic effects across species (e.g., Kehoe & Blass, 1986; for a review, see MacDonald & Leary, 2005). These results not only link the PAG to physical and social pain but also provide evidence that animals respond to extreme social pain in the same manner as they respond to severe physical pain—with physical analgesia.

The findings just reviewed show that threats to the need to belong activate some of the same neural mechanisms as those associated with the detection and regulation of physical pain. Such evidence underscores the importance of sociality in shaping the development of neural structures throughout our evolutionary past. If the social pain system is mapped onto the physical pain system, then perhaps people respond to social pain similarly to the way they respond to physical injury. Just as the body goes numb in response to severe physical trauma, extreme threats of social exclusion may disrupt the emotional system from processing strong emotional responses. If the social pain system activates the same neural mechanisms as those activated by physical injury, then severe social pain will impact the human body in a way similar to how severe physical injury impacts the body.

The Body's Physical Pain Response

A variety of neural factors produce and extinguish the body's pain response. In general, threatening stimuli, whether mechanical or thermal, cause nociceptive (i.e., pain-sensing) neurons to transmit to the dorsal horn of the spinal cord, which elicits the body's pain response (Price, 1988). The central nervous system contains endogenous opioids, called endorphins and enkephalins, each of which is essential for pain reduction. Activation of the midbrain structures, including the PAG, permits the release of these analgesics. When these chemicals are released, they inhibit the pain response. In other words, these endogenous chemicals numb or dull the pain caused by the painful stimuli. By becoming numb to pain, people are able to focus on signs of safety instead of being debilitated by the pain.

The Body's Social Pain Response

If the social pain system is linked to the physical pain system, then the body should respond to severe social pain similar to the way it responds to physical injury; that is, the body should experience tremendous pain from social exclusion, which should be linked to a numbing response to cope with the pain. Because of the overlap between social and physical pain systems, the numbing response to cope with the pain of social exclusion should have consequences for both emotional and physical pain responses. DeWall and Baumeister (2006) tested this hypothesis directly in a series of experiments. During these studies, participants completed a personality questionnaire, in which they received accurate feedback regarding their extroversion score. Participants then received bogus feedback corresponding to one of four conditions, in which they were randomly placed. Those in the exclusion condition (future alone) were told that they had the personality type that would cause them to be alone later in life. Those in the accepted condition (future belonging) were told that they could expect many positive and lasting relationships throughout their lives. Participants in an additional control group were told that they would be accident-prone in the future, which would result in many hospital visits (misfortune control). The misfortune group was created to ensure that any differences associated with exclusion were, in fact, due to exclusion and not a response to bad news. The last condition consisted of participants who were not given additional information other than their extroversion score (no-feedback control).

Before exposure to the experimental manipulation, participants provided baseline measures of pain tolerance and threshold using a pressure algometer. For pain tolerance, participants were instructed to say "stop" when the pressure became too uncomfortable to continue. Pain threshold was measured by asking participants to indicate when they first felt pain from the pressure. After baseline measures were taken, the participants received the exclusion manipulation and then completed additional measures of pain tolerance and threshold. As predicted, excluded participants showed significantly higher pain thresholds than did participants in the control conditions. Pain threshold increased from baseline measures for excluded participants only, suggesting an absolute change in physical pain sensitivity instead of merely a relative difference compared with the control conditions. Future alone participants also demonstrated higher levels of pain tolerance and an increase in pain tolerance from baseline relative to participants in the control conditions. These results suggest that social exclusion produces analgesic effects on physical pain.

In a follow-up study, DeWall and Baumeister (2006) then examined whether the physical analgesia produced by exclusion was related to emotional insensitivity. Participants again completed baseline pain threshold and tolerance measures and were placed in the same experimental groups as previously described. They then completed measures of affective forecasting. Participants were asked to predict how happy they would feel if their school's football team won or lost a game against a local rival. If social exclusion impairs emotional responding, then the participants should be less sensitive to their emotions. After completing the affective forecasting measures, participants completed additional measures of pain threshold and tolerance.

As predicted, future alone participants showed neutral responses to both game outcomes, whereas the control groups elicited stronger emotional responses to a victory and a defeat. Excluded participants also reported higher levels of happiness in response to a defeat and lower levels of happiness in response to a win when compared with the control groups. Pain threshold and tolerance were significant predictors of the emotional forecasting scores. Such evidence suggests that social exclusion produces both physical and emotional insensitivity, providing support for the hypothesis that there is important overlap between the social and physical pain systems.

DeWall and Baumeister (2006) then tested whether the emotional insensitivity exhibited in excluded individuals would make them less capable of responding to a distressed other relative to nonexcluded individuals. Participants were asked to read and respond to an essay regarding romantic rejection after receiving their bogus feedback. Next, participants rated how empathetic they felt toward the distressed confederate. Participants then completed their measures of pain threshold and tolerance. Replicating the prior results, future alone participants exhibited higher pain threshold and tolerance than did the control conditions. Compared with accepted and control participants, excluded participants also expressed less interpersonal empathy toward the romantically rejected target character. The pain threshold and tolerance measures significantly predicted the empathy index, which suggests that the loss of empathetic concern was related to physical insensitivity.

To test whether this effect was simply due to participants responding to someone who had also experienced social exclusion, DeWall and Baumeister (2006) conducted a replication experiment in which participants were given the opportunity to empathize with a student who had experienced a physical injury. Results showed that participants in the rejection condition reported lower levels of empathetic concern toward the suffering student compared with accepted and control participants. This experiment suggests that social exclusion causes widespread emotional insensitivity to others' suffering, regardless of whether the suffering person has experienced social or physical injury.

CAN ACETAMINOPHEN REDUCE PAINFUL EMOTIONS?

The previous sections suggest that social and physical pain share common neural overlap. People who experience some form of social exclusion show physical and emotional responses that are commonly linked with experiencing physical pain, such as increased blood flow to brain regions linked to physical pain and physical analgesia. If social and physical pain are closely interlinked, then dulling physical pain sensitivity should influence sensitivity to socially painful emotions. The following sections review recent evidence regarding the role of acetaminophen in reducing socially painful emotions.

Acetaminophen is a common, over-the-counter painkiller that is the active ingredient in regular Tylenol. In some countries, the same drug is referred to as paracetamol and is the active ingredient in Panadol. However, before we discuss how acetaminophen influences socially painful emotions, it is necessary to review briefly how acetaminophen functions. Acetaminophen is unlike nonsteroidal anti-inflammatory drugs because it is considered to have no anti-inflammatory activity. In addition, no serious side effects for the heart, gastrointestinal, or respiratory systems are connected to the use of acetaminophen (Bertolini et al., 2007). The past 5 years have witnessed a growing body of evidence that suggests that the analgesic effect of acetaminophen is due to the indirect activation of cannabinoid (CB_1) receptors (Bertolini et al., 2007; Zygmunt, Chuang, Movahed, Julius, & Högestätt, 2000). Mallet et al. (2009) argued that acetaminophen-induced analgesia involves a specific sequence of chemical changes.

First, fatty acid amide hydrolase is required to metabolize acetaminophen into AM404. Next, there is indirect involvement of CB_1 receptors by AM404. AM404 inhibits the cellular uptake of anandamide (another endogenous cannabinoid), thereby causing the body to make more of this chemical, raising its concentration in the synapse (Zygmunt et al., 2000). The increased levels of endogenous cannabinoids are in part responsible for the analgesic effects of acetaminophen. This process of events limits the spinal cord's ability to sense physical pain. In contrast, other pain medications, such as ibuprofen, act locally at the site of inflammation. Acetaminophen's direct action on the spinal cord means that its analgesic effect is focused on the central nervous system and not the site of injury. Thus, acetaminophen inhibits the cellular uptake of an endogenous cannabinoid, which causes the body to make more of this chemical, which in turn causes general analgesia.

The Effect of Acetaminophen on Socially Painful Emotions

The effect of acetaminophen on the central nervous system suggests that it may have an important role in reducing the emotional pain associated with affectively painful events such as social exclusion. Experiencing physical pain involves two physiological pain systems: pain sensation and pain affect (Price, 2000). Whereas analgesics that act locally at the site of injury (e.g., ibuprofen) reduce pain sensation, analgesics that act in the central nervous system (e.g., acetaminophen) should reduce the emotional distress that accompanies pain affect (Eisenberger & Lieberman, 2004). Hence, for the purposes of this chapter's discussion, acetaminophen should reduce the emotional distress linked with socially painful events such as social exclusion, but acetaminophen should not disrupt the ability people have to identify and sense that they are experiencing social pain because acetaminophen is mainly dulling pain affect rather than pain sensation.

We set out to test the effect of acetaminophen on socially painful emotions by targeting an emotion that is linked closely to social pain: hurt feelings (Leary, Springer, Negel, Ansell, & Evans, 1998; MacDonald, Kingsbury,

& Shaw, 2005). *Hurt feelings* refer to the acute emotional distress felt in response to feeling less valued by a relational partner (friend, colleague, romantic partner) than one desires (Leary & Springer, 2001). People experience minor instances of relationship devaluation each day (Nezlek, Williams, & Wheeler, 2008), which can build up to create a sense of hurt feelings. If acetaminophen reduces the emotional distress that accompanies pain affect, then people who take a daily dose of acetaminophen, compared with placebo, should experience lower levels of hurt feelings.

To test this hypothesis, DeWall and colleagues (2007) conducted an experimental, experience-sampling study in which participants were assigned randomly to ingest either acetaminophen or a placebo pill filled with cornstarch over the course of 21 days. Those in the experimental condition took 500 mg of acetaminophen in the morning and before bed (totaling 1,000 mg or one fourth of the maximum daily dose). At the end of each day, participants reported how much their feelings had been hurt that day.

As expected, acetaminophen reduced hurt feelings over the course of the 3-week study. After consuming acetaminophen for only 14 days, participants reported lower levels of daily hurt feelings relative to participants who took the placebo. The effect of acetaminophen reducing hurt feelings grew stronger each day until the end of the study. Although participants consumed only one fourth of the maximum daily dose, the size of the difference in hurt feelings between participants who took acetaminophen and those who took the placebo met criteria used to describe medium effect sizes (Cohen, 1977). These results offer initial evidence that acetaminophen reduces emotional distress that accompanies the daily painful affect that is linked to social exclusion.

Can Acetaminophen Increase State Self-Esteem and Reduce Emotional Instability Among Chronically Anxious People?

In light of the rewards of social inclusion, people should have a sensitive detection mechanism that alerts them to cues for social exclusion. Leary, Tambor, Terdal, and Downs (1995) argued that people have a "sociometer" that monitors inclusion or exclusion cues and alerts the individual to perceived exclusion through hurt feelings and other forms of negative affect. Vigilance to potential signs of social threat represents a beneficial strategy in that it wards off the negative consequences of social exclusion. By recognizing that certain behaviors cause others to show signs of social disapproval (e.g., through a negative facial expression or avoidant body posture), people can change how they behave to increase their chances of gaining social acceptance.

Yet, vigilance regarding cues signaling social exclusion appears to benefit people only in relatively small doses. Indeed, hypersensitivity to social threats is associated with the development and maintenance of anxiety disorders (Bradley, Mogg, & Millar, 2000; Fox, 1993). Bar-Haim and colleagues'

(2007) meta-analytic findings demonstrated across various experimental measures that anxious individuals, compared with nonanxious individuals, showed greater threat-related bias. Highly anxious people are also hypersensitive to physical pain, as shown by their relatively low physical pain thresholds (Vassend, 1993; Widerström-Noga et al., 1998). People who experience chronic physical pain have a heightened risk of diagnosis of anxiety disorders (McWilliams, Cox, & Enns, 2003). These findings suggest that highly anxious people are sensitive to social and physical pain.

Because of their heightened sensitivity to social and physical pain, it may be difficult for highly anxious people to feel valued in their social interactions. Being constantly on guard for social threat may also lead highly anxious people to experience unstable emotions. Indeed, there is some evidence suggesting that trait anxiety is negatively correlated with social state self-esteem (Heatherton & Polivy, 1991) and positively correlated with emotional instability (Carels, Blumenthal, & Sherwood, 2000). Ingesting acetaminophen may dull sensitivity to social threat cues among highly anxious people, leading them to experience higher levels of social state self-esteem and lower levels of emotional instability relative to anxious people who take placebo. People who are relatively low in anxiety, in contrast, have relatively low sensitivity to social threat and therefore should not experience changes in their social state self-esteem or emotional instability regardless of whether they consume acetaminophen or placebo.

This hypothesis was tested by assigning participants to consume a daily dose of acetaminophen or placebo each day for 21 days, in addition to completing the State Self-Esteem Scale (SSES; Heatherton & Polivy, 1991), the Brief Mood Introspection Scale (BMIS; Mayer & Gaschke, 1988), the "today" version of the Hurt Feelings Scale (Leary & Springer, 2001), and a three-item hostile affect scale (composed of responses to the items "hostile," "angry," and "frustrated") at the end of each day (DeWall, MacDonald, Webster, Tice, & Baumeister, 2007). The SSES contains subscales for social, performance, and appearance state self-esteem. The BMIS contains mood valence and arousal subscales. Before the study began, participants completed the trait version of the State-Trait Anxiety Inventory (STAI; Spielberger et al., 1979). Because acetaminophen reduces the painful affect that is linked with socially painful emotions, it was predicted that the effect of acetaminophen on increasing state self-esteem among highly anxious people would be specific to the social subscale.

Results showed that acetaminophen enhanced social state self-esteem over time among highly anxious participants. Whereas highly anxious participants (i.e., those who scored 1 standard deviation above the mean on the STAI) who took acetaminophen showed a significant increase in social state self-esteem over time, those who took the placebo did not show any change in their social state self-esteem over the course of the study. Participants who were relatively low in anxiety (i.e., those who scored 1 standard deviation below the mean on the STAI) did not report levels of social state self-esteem that changed over time whether they took acetaminophen or placebo. As predicted, we found no significant changes for either performance or appearance state self-esteem subscales (DeWall et al., 2007).

Acetaminophen also eliminated the relationship between trait anxiety and emotional instability. Following procedures from Kernis and colleagues (1989; see also Webster, Kirkpatrick, Nezlek, Smith, & Paddock, 2007), we constructed instability coefficients by calculating a standard deviation for each participant's self-report emotion measure across the days for which data were provided. Among people who took placebo, trait anxiety was positively correlated with each emotional instability measure (i.e., hurt feelings, mood valence, arousal, hostility). This study replicates prior work showing a positive relationship between anxiety and emotional instability (e.g., Carels et al., 2000). In contrast, trait anxiety had no significant relationship to any of the emotional instability measures among people who took acetaminophen.

These findings offer additional evidence that acetaminophen impacts emotional responses linked to social pain. Highly anxious people are hypersensitive to social and physical pain, which impacts their feeling of social value and emotional stability. Reducing their sensitivity to physical pain also influenced their sensitivity to social pain, which led anxious participants to report levels of social state self-esteem that increased over the course of the 21-day study. Participants who were relatively low in anxiety did not show changes in their social state self-esteem over time as a function of taking acetaminophen, presumably because they tend to have healthy levels of sensitivity to social and physical pain. Acetaminophen also reduced the link between trait anxiety and emotional instability, whereas the anxiety–emotional instability relationship remained consistent and strong among people who took placebo.

Will Acetaminophen Reduce Coping With the Pain of Chronic Belonging Deficits?

People experience acute and chronic social disconnection. Both types of disconnection thwart the need to belong and therefore represent socially painful events. Whereas the previously reviewed evidence focused primarily on how people respond to acute threats of social disconnection, an additional series of studies tested whether acetaminophen would reduce coping responses among people who experience chronic deficits in their belongingness (DeWall, Stillman, & Finkel, 2008). As with any fundamental need, deprivation increases desire. Just as hunger increases the desire to gain sustenance, chronic deficits in belongingness increase the desire to gain affiliation (e.g., Maner et al., 2007). We hypothesized that chronic belongingness deficits motivate people to create signs of psychological closeness with others where none exist, presumably as a strategy designed to cope with the pain of social disconnection.

We developed a drawing exercise that served as the measure of non-conscious coping with the pain of chronic belongingness deficits. Participants were given a sheet of paper and were instructed to draw five objects: a tree, a house, a car, and two people. The experimenter told participants they must have all five objects in their drawing but they could place them wherever they wanted. We predicted that participants who experienced chronic belongingness deficits would have a relatively strong motivation for psychological closeness, which in turn would lead them to construct drawings in which people were physically close together. Because of their stage of psychosocial development, establishing a romantic relationship is a highly salient goal for college students (Erikson, 1950). Therefore, we anticipated that our single, college-age participants would experience a higher level of chronic belongingness deficits relative to their romantically attached counterparts. As a result, single college students should have a heightened desire for social connectedness compared with romantically attached college students. The main prediction was that chronic belongingness deficits would motivate people to construct drawings in which people are physically close to each other, but that participants who took acetaminophen would not show this nonconscious coping strategy.

We (DeWall et al., in press) conducted an initial study to determine whether single, compared with romantically attached, participants would show the predicted motivated drawing effect. Participants first reported whether they were currently involved in a romantic relationship. Next, participants completed the drawing exercise in which they drew a picture containing one tree, one car, one house, and two people. The distance between the two people was then measured in millimeters as a measure of the desire for social connection. As predicted, single participants drew the two people closer together compared with romantically attached participants. Thus, results from an initial study suggest that drawing can be used as an implicit measure of the desire for closeness with others.

The purpose of the next study was to test the hypothesis that decreasing sensitivity to daily physical pain (via a regular dose of acetaminophen) would reduce the motivated drawing effect among single participants. Participants consumed a daily dose of acetaminophen or placebo for 21 days. On day 21, participants returned to the laboratory and completed the same drawing task used in the previous study. Results showed that among participants who took placebo, single participants drew the two people in their drawings closer together than did romantically attached participants. Taking a daily dose of acetaminophen eliminated this effect. Among participants who took acetaminophen, single and romantically attached participants did not differ in terms of the amount of distance between the two people with their drawings.

These results provide further evidence that social disconnection is painful. People who experience chronic belongingness deficits have a relatively strong desire for psychological closeness with others. This motivation for psychological closeness, in turn, has implications for the amount of physical closeness they include between two people in an impromptu drawing exercise. Numbing people to daily physical pain eliminated this nonconscious coping response. In light of the previously reviewed literature on the relationship between social and physical pain systems (e.g., Eisenberger et al., 2003; MacDonald & Leary, 2005), these findings suggest that the motivated drawing effect relates to the pain of social disconnection.

CONCLUSIONS

Most living things have fundamental desires to seek pleasure and to avoid pain (Bentham, 1823). The current findings suggest that being robbed of the pleasure of social belongingness is painful. As well, people's bodies respond to social disconnection in much the same way they respond to physical pain. People who experience a severe threat to their belongingness status show numbing responses that closely resemble reactions to severe physical injury. Social pain results in emotional and physical insensitivity, which supports the proposed link between the two types of pain systems. Yet such a link has implications for the treatment of psychological pain. Over-the-counter medications intended to treat physical injury or soreness also have the effect of dulling social hurt, thereby reducing the need to cope with the disconnection. Understanding the intricacies of the social–physical pain system will help further an understanding of the implications that belongingness has on daily health.

REFERENCES

Bar-Haim, Y., Lamy, D., Pergamin, L., Bakermans-Kranenburg, M. J., & van IJzendoorn, M. H. (2007). Threat-related attentional bias in anxious and nonanxious individuals: A meta-analytic study. *Psychological Bulletin, 133,* 1–24. doi:10.1037/0033-2909.133.1.1

Baumeister, R. F. (1990). Suicide as escape from the self. *Psychological Review, 97,* 90–113. doi:10.1037/0033-295X.97.1.90

Baumeister, R. F., DeWall, C. N., Ciarocco, N. J., & Twenge, J. M. (2005). Social exclusion impairs self-regulation. *Journal of Personality and Social Psychology, 88,* 589–604. doi:10.1037/0022-3514.88.4.589

Baumeister, R. F., & Leary, M. R. (1995). The need to belong: Desire for interpersonal attachments as a fundamental human motivation. *Psychological Bulletin, 117,* 497–529. doi:10.1037/0033-2909.117.3.497

Baumeister, R. F., Twenge, J. M., & Nuss, C. K. (2002). Effects of social exclusion on cognitive processes: Anticipated aloneness reduces intelligent thought. *Journal of Personality and Social Psychology, 83*, 817–827. doi:10.1037/0022-3514.83.4.817

Bentham, J. (1823). *An introduction to the principles of morals and legislation*. London, England: Pickering.

Bertolini, A., Ferrari, A., Ottani, A., Guerzoni, S., Tacchi, R., & Leone, S. (2007). Paracetamol: New vistas of an old drug. *CNS Drug Reviews, 12*, 250–275. doi:10.1111/j.1527-3458.2006.00250.x

Bradley, B. P., Mogg, K., & Millar, N. (2000). Covert and overt orienting of attention to emotional faces in anxiety. *Cognition and Emotion, 14*, 789–808. doi:10.1080/02699930050156636

Buckley, K. E., Winkel, R. E., & Leary, M. R. (2004). Reactions to acceptance and rejection: Effects of level and sequence of relational evaluation. *Journal of Experimental Social Psychology, 40*, 14–28. doi:10.1016/S0022-1031(03)00064-7

Bush, G., Luu, P., & Posner, M. I. (2000). Cognitive and emotional influences in anterior cingulate cortex. *Trends in Cognitive Sciences, 4*, 215–222. doi:10.1016/S1364-6613(00)01483-2

Cacioppo, J. T., Hawkley, L. C., Crawford, L. E., Ernst, J. M., Burleson, M. H., Kowalski, R., . . . Berntson, G. G. (2002). Loneliness and health: Potential mechanisms. *Psychosomatic Medicine, 64*, 407–417.

Carels, R. A., Blumenthal, J. A., & Sherwood, A. (2000). Emotional responsivity during daily life: Relationship to psychosocial functioning and ambulatory blood pressure. *International Journal of Psychophysiology, 36*, 25–33. doi:10.1016/S0167-8760(99)00101-4

Cohen, J. (1977). *Statistical power analysis for the behavioral sciences*. New York, NY: Academic Press.

Craig, A. D., & Dostrovsky, J. O. (1999). Medulla to thalamus. In P. Wall & R. Melzack (Eds.), *Textbook of pain* (pp. 183–214). New York, NY: Churchill Livingstone.

DeWall, C. N., & Baumeister, R. F. (2006). Alone but feeling no pain: Effects of social exclusion on physical pain tolerance and pain threshold, affective forecasting, and interpersonal empathetic concern. *Journal of Personality and Social Psychology, 91*, 1–15. doi:10.1037/0022-3514.91.1.1

DeWall, C. N., MacDonald, G., Webster, G. D., Tice, D. M., & Baumeister, R. F. (2007). *Acetaminophen increases social self-esteem among the anxious: An experimental experience-sampling study*. Manuscript in preparation.

DeWall, C. N., MacDonald, G., Webster, G. D., Masten, C., Baumeister, R. F., Powell, C., . . . Eisenberger, N. I. (in press). Tylenol reduces social pain: Behavioral and neural evidence. *Psychological Science*.

DeWall, C. N., Stillman, T. F., & Finkel, E. J. (2008). *Drawing as an implicit window into the motivated mind: Measuring the desire for social connection, in millimeters*. Manuscript submitted for publication.

Eisenberger, N. I., & Lieberman, M. D. (2004). Why rejection hurts: A common neural alarm system for physical and social pain. *Trends in Cognitive Sciences, 8*, 294–300. doi:10.1016/j.tics.2004.05.010

Eisenberger, N. I., Lieberman, M. D., & Williams, K. D. (2003, October 10). Does rejection hurt? An fMRI study of social exclusion. *Science, 302*, 290–292. doi:10.1126/science.1089134

Eisenberger, N. I., Taylor, S. E., Gable, S. L., Hilmert, C. J., & Lieberman, M. D. (2007). Neural pathways link social support to attenuated neuroendocrine stress responses. *NeuroImage, 35*, 1601–1612.

Erikson, E. H. (1950). *Childhood and society.* New York, NY: Norton.

Fox, E. (1993). Allocation of visual attention and anxiety. *Cognition and Emotion, 7*, 207–215. doi:10.1080/02699939308409185

Hawkley, L. C., Burleson, M. H., Berntson, G. G., & Cacioppo, J. T. (2003). Loneliness in everyday life: Cardiovascular activity, psychosocial context, and health behaviors. *Journal of Personality and Social Psychology, 85*, 105–120. doi:10.1037/0022-3514.85.1.105

Heatherton, T. F., & Polivy, J. (1991). Development and validation of a scale for measuring state self-esteem. *Journal of Personality and Social Psychology, 60*, 895–910. doi:10.1037/0022-3514.60.6.895

Herman, B. H., & Panksepp, J. (1978). Effects of morphine and nalozone on separation distress and approach attachment: Evidence for opiate mediation of social affect. *Pharmacology, Biochemistry, and Behavior, 9*, 213–220. doi:10.1016/0091-3057(78)90167-3

Kehoe, P., & Blass, E. M. (1986). Opioid-mediation of separation distress in 10-day-old rats: Reversal of stress with maternal stimuli. *Developmental Psychobiology, 19*, 385–398. doi:10.1002/dev.420190410

Kernis, M. H., Brockner, J., & Frankel, B. S. (1989). Self-esteem and reactions to failure: The mediating effect of overgeneralization. *Journal of Personality and Social Psychology, 57*, 707–714. doi:10.1037/0022-3514.57.4.707

Kirkpatrick, L. A., Waugh, C. E., Valencia, A., & Webster, G. D. (2002). The functional domain specificity of self-esteem and the differential prediction of aggression. *Journal of Personality and Social Psychology, 82*, 756–767. doi:10.1037/0022-3514.82.5.756

Leary, M. R., & Springer, C. A. (2001). Hurt feelings: The neglected emotion. In R. M. Kowalski (Ed.), *Behaving badly: Aversive behaviors in interpersonal relationships* (pp. 151–175). Washington, DC: American Psychological Association. doi:10.1037/10365-006

Leary, M. R., Springer, C. A., Negel, L., Ansell, E., & Evans, K. (1998). The causes, phenomenology, and consequences of hurt feelings. *Journal of Personality and Social Psychology, 74*, 1225–1237. doi:10.1037/0022-3514.74.5.1225

Leary, M. R., Tambor, E. S., Terdal, S. K., & Downs, D. L. (1995). Self-esteem as an interpersonal monitor: The sociometer hypothesis. *Journal of Personality and Social Psychology, 68*, 518–530. doi:10.1037/0022-3514.68.3.518

MacDonald, G., Kingsbury, R., & Shaw, S. (2005). Adding insult to injury: Social pain theory and response to social exclusion. In K. Williams, J. Forgas, & W. von Hippel (Eds.), *The social outcast: Ostracism, social exclusion, rejection, & bullying* (pp. 77–90). New York, NY: Psychology Press.

MacDonald, G., & Leary, M. R. (2005). Why does social exclusion hurt? The relationship between social and physical pain. *Psychological Bulletin, 131,* 202–223. doi:10.1037/0033-2909.131.2.202

Mallet, C., Daulhac, L., Bonnefont, J., Ledent, C., Etienne, M., Chapuy, E., . . . Eschalier, A. (2009). Endocannabinoid and serotonergic systems are needed for acetaminophen-induced analgesia. *Pain, 139,* 190–200.

Maner, J. K., DeWall, C. N., Baumeister, R. F., & Schaller, M. (2007). Does social exclusion motivate interpersonal reconnection? Resolving the "porcupine problem." *Journal of Personality and Social Psychology, 92,* 42–55. doi:10.1037/0022-3514.92.1.42

Mayer, J. D., & Gaschke, Y. N. (1988). The experience and meta-experience of mood. *Journal of Personality and Social Psychology, 55,* 102–111. doi:10.1037/0022-3514.55.1.102

McWilliams, L. A., Cox, B. J., & Enns, M. W. (2003). Mood and anxiety disorders associated with chronic pain: An examination in a nationally representative sample. *Pain, 106,* 127–133. doi:10.1016/S0304-3959(03)00301-4

Nelson, E. E., & Panksepp, J. (1998). Brain substrates of infant–mother attachment: Contributions of opioids, oxytocin, and norepinephrine. *Neuroscience and Biobehavioral Reviews, 22,* 437–452. doi:10.1016/S0149-7634(97)00052-3

Nezlek, J. B., Williams, K. D., & Wheeler, L. (2008). *Ostracism in everyday life.* Manuscript in preparation.

Panksepp, J. (1998). *Affective neuroscience: The foundations of human and animal emotions.* New York, NY: Oxford University Press.

Panksepp, J., Herman, B. H., Conner, R., Bishop, P., & Scott, J. P. (1978). The biology of social attachments: Opiates alleviate separation distress. *Biological Psychiatry, 13,* 607–618.

Panksepp, J., Vilberg, T., Bean, N., Coy, D., & Kastin, A. (1978). Reduction of distress vocalization in chicks by opiate-like peptides. *Brain Research Bulletin, 3,* 663–667. doi:10.1016/0361-9230(78)90014-X

Price, D. D. (1988). *Psychological and neural mechanisms of pain.* New York, NY: Raven Press.

Price, D. D. (2000, June 9). Psychological and neural mechanisms of the affective dimension of pain. *Science, 288,* 1769–1772. doi:10.1126/science.288.5472.1769

Shaver, P., & Buhrmester, D. (1983). Loneliness, sex-role orientation and group life: A social needs perspective. In P. B. Paulus (Ed.), *Basic group processes* (pp. 259–288). New York, NY: Springer-Verlag.

Spielberger, C. D., Jacobs, G., Crane, R., Russel, S., Westberry, L., Barker, E., et al. (1979). *Scoring manual for the State-Trait Personality Inventory.* Tampa: University of South Florida.

Twenge, J. M., Baumeister, R. F., DeWall, C., Ciarocco, N., & Bartels, J. (2007). Social exclusion decreases prosocial behavior. *Journal of Personality and Social Psychology, 92,* 56–66. doi:10.1037/0022-3514.92.1.56

Twenge, J. M., Baumeister, R. F., Tice, D. M., & Stucke, T. S. (2001). If you can't join them, beat them: Effects of social exclusion on aggressive behavior. *Journal of Personality and Social Psychology, 81,* 1058–1069.

Twenge, J. M., Catanese, K. R., & Baumeister, R. F. (2002). Social exclusion causes self-defeating behavior. *Journal of Personality and Social Psychology, 83,* 606–615. doi:10.1037/0022-3514.83.3.606

Twenge, J. M., Catanese, K. R., & Baumeister, R. F. (2003). Social exclusion and the deconstructed state: Time perception, meaninglessness, lethargy, lack of emotion, & self-awareness. *Journal of Personality and Social Psychology, 85,* 409–423. doi:10.1037/0022-3514.85.3.409

Twenge, J. M., Zhang, L., Catanese, K. R., Dolan-Pascoe, B., Lyche, L. F., & Baumeister, R. F. (2007). Replenishing connectedness: Reminders of social activity reduce aggression after social exclusion. *The British Journal of Social Psychology, 46,* 205–224. doi:10.1348/014466605X90793

Vassend, O. (1993). Anxiety, pain, and discomfort associated with dental treatment. *Behaviour Research and Therapy, 31,* 659–666. doi:10.1016/0005-7967(93)90119-F

Warburton, W. A., Williams, K. D., & Cairns, D. R. (2006). When ostracism leads to aggression: The moderating effects of control deprivation. *Journal of Experimental Social Psychology, 42,* 213–220. doi:10.1016/j.jesp.2005.03.005

Webster, G. D., Kirkpatrick, L. A., Nezlek, J. B., Smith, C. V., & Paddock, E. L. (2007). Different slopes for different folks: Self-esteem instability and gender as moderators of the relationship between self-esteem and attitudinal aggression. *Self and Identity, 6,* 74–94. doi:10.1080/15298860600920488

Widerström-Noga, E., Dyrehag, L. E., Borglum-Jensen, L., Ashlund, P. G., Wenneberg, B., & Andersson, S. A. (1998). Pain threshold responses to different modes of sensory stimulation in patients with orofacial muscular pain: Psychologic considerations. *Journal of Orofacial Pain, 12,* 27–34.

Wiedenmayer, C. P., Goodwin, G. A., & Barr, G. A. (2000). The effect of periaqueductal gray lesions on responses to age-specific threats in infant rats. *Brain Research. Developmental Brain Research, 120,* 191–198. doi:10.1016/S0165-3806(00)00009-2

Williams, K. D., Cheung, C. K. T., & Choi, W. (2000). CyberOstracism: Effects of being ignored over the Internet. *Journal of Personality and Social Psychology, 79,* 748–762. doi:10.1037/0022-3514.79.5.748

Williams, K. D., & Sommer, K. L. (1997). Social ostracism by coworkers: Does rejection lead to social loafing or compensation. *Personality and Social Psychology Bulletin, 23,* 693–706. doi:10.1177/0146167297237003

Zygmunt, P. M., Chuang, H., Movahed, P., Julius, D., & Högestätt, E. (2000). The anandamide transport inhibitor AM404 activates vanilloid receptors. *European Journal of Pharmacology, 396,* 39–42. doi:10.1016/S0014-2999(00)00207-7

6

DEFENSIVE AVOIDANCE OF SOCIAL PAIN VIA PERCEPTIONS OF SOCIAL THREAT AND REWARD

GEOFF MacDONALD, TERRY K. BORSOOK,
AND STEPHANIE S. SPIELMANN

Asking a potential romantic partner for a date is a common experience that provides insight into important fundamentals of social perceptions. On the one hand, asking for the date is likely to be motivated by the perceived benefits that a "yes" would bring, such as emotional and physical intimacy. On the other hand, hesitation in asking for the date is likely to be motivated by the perceived harm that would result from a "no," such as a damaged ego or reputation. This example highlights how, in regulating social behavior, people are likely to take into account both the potential rewards that a relationship offers as well as the potential threats that may manifest in pursuing that relationship.

In this chapter, we describe the research program being undertaken in our lab, a program that is designed to systematically examine the nature and functional importance of perceptions of social threats and social rewards. We begin by describing our conceptualization of social threats as primarily focused on the fear of rejection and social rewards as primarily focused on feelings of interpersonal connection. We also distinguish social threats and rewards from the related constructs of social avoidance and approach goals. Next, we discuss work validating new measures of social threat and reward and showing that these constructs appear to influence social outcomes. In particular, we describe research suggesting that perceptions of social reward are especially likely to influence social outcomes following socially painful experiences. We then elaborate on why researchers interested in social pain should be mindful of the distinction between social threats and rewards. In particular, we argue that both rejection and lost connection are experienced as painful and, as a result, social threat and reward perceptions can be defensively manipulated to minimize the experience of such pain in a manner that is predicted by measures of adult attachment.

CONCEPTUALIZING SOCIAL THREAT AND REWARD

In developing a scale to measure perceptions of social threat and reward (MacDonald, Tackett, & Borsook, 2009), we conceptualized *social threat* as evaluations of the degree to which the social environment contains signals of the potential for negative evaluation and rejection by others. Several researchers consider negative evaluation and rejection to be the primary risks of social interaction (e.g., Dickerson & Kemeny, 2004; MacDonald & Leary, 2005; Murray, Holmes, & Collins, 2006). Negative evaluation and rejection particularly threaten an individual's sense of belonging, a fundamental need tied to physical and psychological well-being (Baumeister & Leary, 1995). In our preliminary research to develop our scales, participants evaluated the potential for social threat in the context of meeting a stranger. Factor analytic procedures suggested the core items of the social threat scale included evaluations of the potential for being unliked, committing a social faux pas, and experiencing embarrassment or social anxiety (e.g., "I'm concerned my partner won't like me very much"). As a whole, the social threat scale assessed the potential for negative feelings resulting from interpersonal disapproval.

Social reward was conceptualized as evaluations of the degree to which the social environment contains signals of the potential to develop intimacy and connection with others. Laurenceau and Kleinman (2006) described *intimacy* as feelings of connectedness resulting from a process of self-disclosure that is met with responsiveness by a relational partner. These authors argued that the desire for experiences of warmth and closeness with others is a primary human motive. In our view, feelings of intimacy are the fundamental reward of close relationships. In our research context of meeting a stranger, factor analysis suggested that the social reward scale formed a factor separate from the social threat scale and included items relating to the potential for developing meaningful connection, anticipation of comfortable self-disclosure, expectations for liking the partner, interest in learning about the partner, and the possibility of making a new friend (e.g., "I think I could develop a meaningful connection with my interaction partner"). Overall, these items assessed the potential for knowing and being known, the basis for developing intimacy.

RELATION OF SOCIAL THREAT–REWARD TO SOCIAL AVOIDANCE–APPROACH GOALS

Research across species and behavioral domains has suggested that evaluations of the potential for threat and reward are a fundamental aspect of behavior regulation. For example, according to Gray and McNaughton's (2000) model, behavior regulation in human and nonhuman animals involves three separate but interacting physiological systems. The fight–flight–freeze system is associated with fearful emotions and motivates avoidance and escape of threat. The behavioral approach system (BAS) is associated with anticipatory pleasure (Corr, 2005) and motivates approach behavior toward reward. Finally, the behavioral inhibition system (BIS) serves, in large part, to resolve competing avoidance and approach motivations in response to simultaneous perceptions of threat and reward (the BIS also has a role in resolving approach–approach and avoid–avoid conflicts). The process of such conflict resolution is related to an affective experience of anxiety, motivating an assessment of risk that is "experienced as worry and rumination, and a feeling of possible danger or loss" (Corr, 2005, p. 233).

Previous research investigating social behavior in the context of these more general behavior regulation systems has focused on avoidance and approach social motivations and goals (Gable, 2006; Gable & Strachman, 2008; Impett, Gable, & Peplau, 2005; Locke, 2008; Strachman & Gable, 2006) rather than perceptions of threats and rewards, per se. Social avoidance goals are aimed at averting undesired end-states such as rejection or conflict whereas social approach goals are focused on the realization of desired end-states such as obtaining closeness and intimacy (Gable & Strachman, 2008). Gable and colleagues' research has provided evidence that those with stronger social avoidance goals (e.g., the goal to avoid conflicts) react more strongly to negative social events and experience poorer outcomes in their close relationships (Gable, 2006; Impett et al., 2005). On the other hand, those with stronger social approach goals (e.g., the goal to make new friends) tend to experience a greater number of positive social events and experience better outcomes in close relationships.

Although functionally related, social threat–reward perceptions are conceptually distinct from and not reducible to social avoidance or approach drives. For example, knowing that an individual holds a goal to make new friends does not allow a prediction of whom that individual will approach for friendship. One crucial piece of information needed to make such a prediction would seem to be the potential reward value that individual sees in each candidate for friendship. Indeed, research has shown that holding an approach goal does not lead to evaluating an interaction partner more positively (Strachman & Gable, 2006), suggesting that approach goals and assessments of the reward value of the social environment are independent. In fact, as is discussed in the next section, social approach goals (e.g., the goal to make new friends) should be particularly likely to energize behavior when experienced in combination with perceptions of the potential for social reward (e.g., seeing someone as a good candidate for friendship). Of note, however, Strachman and Gable's (2006) research did show that holding avoidance goals led to more negative evaluations of an interaction partner, suggesting that avoidance goals and threat perception may not be as independent.

VALIDATING THE SOCIAL THREAT AND REWARD SCALES

In two studies examining the new social threat and reward scales described earlier, participants believed they would interact with another participant after completing a questionnaire package that included the social threat and reward measures (no interaction actually took place; MacDonald et al., 2009). In both studies, social threat and reward perceptions were not significantly correlated despite sample sizes of more than 140 participants in each (MacDonald et al., 2009).

In both studies, higher levels of perceived social threat potential predicted lower levels of anticipated enjoyment of the interaction. It is not surprising that these studies also revealed that social threat scores were associated with a number of individual difference variables employed in past research to investigate sensitivity to interpersonal rejection. In Study 1, higher social threat scores were strongly associated with higher fear of negative evaluation (Leary, 1983), rejection sensitivity (Downey & Feldman, 1996), hurt feelings proneness (Leary & Springer, 2001), loneliness (Russell, 1996), and the need to belong (Leary, Kelly, Cottrell, & Schreindorfer, 2007). More threat perception was also associated with lower levels of trait self-esteem (Rosenberg, 1979) and perceived social support (Cohen & Hoberman, 1983). In addition to these interpersonal variables, perceptions of social threat were associated with higher general avoidance motivation and lower general approach motivation as measured by the BIS and BAS scales, respectively (Carver & White, 1994). In Study 2, social threat perceptions were shown to be correlated negatively with the approach-motivation variable of promotion focus (Higgins et al., 2001) as well as the Big Five personality measures of Extraversion and Conscientiousness (John & Srivastava, 1999). Social threat perceptions were also positively correlated with the personality dimension of neuroticism. Overall, the new social threat scale appears to be clearly associated with sensitivity to social and general threats.

Across both studies, higher levels of perceived potential for social reward were related to greater anticipated enjoyment of the interaction. However, of the individual differences in social sensitivity included in Study 1, only loneliness was shown to be significantly (and negatively) related to social reward scores. Social reward perceptions were also related negatively to general avoidance motivation (BIS) and positively to general approach motivation (BAS), although the latter effect did not replicate in Study 2. Study 2 revealed that social reward perceptions were related to higher levels of the Big Five personality dimensions of Extraversion and Agreeableness as well as lower levels of neuroticism. In sum, the evidence suggests that perceptions of social reward are related to higher levels of general positive emotionality and lower levels of general negative emotionality. However, the data also suggest that variables typically employed to study social sensitivity (e.g., rejection sensitivity) cannot account for social reward perceptions and thus may be insensitive to the role that perceptions of the potential for connection play in the regulation of social behavior.

To extend our validation of the social threat and reward scales beyond outcomes measured by self-report questionnaires, our lab has also investigated the relation of these new scales to social behavior (MacDonald et al., 2009). We reasoned that, at least in our research context, perceptions of social threat potential may promote making a good first impression on others. That is, when meeting a stranger, those who perceive higher potential for rejection may work harder to produce a good first impression to keep negative evaluation at bay. For example, Heatherton and Vohs (2000) showed that individuals lower in self-esteem (which our Study 1 showed is related to higher social threat perception) who had just experienced a failure were evaluated as more likable by an interaction partner than were those with high self-esteem. This finding suggests the possibility that individuals experiencing strong perceptions of social threat may behave prosocially to avoid social injury via rejection from others. This hypothesis may seem somewhat counterintuitive given the voluminous literature suggesting that interpersonally insecure individuals often behave in ways that are destructive to relationships because of self-fulfilling beliefs that others evaluate them negatively (e.g., Downey, Feldman, & Ayduk, 2000; Murray, Bellavia, Rose, & Griffin, 2003). However, because strangers do not know one's faults, insecure individuals may be more confident that a positive impression can be made on a new interaction partner, leading to prosocial behavior in an attempt to minimize social threats (MacDonald & Leary, 2002).

Our expectations for the effects of social reward were more nuanced. As suggested earlier, we hypothesized that social reward perceptions may be particularly likely to influence social behavior when the goal of approaching connectedness is activated. That is, because the activation of approach motivations energizes behavior with the goal of obtaining potential rewards (Carver et al., 2000), those who both have a goal of connecting with others and see the upcoming interaction as holding strong potential for connection may be the most likely to work to make a good first impression. Past research has suggested that the experience of social pain may well activate the goal to connect with others. Research suggests that social pain activates social avoidance motivations as well (MacDonald, 2009). For example, socially excluded individuals exhibit lower levels of prosocial behavior (Twenge, Baumeister, DeWall, Ciarocco, & Bartels, 2007) and higher levels of aggressiveness (Leary, Twenge, & Quinlivan, 2006). However, as we did not expect social avoidance motivation to interact with perceptions of social reward in energizing prosocial behavior, the focus here is on the social approach implications of social pain. Maner, DeWall, Baumeister, and Schaller (2007) argued that social exclusion leads to a perception that the goal of achieving intimacy has been blocked, which leads to a heightened desire to pursue connection. For example, experiences of social pain have been shown to lead to seeking out new relationships (Leary & Springer, 2001) and increased interest in meeting potential new friends (Maner et al., 2007). Further, Murray, Derrick, Leder, and Holmes (2008) showed that recalled rejection experiences lead to faster reaction times to connectedness-related words and stronger endorsement of connectedness goals. This analysis suggests that, following a socially painful experience, those who perceive higher potential for social reward in an interaction should be especially likely to behave prosocially. That is, prosocial behavior should be especially likely when strong potential for connection is perceived and the motivation to pursue connection is high as a result of social pain.

We tested these hypotheses in our second study of social threat and reward perceptions (MacDonald et al., 2009). Participants were told that before meeting their interaction partner, they would exchange video greetings with the other participant. Prior to completing the social threat–reward measures and recording their video greeting, participants were randomly assigned to one of three experimental conditions. In the social pain condition, participants were asked to describe and relive a past betrayal episode, a procedure shown to lead to the current experience of emotional pain (Chen, Williams, Fitness, & Newton, 2008). Those randomly assigned to the physical pain condition were asked to relive a past incident of physical injury. Participants in the control condition did not complete a reliving task before completing the social threat–reward measures and video greeting. Consistent with past research (Chen et al., 2008), those who relived a betrayal incident reported significantly more current pain experience than did those who relived a physical injury (no measure of current pain was taken in the control condition). The video greetings recorded by participants were evaluated by five raters who were blind to condition.

Neither perceptions of social threat nor perceptions of social reward significantly differed across experimental condition. Thus, perceptions of the potential for threat and reward were seemingly uninfluenced by the experience of social pain. As predicted, those who perceived higher levels of social threat potential in the interaction received more positive evaluations from the raters, an effect that was not qualified by experimental condition. This result suggests that those more concerned about the potential threat of rejection behave more prosocially to avoid that threat being realized. At least in this particular context, these efforts appear to have been successful.

Perceptions of the potential for social reward were not significantly related to positive evaluations in either the control or physical pain condition. However, among participants who were experiencing relatively high levels of social pain following the reliving of a betrayal, higher social reward scores were significantly related to more positive evaluations from the raters. These data suggest that when the goal of pursuing connection is activated by a socially painful experience, those who see the most potential for intimacy display the highest levels of prosocial behavior. Under these conditions, perceptions of the potential for social reward appear to have led to a self-fulfilling prophecy. That is, those socially pained participants who believed that connection was a realistic possibility seem to have created the very conditions that would appear to facilitate intimacy (i.e., positive interpersonal evaluations).

Overall, then, our research suggests that the effects of social threat and reward perceptions are not just intrapsychic but serve to influence the social environment as well. Those who perceive high social threat potential appeared to greet novel interaction partners with prosocial behavior that, at least initially, may reduce the degree of rejection threat. At the same time, perceptions of the potential for social reward appeared to function as a latent resource for promoting connection that came online particularly during the experience of social pain. This latter finding is particularly important in demonstrating the value added by an understanding of social reward perceptions as both separate from and interacting with social approach goals.

REJECTION AND LOST CONNECTION AS CAUSES OF EMOTIONAL PAIN

MacDonald (2009) distinguished between two types of social exclusion: rejection and noninclusion. *Rejection* involves signals of the presence of negative social evaluation. Examples of rejecting experiences include criticism, betrayal, and explicit statements of exclusion. It is not surprising that research has shown that the threats to social connection posed by rejection are experienced as emotionally painful (Leary, Springer, Negel, Ansell, & Evans, 1998). For example, in one study, participants randomly assigned to receive rejecting messages reported higher levels of hurt feelings than did those who received neutral or accepting messages (Buckley, Winkel, & Leary, 2004). That rejection is associated with responses mediated by physical pain systems is attested to by research connecting exclusion to physical numbness. Acute physical injury has been shown to lead to analgesia or decreased physical pain (Gray & McNaughton, 2000). Similarly, individuals randomly assigned to experience the social injury of being told they would have a lonely life demonstrated reduced pain sensitivity (DeWall & Baumeister, 2006). Combined with work showing that nonhuman animals that are isolated from conspecifics experience analgesia (e.g., Konecka & Sroczynska, 1990), these results suggest that the realization of social threat triggers physical pain–related mechanisms.

Noninclusion is a form of social exclusion that involves the loss of or the failure to obtain relationship rewards such as intimacy and validation (MacDonald, 2009). For example, being ignored or ostracized (experiences that involve the withholding of social rewards rather than the delivery of social threats) leads to emotional pain in the form of hurt feelings (Leary & Springer, 2001; Williams, 2000). Further, research has suggested that the effects of rejection and noninclusion on emotional pain are independent and additive. In one study, participants received either a constantly negative evaluation from another "participant" (in fact, delivered by a computer program) or an evaluation that changed from positive to negative over time (Buckley et al., 2004). Participants who experienced the constant punishment of negative evaluation reported lower levels of hurt feelings than did those who both lost the social reward of acceptance and received the social punishment of negative evaluation. That is, the addition of lost social reward to experienced social threat appeared to lead to higher degrees of social pain.

As with threat, nonhuman animal research has suggested that lost or unrealized rewards can be painful. For example, an unexpected downshift in degree of sucrose in a sucrose solution facilitates the same escape and startle responses in rats that are promoted by physical injury (Papini, Wood, Daniel, & Norris, 2006). Also, similar to the analgesic response to physical injury and social isolation, rats show decreased pain sensitivity following reward loss (Mustaca & Papini, 2005). Work in our lab has extended these analgesia findings to the realm of human social behavior (Borsook & MacDonald, 2008). Participants in our study began with a baseline test of pain sensitivity, then engaged in a social interaction with a person they believed was another participant. In fact, this "participant" was a confederate (a trained professional actress) who was randomly assigned to interact in one of two ways (those in a third, control condition did not meet the confederate or have an interaction). In the positive interaction condition, the confederate was engaging, validating, and warm. In the indifferent interaction condition, the confederate was not negative or hostile but failed to provide cues of intimacy or connection to the participant (e.g., little eye contact, brief answers to questions). Results showed that participants in the indifferent interaction condition experienced a significant decrease in pain sensitivity. No change in pain sensitivity was found in either the control or positive interaction condition. These results suggest that, as with the delivery of social threats, the withholding of social rewards can be experienced as injurious and thus activate physical pain related systems.

ADULT ATTACHMENT, SOCIAL THREAT OR REWARD, AND THE DEFENSIVE AVOIDANCE OF SOCIAL PAIN

The notion that both rejection and social loss are emotionally painful suggests two defensive strategies that individuals may use to avoid social pain: overestimating the potential for social threat and underestimating the potential for social reward. In this section, we describe research in our lab suggesting that anxiously attached individuals are relatively likely to engage in the pain-avoidance strategy of strong expectation of threat, whereas avoidantly attached individuals are relatively likely to engage in the pain-avoidance strategy of low expectation of reward.

Because perceptions of social threat signal the potential for social injury, attending to realistic signs of social threat is likely to be helpful in avoiding socially painful situations. However, in an attempt to more thoroughly minimize exposure to rejection, an individual may exaggerate and distort social threat perceptions. Although such a strategy of overestimating the degree of social threat may better ensure that rejecting situations do not go undetected, the cost of this strategy is likely to be withdrawn or defensive social behavior even in relatively nonthreatening environments. In this way, heightened social threat perception can become a self-fulfilling prophecy. Indeed, highly rejection sensitive individuals have been shown to behave in ways that increase the likelihood of rejection because of their hypervigilance for threat (Downey et al., 2000; Murray et al., 2003).

Less explored in the literature is the notion that another means for defensively avoiding social pain may be minimizing one's perceptions of social reward potential. By limiting one's expectations regarding the potential for intimacy, one is less likely to experience the social pain associated with disappointment, frustration, or loss. The cost of such a strategy would appear to be lost opportunity for social connection by missing signs of the potential for intimacy.

Bowlby (1973) described the attachment system as functioning to promote proximity between a child and his or her caregiver. A large volume of literature now makes clear that attachment mechanisms operate throughout the life span, focusing on attachment figures such as romantic partners (Mikulincer & Shaver, 2007). Functioning optimally, the attachment system is activated by signs of threat and motivates an individual to signal emotional distress to a caring other who can provide comfort, protection, and support (Shaver & Mikulincer, 2002). Receipt of such care relieves the individual's emotional distress and promotes a sense of bonding to the provider of care. A history of receiving responsive care in potentially threatening situations provides individuals with a sense that emotional distress is manageable and that attachment figures are a resource that can be called on in times of need. Because of their confidence in their ability to respond effectively to distressing situations, securely attached individuals tend to be relatively realistic in their assessment of potential threat (Mikulincer & Shaver, 2007).

However, attachment research has identified two stable profiles of insecurely attached individuals who tend to distort general perceptions of threat in their environments. Although individuals high in anxious attachment strongly crave acceptance and validation from others, they tend to be chronically rejection sensitive and are thus hypervigilant for potential signs of exclusion (Mikulincer & Shaver, 2007). As a result, these individuals tend to overestimate the potential for rejection, which suggests that anxious attachment may be related to the social pain avoidance strategy of exaggerated perceptions of social threat.

Individuals high in avoidant attachment tend to not value relationships highly and claim to prefer independence (Mikulincer & Shaver, 2007). However, research suggests that this stance of self-reliance is a defensive response to fears of rejection and abandonment. Further, these individuals are uncomfortable with the experience of emotional distress because the acknowledgment of such distress would activate attachment systems, motivate the need for closeness, and potentiate the rejection they fear. As a result, avoidantly attached individuals cognitively suppress rather than acknowledge distressing feelings. Avoidantly attached individuals' fear of abandonment and discomfort with distress would seem to provide the motivation to be hypervigilant for social threat to avoid social pain. However, this strategy necessitates acknowledging feelings of threat, something that should be overwhelming for avoidants and thus blocked through cognitive suppression.

We propose that a strategy more likely to be used by avoidantly attached individuals to avoid social pain (at least at the conscious level) may instead be the underestimation of potential social reward. By perceiving social situations as lacking the potential for meaningful connection, individuals high in avoidant attachment reduce the possibility of social pain from frustration or loss. Indeed, avoidant persons have been shown to inhibit feelings of dependence on others (Mikulincer & Shaver, 2007), which suggests a minimization of what they stand to lose in a close relationship. In addition, low perceptions of social reward can help minimize exposure to potentially rejecting situations without the need to acknowledge a fear of rejection. That is, avoidantly attached individuals can withdraw from a social situation with the rationalization that they have little to gain from it, rather than the acknowledgment that they are afraid they will be unliked. That such a strategy may lead to missed social opportunities should be a minimal cost for avoidantly attached individuals whose identities are founded on notions of separateness and independence. Thus, by minimizing perceptions of social reward potential, avoidantly attached individuals may avoid social pain both by minimizing the potential for loss and by providing an excuse for withdrawal from potentially rejecting relationships.

We examined the associations between the attachment dimensions and perceptions of social threat or reward in our research context of interaction with a novel and unknown social partner (MacDonald et al., 2009). Past research has shown that anxious and avoidant attachment are significantly related to general avoidance and approach motivation, respectively (Meyer, Olivier, & Roth, 2005). Thus, to examine whether any relations between the attachment dimensions and social threat or reward perceptions were merely a function of broader approach and avoidance tendencies, we conducted our analyses in Study 1 with the BIS and BAS scales as control variables. Consistent with hypotheses, higher levels of anxious attachment significantly predicted higher levels of social threat perception, whereas the relation between avoidant attachment and social threat was not significant. In the analysis of social reward perception, higher levels of avoidant attachment were a significant, negative predictor. It is interesting that anxious attachment also emerged as a significant, positive predictor of perceptions of social reward in this analysis.

We attempted to replicate these findings in Study 2. To be more comprehensive, we not only used the BIS and BAS scales as a means to control for general avoidance or approach motivation but also included measures of prevention and promotion focus. In addition, to examine whether the link between attachment and social threat and reward perceptions could be attributed to more general personality variables, we included the Big Five personality measures as controls. These analyses revealed that higher levels of anxious attachment again significantly and positively predicted greater perceptions of social threat, whereas avoidant attachment was a nonsignificant predictor. Social reward was again significantly and negatively predicted by avoidant attachment, whereas anxious attachment was a significant, positive predictor of social reward.

Overall, our predictions were strongly supported in this research. Individuals higher in anxious attachment perceived higher degrees of social threat before meeting a stranger. Although this finding is largely a confirmation of existing research, it is interesting to note that this relation could not be accounted for by an exhaustive set of general motivational and personality variables. In addition, individuals higher in anxious attachment were also shown to perceive greater potential for social reward. Supplementary analyses revealed that this effect appeared to emerge particularly when general avoidance motivation as measured by the BIS scale was entered into the equation. In particular, higher levels of BIS were related to lower levels of perceived social reward in this set of analyses. This finding suggests an internal conflict for anxiously attached individuals such that their general sensitivity to threat (which appears to inhibit perceptions of the potential for connection) conflicts with their strong reliance on others for validation and reassurance (which appears to promote perceptions of the potential for connection). Anxiously attached individuals have been described as experiencing an approach–avoid conflict where fears of rejection are at odds with their desire for connection (Mikulincer & Shaver, 2007). The present results suggest the possibility of an additional approach–do not approach conflict involving simultaneous perceptions of high and low potential for social reward.

Supportive of our key hypothesis, the research indicated that individuals higher in avoidant attachment perceived lower potential for social reward in the interaction. This finding suggests that avoidantly attached individuals circumvent the possibility of social pain not by focusing on potential threats but by keeping their hopes for intimacy low. Although this interpretation of the results suggests that low social reward perceptions are a defensive strategy employed by avoidantly attached individuals, an alternative interpretation is that avoidantly attached individuals are simply less sensitive to rewards in their social environment. One argument against this alternative interpretation is that the relation between high avoidant attachment and low social reward remained significant when controlling for general motivational and personality measures (which should account to a large degree for general reward sensitivity and positive affectivity). Further, past research has shown that individuals high in dismissive attachment (i.e., high in avoidant attachment and low in anxious attachment) experience higher levels of positive affect and self-esteem than do more securely attached individuals upon learning they are liked by others or will have successful interpersonal futures (Carvallo & Gabriel, 2006). This work suggests that avoidantly attached individuals are indeed capable of experiencing positive feelings in response to positive social circumstances.

Although this past work demonstrates that avoidantly attached individuals are as capable as others of experiencing positive feelings at the idea of being accepted, it does not show that avoidantly attached individuals are as capable of feeling socially connected in real social situations. Thus, the possibility remains that avoidantly attached individuals do not anticipate feelings of social reward because of a realistic expectation that they will feel relatively low levels of interpersonal connection with their interaction partner. To account for this possibility, we tested whether those high in avoidant attachment were sensitive to feelings of connection in a follow-up study. We reasoned that if avoidantly attached individuals were simply deficient at experiencing intimacy, then they should experience low levels of connection even in interaction with a highly rewarding partner. On the other hand, if the defensive strategy of low reward perceptions leaves their need to belong strongly unfulfilled (Carvallo & Gabriel, 2006), not only may those high in avoidant attachment experience connection equal to that of low avoidants in response to a rewarding partner, but high avoidants may even experience a stronger sense of connection. That is, those who starve themselves of social connection to avoid social pain may especially relish the rare times when the strong pull of an unusually warm person draws them out of their shell and into an open and validating interaction.

In Study 3 (MacDonald et al., 2009), then, participants engaged in an interaction with our trained confederate–actress. As described earlier, those randomly assigned to the positive interaction condition experienced the confederate as warm, open, and validating. Those assigned to the indifferent interaction condition experienced the confederate as uninterested but not rejecting. Immediately following the interaction, both the participant and the confederate evaluated the degree of connection they felt with each other (the confederate could not be blind to condition but was blind to participants' attachment scores). In the indifferent interaction condition, avoidant attachment was a significant, negative predictor of participants' feelings of connection to the confederate. In the positive interaction condition, however, higher levels of avoidant attachment significantly predicted stronger feelings of connection to the confederate. This latter finding appeared to be validated by the confederate's own feelings of connection. Although avoidant attachment was not related to the confederate's feelings of connection in the indifferent interaction condition, higher avoidant attachment was significantly related to stronger feelings of connection in the positive interaction condition.

This study suggests that the relatively low social reward perceptions of those high in avoidant attachment are not a result of an inability to detect reward in the social environment. In fact, if anything, avoidantly attached individuals appeared hypersensitive to the degree of reward in the social environment. In an interaction with a partner who offered lower levels of intimacy, avoidantly attached individuals felt less of a sense of connection than did those lower in avoidant attachment. Conversely, in an interaction with a highly rewarding partner, those higher in avoidant attachment felt a stronger sense of connection than did those lower in avoidant attachment. That the confederate also experienced stronger feelings of connection to avoidants in the high reward condition suggests that these participants' feelings of intimacy were not merely an intrapersonal phenomenon but something that affected their interpersonal behavior. These data are consistent with the hypothesis that low expectation of social reward is not due to a lack of reward sensitivity but is rather a defensive strategy employed by individuals high in avoidant attachment that protects them from pain but leaves them starving for connection.

CONCLUSIONS

Gable and Strachman (2008) noted that although research has long considered social avoidance and approach motivations in isolation, a full understanding of the regulation of social behavior can result only from work such as theirs that investigates these factors in tandem. Our program of research is beginning to suggest that understanding the positives and negatives that underlie social behavior will also necessitate a simultaneous consideration of social threat and reward perceptions. The research described in this chapter demonstrates that perceptions of the potential for rejection and connection can be independent of one another, relate predictably to a range of individual differences, and have measurable implications for social outcomes. Perceptions of potential for social threat correlate strongly with standard social sensitivity measures and appear to motivate prosocial behavior aimed at avoiding negative evaluation. Perceptions of the potential for social connection, on the other hand, are poorly captured by existing social sensitivity measures. Whereas those who perceived more potential for social reward were not more liked by others under baseline conditions, when social approach goals were seemingly activated by social pain, higher social reward perception predicted being more liked.

Perceptions of social threat and reward also appear important for understanding how insecure individuals defend themselves against the experience of social pain. Anxiously attached individuals evaluate social interaction as potentially threatening, consistent with the notion that anxious attachment promotes a hypervigilance for signs of rejection. Although such a strategy may ensure that cues predictive of social pain are not missed, research has suggested that the defensive and hostile reactions this strategy engenders too often lead to rejection in a self-fulfilling manner (Mikulincer & Shaver, 2007).

More novel to the literature, understanding that the loss of social rewards can also be painful suggests that limiting social reward perceptions can minimize exposure to social pain by leaving an individual with nothing to lose. Indeed, our work suggests that avoidantly attached individuals defensively underestimate the potential for social reward. This is not simply because those higher in avoidant attachment are universally insensitive to the presence of reward. After interacting with a highly rewarding social partner, those high in avoidance felt more connected to a new acquaintance than did those low in avoidance, a finding confirmed by their partner's own ratings of connection. This pattern suggests that those high in avoidant attachment essentially starve themselves of connection through their low reward perceptions, such that when they do encounter an undeniably warm and validating other they are especially taken by feelings of intimacy.

In light of the validity of the distinction between social threats and social rewards, future research will need to investigate what implications this distinction has in the context of socially painful situations. Research is already beginning to suggest that the presence of social threats and the absence of social rewards may have different motivational consequences. Molden, Lucas, Gardner, Dean, and Knowles (2009) reasoned that being actively rejected (which provides a clear signal of social threat) should result in motivation to prevent further social losses whereas being ignored (which provides a signal of lack of social reward) should result in motivation to promote social gains. Their research confirmed these hypotheses, showing that experiences of rejection lead to higher levels of social withdrawal whereas experiences of being ignored lead to higher levels of social engagement.

Our more general view is that researchers in areas related to social exclusion have not thoroughly explored the importance of social opportunities for the resolution of social pain. For example, anxiously attached individuals have been shown to be more likely to remain emotionally attached to ex-partners following relationship dissolution than are more secure individuals (e.g., Sbarra, 2006). This finding seems hard to explain in terms of social threat because anxiously attached individuals often continue to pine even for those who rejected them. Instead, our research has suggested that perceived potential for social connection may be what drives anxiously attached individuals' emotional ties. Spielmann, MacDonald, and Wilson (2009) demonstrated experimentally that perceiving more potential for new romantic opportunities significantly increases the chances that anxiously attached individuals will let go of feelings for their past partners. That is, perceived potential for social connection appears to be key in detachment from sources of pain, at least within the context of romantic relationships.

Of course, to this point our research on social rewards and threats has been conducted only in the context of interactions with strangers, leaving many questions currently unanswered. For example, although orthogonal in the context of interactions with strangers, perhaps perceptions of social threat and reward potential in more established relationships are not uncorrelated. Whereas rejection by a stranger does not lead to a loss of connection (as there is no existing intimacy), rejection by a spouse is more closely tied to the loss of important bonds. In more general terms, perhaps the dynamics of social threat and reward perceptions would differ when a known social entity is evaluated. Thus far, participants in our research have evaluated social threat and reward potential with no knowledge of any specifics of their interaction partner. In this sense, our participants are making evaluations of situations that are somewhat akin to projective tests, rather than making evaluations of the perceived characteristics of individuals. It is also unclear whether the effects of social threat and reward perceptions on interpersonal liking would change beyond first impressions, as an interaction progressed. For example, perceiving potential for reward in an interaction may affect social outcomes not just by the presentation one makes to others but by the behavior that one draws out of others. Those who expect interpersonal connection may ask questions that draw out greater depth of self-disclosure, thus promoting intimacy.

It is clear, then, that the research presented in this chapter represents only a tentative step toward a more complete understanding of the role of social threat and reward perception in the regulation of social behavior. Nevertheless, we hope that this work does make clear to researchers interested in social pain that such pain can come both from experiences of rejection and the loss of connection. Although loss as a source of social pain has been less discussed, at least within social psychology, it would appear that those high in avoidant attachment are familiar enough with such pain to defend against it with distorted perceptions of low social reward. In light of the separate physiological underpinnings of avoidance and approach motivations, it appears that future research at both the social and physiological level would benefit from carefully distinguishing between the pain of rejection and loss.

REFERENCES

Baumeister, R. F., & Leary, M. R. (1995). The need to belong: Desire for interpersonal attachments as a fundamental human motivation. *Psychological Bulletin*, *117*, 497–529. doi:10.1037/0033-2909.117.3.497

Borsook, T., & MacDonald, G. (2008). *Mild social exclusion causes analgesia*. Unpublished manuscript.

Bowlby, J. (1973). *Attachment and loss* (Vol. 2). New York, NY: Basic Books.

Buckley, K. E., Winkel, R. E., & Leary, M. R. (2004). Reactions to acceptance and rejection: Effects of level and sequence of relational evaluation. *Journal of Experimental Social Psychology*, *40*, 14–28. doi:10.1016/S0022-1031(03)00064-7

Carvallo, M., & Gabriel, S. (2006). No man is an island: The need to belong and dismissive avoidant attachment style. *Personality and Social Psychology Bulletin*, *32*, 697–709. doi:10.1177/0146167205285451

Carver, C. S., Sutton, S. K., & Scheier, M. F. (2000). Action, emotion, and personality: Emerging conceptual integration. *Personality and Social Psychology Bulletin, 26*, 741–751. doi:10.1177/0146167200268008

Carver, C. S., & White, T. L. (1994). Behavioral inhibition, behavioral activation, and affective responses to impending reward and punishment: The BIS/BAS scales. *Journal of Personality and Social Psychology, 67*, 319–333. doi:10.1037/0022-3514.67.2.319

Chen, Z., Williams, K. D., Fitness, J., & Newton, N. C. (2008). When hurt will not heal: Exploring the capacity to relive social and physical pain. *Psychological Science, 19*, 789–795. doi:10.1111/j.1467-9280.2008.02158.x

Cohen, S., & Hoberman, H. M. (1983). Positive events and social supports as buffers of life change stress. *Journal of Applied Social Psychology, 13*, 99–125. doi:10.1111/j.1559-1816.1983.tb02325.x

Corr, P. J. (2005). Social exclusion and the hierarchical defense system: Comment on MacDonald and Leary (2005). *Psychological Bulletin, 131*, 231–236. doi:10.1037/0033-2909.131.2.231

DeWall, C. N., & Baumeister, R. F. (2006). Alone but feeling no pain: Effects of social exclusion on physical pain tolerance and pain threshold, affective forecasting, and interpersonal empathy. *Journal of Personality and Social Psychology, 91*, 1–15. doi:10.1037/0022-3514.91.1.1

Dickerson, S. S., & Kemeny, M. E. (2004). Acute stressors and cortisol responses: A theoretical integration and synthesis of laboratory research. *Psychological Bulletin, 130*, 355–391. doi:10.1037/0033-2909.130.3.355

Downey, G., & Feldman, S. I. (1996). Implications of rejection sensitivity for intimate relationships. *Journal of Personality and Social Psychology, 70*, 1327–1343. doi:10.1037/0022-3514.70.6.1327

Downey, G., Feldman, S. I., & Ayduk, O. (2000). Rejection sensitivity and male violence in romantic relationships. *Personal Relationships, 7*, 45–61. doi:10.1111/j.1475-6811.2000.tb00003.x

Gable, S. L. (2006). Approach and avoidance social motives and goals. *Journal of Personality, 74*, 175–222. doi:10.1111/j.1467-6494.2005.00373.x

Gable, S. L., & Strachman, A. (2008). Approaching social rewards and avoiding social punishments: Appetitive and aversive social motivation. In J. Shah & W. Gardner (Eds.), *Handbook of motivation science* (pp. 561–575). New York, NY: Guilford Press.

Gray, J. A., & McNaughton, N. (2000). *The neuropsychology of anxiety*. New York, NY: Oxford University Press.

Heatherton, T. F., & Vohs, K. D. (2000). Interpersonal evaluations following threats to self: Role of self-esteem. *Journal of Personality and Social Psychology, 78*, 725–736. doi:10.1037/0022-3514.78.4.725

Higgins, E. T., Friedman, R. S., Harlow, R. E., Idson, L. C., Ayduk, O. N., & Taylor, A. (2001). Achievement orientations from subjective histories of success:

Promotion pride versus prevention pride. *European Journal of Social Psychology*, *31*, 3–23. doi:10.1002/ejsp.27

Impett, E. A., Gable, S. L., & Peplau, L. A. (2005). Giving up and giving in: The costs and benefits of daily sacrifice in intimate relationships. *Journal of Personality and Social Psychology*, *89*, 465–482.

John, O. P., & Srivastava, S. (1999). The Big Five trait taxonomy: History, measurement, and theoretical perspectives. In L. A. Pervin & O. P. John (Eds.), *Handbook of personality: Theory and research* (2nd ed., pp. 102–138). New York, NY: Guilford Press.

Konecka, A. M., & Sroczynska, I. (1990). Stressors and pain sensitivity in CFW mice: Role of opioid peptides. *Archives Internationales de Physiologie et de Biochimie*, *98*, 245–252. doi:10.3109/13813459009113984

Laurenceau, J. P., & Kleinman, B. M. (2006). Intimacy in personal relationships. In A. L. Vangelisti & D. Perlman (Eds.), *The Cambridge handbook of personal relationships* (pp. 637–653). New York, NY: Cambridge University Press.

Leary, M. R. (1983). A brief version of the fear of negative evaluation scale. *Personality and Social Psychology Bulletin*, *9*, 371–375. doi:10.1177/0146167283093007

Leary, M. R., Kelly, K. M., Cottrell, C. A., & Schreindorfer, L. S. (2007). *Individual differences in the need to belong: Mapping the nomological network*. Unpublished manuscript.

Leary, M. R., & Springer, C. A. (2001). Hurt feelings: The neglected emotion. In R. Kowalski (Ed.), *Aversive behaviors in interpersonal relationships* (pp. 151–175). Washington, DC: American Psychological Association. doi:10.1037/10365-006

Leary, M. R., Springer, C. A., Negel, L., Ansell, E., & Evans, K. (1998). The causes, phenomenology, and consequences of hurt feelings. *Journal of Personality and Social Psychology*, *74*, 1225–1237. doi:10.1037/0022-3514.74.5.1225

Leary, M. R., Twenge, J. M., & Quinlivan, E. (2006). Interpersonal rejection as a determinant of anger and aggression. *Personality and Social Psychology Review*, *10*, 111–132. doi:10.1207/s15327957pspr1002_2

Locke, K. D. (2008). Attachment styles and interpersonal approach and avoidance goals in everyday couple interactions. *Personal Relationships*, *15*, 359–374. doi:10.1111/j.1475-6811.2008.00203.x

MacDonald, G. (2009). Social pain and hurt feelings. In P. Corr & G. Matthews (Eds.), *The Cambridge handbook of personality* (pp. 541–555). Cambridge, England: Cambridge University Press.

MacDonald, G., & Leary, M. R. (2002, February). *The devil that knows you: Self-esteem and feeling known in interpersonal evaluation*. Poster presented at the Society for Personality and Social Psychology Conference, Savannah, GA.

MacDonald, G., & Leary, M. R. (2005). Why does social exclusion hurt? The relationship between social and physical pain. *Psychological Bulletin*, *131*, 202–223. doi:10.1037/0033-2909.131.2.202

MacDonald, G., Tackett, J. L., & Borsook, T. K. (2009). *Attachment, social threat, and social reward*. Unpublished manuscript.

Maner, J. K., DeWall, C. N., Baumeister, R. F., & Schaller, M. (2007). Does social exclusion motivate interpersonal reconnection? Resolving the "porcupine problem." *Journal of Personality and Social Psychology, 92*, 42–55. doi:10.1037/0022-3514.92.1.42

Meyer, B., Olivier, L., & Roth, D. A. (2005). Please don't leave me! BIS/BAS, attachment styles, and responses to a relationship threat. *Personality and Individual Differences, 38*, 151–162. doi:10.1016/j.paid.2004.03.016

Mikulincer, M., & Shaver, P. R. (2007). *Attachment in adulthood: Structure, dynamics, and change*. New York, NY: Guilford Press.

Molden, D. C., Lucas, G. M., Gardner, W. L., Dean, K., & Knowles, M. L. (2009). Motivations for prevention or promotion following social exclusion: Being rejected versus being ignored. *Journal of Personality and Social Psychology, 96*, 415–431.

Murray, S. L., Bellavia, G. M., Rose, P., & Griffin, D. W. (2003). Once hurt, twice hurtful: How perceived regard regulates daily marital interactions. *Journal of Personality and Social Psychology, 84*, 126–147. doi:10.1037/0022-3514.84.1.126

Murray, S. L., Derrick, J. L., Leder, S., & Holmes, J. G. (2008). Balancing connectedness and self-protection goals in close relationships: A levels-of-processing perspective on risk regulation. *Journal of Personality and Social Psychology, 94*, 429–459. doi:10.1037/0022-3514.94.3.429

Murray, S. L., Holmes, J. G., & Collins, N. L. (2006). Optimizing assurance: The risk regulation system in relationships. *Psychological Bulletin, 132*, 641–666. doi:10.1037/0033-2909.132.5.641

Mustaca, A. E., & Papini, M. R. (2005). Consummatory successive negative contrast induces hypoalgesia. *International Journal of Comparative Psychology, 18*, 333–339.

Papini, M. R., Wood, M., Daniel, A. M., & Norris, J. N. (2006). Reward loss as psychological pain. *International Journal of Psychology & Psychological Therapy, 6*, 189–213.

Rosenberg, M. (1979). *Conceiving the self*. New York, NY: Basic Books.

Russell, D. W. (1996). UCLA Loneliness Scale (Version 3): Reliability, validity, and factor structure. *Journal of Personality Assessment, 66*, 20–40. doi:10.1207/s15327752jpa6601_2

Sbarra, D. A. (2006). Predicting the onset of emotional recovery following nonmarital relationship dissolution: Survival analyses of sadness and anger. *Personality and Social Psychology Bulletin, 32*, 298–312. doi:10.1177/0146167205280913

Shaver, P. R., & Mikulincer, M. (2002). Attachment-related psychodynamics. *Attachment & Human Development, 4*, 133–161. doi:10.1080/14616730210154171

Spielmann, S. S., MacDonald, G., & Wilson, A. E. (2009). On the rebound: Focusing on someone new helps anxiously attached individuals let go of ex-partners. *Personality and Social Psychology Bulletin, 35*, 1382–1394. doi:10.1177/0146167209341580

Strachman, A., & Gable, S. L. (2006). What you want (and do not want) affects what you see (and do not see): Avoidance social goals and social events. *Personality and Social Psychology Bulletin, 32,* 1446–1458. doi:10.1177/0146167206291007

Twenge, J. M., Baumeister, R. F., DeWall, C. N., Ciarocco, N. J., & Bartels, J. M. (2007). Social exclusion decreases prosocial behavior. *Journal of Personality and Social Psychology, 92,* 56–66. doi:10.1037/0022-3514.92.1.56

Williams, K. D. (2000). *Ostracism: The power of silence.* New York, NY: Guilford Press.

7

SOCIAL PAIN IS EASILY RELIVED AND PRELIVED, BUT PHYSICAL PAIN IS NOT

ZHANSHENG CHEN AND KIPLING D. WILLIAMS

No man is an island, entire of itself; every man is a piece of the continent, a part of the main. If a clod be washed away by the sea, Europe is the less, as well as if a promontory were, as well as if a manor of thy friend's or of thine own were. Any man's death diminishes me, because I am involved in mankind; and therefore never send to know for whom the bell tolls; it tolls for thee.

—John Donne

If no one turned round when we entered, answered when we spoke, or minded what we did, but if every person we met "cut us dead," and acted as if we were non-existing things, a kind of rage and impotent despair would ere long well up in us, from which the cruelest bodily tortures would be a relief.

—William James

Donne's (1624/1959) meditation emphasized two features of human beings. The first is that human beings are not isolated from each other but interconnected. Therefore, threats to social bonds can lead to emotional suffering. The negative emotions arising from the threat to social inclusion status (e.g., ostracism or social exclusion, rejection, death of a loved one) have been referred to as *social pain* (Eisenberger & Lieberman, 2004; MacDonald & Leary, 2005; Panksepp, 1998). The second feature is that all human beings will have to face inevitable mortality. Because human beings are interconnected with others, the death of others means the loss of social bonds for individuals and thus can lead to negative emotions. Indeed, research indicates that the death of a close other (e.g., a spouse, a close friend) is among the most stressful life events (Weiss, 1979). James (1890/1950) further suggested that social pain could be more devastating than physical pain. Consistent with James's suggestion, in this chapter we argue that an important difference exists between social pain and physical pain. We suggest that although both social pain and physical pain are agonizingly intense, physical pain is typically short-lived, whereas social pain may last forever. In addition, this chapter shows that social pain can be more easily experienced, compared with physical pain, by imagining future scenarios. These differences between social and physical pain have important theoretical and methodological implications.

OVERLAP BETWEEN SOCIAL PAIN AND PHYSICAL PAIN

Consistent with Donne's (1624/1959) quote that "no man is an island," research in social psychology over the past half century has provided substantial evidence that human beings form social bonds with others quickly and easily (Baumeister & Leary, 1995; Sherif, Harvey, White, Hood, & Sherif, 1961/1988; Tajfel, 1970; Tajfel, Flament, Billig, & Bundy, 1971). For example, previously unacquainted boys can form strong ties with their randomly assigned groups (Sherif et al., 1961/1988). Furthermore, Tajfel and colleagues (Tajfel, 1970; Tajfel et al., 1971) found that once people were assigned to an arbitrary category, they began to help other members in the same category. People showed this ingroup favoritism even when they were clearly told that the groups were assigned by lottery (Locksley, Ortiz, & Hepburn, 1980). Indeed, people seem to like whomever they spend time with, even if these are members of a previously disliked or stereotyped outgroup (Wilder & Thompson, 1980).

When compared with connections with strangers, social bonds with important others should be more critical for an individual's survival. Theorists have emphasized the importance of these social bonds by treating belonging as a basic human need (Baumeister & Leary, 1995; Bowlby, 1959; Maslow, 1968). For example, Maslow (1968) suggested that belongingness needs would emerge once the physiological needs (e.g., needs for food, water, sex) and the safety needs (e.g., security of health, employment) of an individual are satisfied. According to Baumeister and Leary's (1995) belongingness hypothesis, human beings have a pervasive drive to form and maintain at least a minimum quality of interpersonal relationships. People need to have frequent personal contacts with significant others, and they need to perceive these interpersonal bonds as stable, positive, and lasting. Baumeister and Leary (1995) even suggested that "belongingness can be almost as compelling a need as food" (p. 498) and that "much of what human beings do is done in the service of belongingness" (p. 498).

Forming social bonds is critical for the survival of human beings, and it is not surprising that research from different disciplines, including social psychology, developmental psychology, personality psychology, and social neuroscience, has generated converging evidence suggesting that people experience pain and emotional distress when facing social rejection and exclusion (MacDonald & Leary, 2005; Williams, 2001, 2007; Williams, Cheung, & Choi, 2000; Williams, Forgas, & von Hippel, 2005). For instance, when separated from caregivers, human infants immediately experience separation anxiety (Robertson & Bowlby, 1952), which is part of infants' sets of instinctual responses (e.g., sucking, clinging, smiling, crying) that function to bind each infant to its caregiver (Bowlby, 1958, 1959, 1960). In addition, excessive separation anxiety can be caused by adverse experiences, such as repeated threats of abandonment or rejection (Bowlby, 1959). Similar to infants' separation anxiety, adults experience anxiety and hurt feelings when separated from their romantic partners. Many researchers argue that romantic love in adulthood is an attachment process through which affectionate bonds with romantic partners are formed (Bartholomew & Horowitz, 1991; Hazan & Shaver, 1987, 1994).

In this chapter, we use the term *social pain* to refer to the emotional reaction to perceptions of social exclusion or ostracism, rejection, and relational devaluation. Social pain is a relatively new term, and although it is used consistently among researchers, some definitional variability exists. For example, Panksepp and colleagues (Nelson & Panksepp, 1998; Panksepp, 1998) referred to the emotional distress during social separation as social pain. MacDonald and Leary (2005) extended social pain to describe an emotional reaction to the perception that one is being excluded from desired relationships or being devalued by desired relationship partners or groups. Similarly, Eisenberger and Lieberman (2004) defined social pain as the distressing experience arising from the perception of actual or potential psychological distance from close others or from a social group. Despite differences in their boundaries, these definitions concur that being separated from, or excluded by, close others is the critical stimulus that leads to social pain. In addition, all of these definitions share two underlying assumptions: that human beings have an innate need to form positive and lasting relationships with others and that humans experience emotional distress when these positive and lasting relationships are threatened.

Mounting evidence has been put forth to suggest similarities between social pain and the pain caused by tissue damage (i.e., physical pain; see MacDonald & Leary, 2005). For instance, sudden emotional stress (e.g., death of a loved one) can result in severe heart muscle weakness that mimics a classic heart attack (Wittstein, et al., 2005). This phenomenon is referred to as the *broken heart syndrome*. In a study by Eisenberger, Lieberman, and Williams (2003), participants in a functional magnetic resonance imaging scanner were led to believe that they would be playing an online ball-tossing game (i.e., Cyberball) with two other players. During one stage of the game, participants were included, whereas in another stage of the game, participants were excluded. When participants were ostracized, they showed significantly increased activity in their dorsal anterior cingulate cortices, similar to the significant increase observed during physical pain. In addition, both psychological and linguistic evidence support the overlap between social pain and physical pain (see MacDonald & Leary, 2005). For instance, people use the words *hurt, wounded,* or *crushed* to describe both social and physical pain, and this linguistic link between social and physical pain can be found across a wide variety of languages and cultures (MacDonald & Leary, 2005).

Furthermore, social pain and physical pain are also related to social support in similar ways. In a meta-analysis, Finch, Okun, Pool, and Ruehlman (1999) found that social support was negatively related with psychological distress. As shown in the review by MacDonald and Leary (2005), social support is associated with lower levels of chronic pain, cardiac pain, child labor pain, and postoperative pain; both social exclusion and physical pain are related to the activation of emotional states related to cautious approach (anxiety) and avoidance (fear); and both social pain and physical pain are positively related to depression and aggression.

These similarities between social pain and physical pain have led theorists to argue that the social pain system, which signals threat to an individual's social inclusion status, may overlap with the physical pain system, which alerts individuals to threats in the environment (Eisenberger & Lieberman, 2004; MacDonald & Leary, 2005). For instance, according to MacDonald and Leary's (2005) social pain theory, social animals require a system to punish individuals who do not avoid social exclusion and to motivate quick responses to signs of exclusion. They argue that during the period in evolutionary history when a social exclusion system was developed, physical pain mechanisms already existed and provided its foundation; thus, social exclusion is experienced as painful because reactions to rejection are mediated by aspects of the physical pain system. Similarly, Eisenberger and Lieberman (2004) suggested that physical pain and social pain share neural and computational mechanisms. This shared system is responsible for detecting cues that might be harmful for survival, such as physical danger or social separation, and recruiting attention and coping resources to minimize the threat.

Indeed, most chapters in this volume are directed toward supporting the overlap between social pain and physical pain. Social pain and physical pain may share some of the same mechanisms, but does this overlap mean that social pain and physical pain are essentially the same construct, with the same sensory and psychological features and consequences? In the following section, we present several studies that tested whether social pain can be more easily triggered through cognitive processes than can physical pain. In these studies we focused on how social pain and physical pain differ when people are asked to recall past painful experiences (i.e., pain reliving) and when people are asked to imagine future hurtful events (i.e., pain preliving).

SOCIAL PAIN IS MORE EASILY RELIVED THAN PHYSICAL PAIN

Pain memory research suggests that social pain may be more easily relived than physical pain. A memory of pain includes three components: a pain event memory, a pain experience memory, and the sensory reexperience of pain (Morley, 1993). Pain events (i.e., the circumstance in which the pain is experienced) are highly memorable and likely to be encoded into long-term memory because they are associated with high levels of distress and are relatively infrequent (Robinson & Swanson, 1990). Pain experience refers to the sensory, affective, and intensity qualities of pain (Morley, 1993). Although contextual factors, such as expectations and moods, have been found to influence the accuracy of physical pain experience memory (see Salovey, Sieber, Jobe, & Willis, 1994), people are still able to recall these experiences with accuracy (Erskine, Morley, & Pearce, 1990; Morley, 1993). Research has found similar results for memories surrounding social pain experiences. For example, Safer, Bonanno, and Field (2001) asked participants to report their feelings and thoughts 6 months after the death of their spouses. Four years later, they asked participants to report how they had felt during the first report; they found that the participants accurately recalled their feelings from 4 years earlier. Porter and Peace (2007) further demonstrated that individuals' memories of traumatic social and physical experiences remained unchanged several years later.

Although social pain and physical pain share similarities in pain event memory and pain experience memory, the two types of pain may differ along the sensory reexperience dimension of memory. For example, Morley (1993) asked participants to report their past experiences of physical pain. Almost all of the participants in Morley's study were able to recall experiences in great detail, such as specific events that had occurred and how they had felt; however, none of them reported feelings of pain during the experience. That is, these individuals could recall their past physical pain and remember how painful it was; however, they were not able to relive or reexperience it. Social pain, on the other hand, seems to be different. For example, people 60 years and older reported that they still had negative feelings (e.g., anger, grief) about social pain experiences that had happened in the past (Hansson, Jones, & Fletcher, 1990). Although this study did not directly test whether participants were able to reexperience their original feelings, the fact that they continue to feel negatively about events long ago suggests that social pain can be reexperienced or relived. In sum, these studies suggest that social pain may be more easily and more intensely relived than physical pain.

In a series of studies, we (Chen, 2008; Chen, Williams, Fitness, & Newton, 2008) tested this hypothesis with direct as well as indirect measures of pain. In Study 1 (Chen et al., 2008), we used a within-subjects design and instructed participants to recall a past social pain experience and a past physical pain experience. In Study 2 (Chen et al., 2008), we used a between-subjects design and asked participants to recall either a past social pain experience or a physical pain experience. For each experience, we asked participants to indicate when the events happened and to rate the level of pain that they initially felt when the event happened (i.e., initial pain) on a visual analog scale—the Pain Slide.

Participants were then asked to write in detail what had happened to them and how they had felt during the experience. To facilitate the reliving of past experiences, experimenters reminded participants several times to write as detailed an account of the event as they could. Following the pain reliving, participants were asked to indicate, using the Pain Slide and the McGill Pain Questionnaire (MPQ; Melzack, 1975, 1983), their current feelings of pain during the experiment. Both studies used the major index from the MPQ Pain Rating Index (PRI), which indicates the level of current pain.

Participants in both studies reported that the social pain and physical pain were equally painful when they were initially experienced (as measured by the Pain Slide). More important, both studies found that social pain was relived more intensely than was physical pain (as measured by both the Pain Slide and the PRI scores). Further analysis indicated that the social pain experience and the physical pain experience did not differ on event recency or frequency of recall (e.g., from being shared with other people), and the number of words used to describe both types of experience did not differ. Finally, the differences were not moderated by gender.

In addition to these direct measures of pain, we also used indirect measures to test whether social pain is more intensely relived than is physical pain. Past research has documented that physical pain interrupts, distracts, and demands attention (Price, 1988) and thus impairs cognitive performance (Eccleston & Crombez, 1999). Research recently showed that social pain interrupts and demands attention as well. For example, Baumeister et al. (2002) found significant decrements in cognitive performance for complex cognitive tasks (e.g., effortful logic and reasoning) when people were told that they would end up alone later in life. However, this manipulation had no effect on simple information-processing tasks.

If recalling social pain leads to a higher level of reexperienced pain than does recalling physical pain, one should find a higher degree of impairment, compared with physical pain, on cognitively demanding tasks. Thus, people's performances on cognitive tasks can serve as an indirect measure of pain. We (Chen et al., 2008) recently asked participants to recall a past socially painful event or a past physically painful event and compared their cognitive performances in each of these two conditions. In one study, following pain reliving, participants were asked to work on two separate tasks with different levels of difficulty: a lexical decision task (designated as an easy task during pretesting) and a Stroop task (designated as a difficult task during pretesting; Study 3; Chen et al., 2008). For each item on the lexical decision task, participants were asked to indicate as quickly as possible whether a string of letters was a word or a nonword. During the Stroop task, participants were asked to quickly judge the color in which a word was written, which might be different from the color the word names (e.g., if the word *blue* were presented in red ink, participants should say "red").

To perform accurately on the Stroop test, individuals must suppress, or inhibit, their tendencies to read a word when the semantic meaning of the word differs from the color in which it is written (e.g., word *blue* written in green ink). In contrast, the lexical decision task requires only a comparison between a letter string and vocabulary in memory. In this study, participants in the social pain condition did not differ from participants in the physical pain condition in their performance on the lexical decision task. However, participants in the social pain condition showed impaired performance on the Stroop test compared with those in the physical pain condition. For example, following the social pain recall task, participants responded more slowly on the Stroop test than they did following the physical pain recall task. This outcome suggests that reliving social pain affects performance on cognitively demanding tasks.

In another study (Study 4; Chen et al., 2008), we asked participants to recall a painful event and then work on a remote association test (RAT), which included items pretested as easy and items pretested as difficult. For each item, we presented participants with three words and asked participants to find a fourth word that related to each of the previous three. For example, *house* is the remote associate of the words *paint*, *doll*, and *cat* because it can combine with each to make *house-paint*, *dollhouse*, and *housecat* (for further information on the RAT, see McFarlin & Blascovich, 1984). Participants performed equally well on the easy items following the social pain and physical pain recall tasks. However, participants performed worse on the difficult items following social pain recall compared with physical pain recall. In the previous study, the lexical decision test and the Stroop test required different mental processes; in this study, the easy RAT items and the difficult RAT items involved the same mental processes. Together, these results indicate that social pain reliving makes effortful information processing more difficult, whether this involves the inhibition of automatic tendencies (the Stroop test) or the retrieval of knowledge to solve challenging questions (the difficult RAT items). The finding that ruminating about past socially hurtful events can lead to cognitive deficiencies further suggests that relived social pain is experienced as more painful than relived physical pain.

Chen (2008) also used people's sensitivity to physical pressure as an indirect measure of pain to provide converging evidence for the hypothesized difference between social pain and physical pain. Physical pain signals highly proximal threat, and it activates panic responses, which are accompanied by a set of psychological changes such as increased heart rate, increased blood clotting factor, and decreased sensitivity to physical pain or analgesia (Gray & McNaughton, 2000). Social pain has been shown to lead to a similar analgesic response. For example, DeWall and Baumeister (2006) asked participants to work on a bogus personality test. Following the test, participants were told that they would live alone in the future (future alone condition), have a lot of lasting relationships in the future (future belonging condition), or have a lot of accidents in the future (accident-prone condition). Following the feedback, participants' pain sensitivity, including pain threshold (i.e., the amount of pressure that leads to feelings of pain) and pain tolerance (i.e., the maximum amount of pressure that one can bear), was measured. Participants in the future alone condition were found to have lower scores on both the pain threshold and the pain tolerance measures, compared with participants in the other two conditions. Thus, participants were able to endure higher levels of pain and were less likely to detect the pain caused by physical stimuli, after being told that they would live alone in the future.

If social pain is more easily relived than physical pain, then we would be more likely to observe a decrease in sensitivity to physical stimuli following social pain recall compared with physical pain recall. Thus, Chen (Study 3; 2008) asked participants to recall either a past socially painful event or a past physically painful event. As in previous studies, participants were asked to write down what had happened to them and how they had felt. An experimenter applied pressure to each participant's second, third, and fourth fingers, via a pressure algometer, before and after he or she recalled the painful event. Participants were asked to report when they began to feel pain from the pressure (i.e., pain threshold) and when they could no longer bear the pain caused by the pressure (i.e., pain tolerance). Participants became less sensitive to pressure applied to their fingers following social pain recall, compared with physical pain recall, such that higher amounts of pressure were applied before they began to feel any pain, and they were able to bear higher levels before declaring the pressure too painful.

This study is consistent with a study by DeWall and Baumeister (2006) but differs from some recent studies by MacDonald and colleagues (MacDonald, 2008; MacDonald, Kingsbury, & Shaw, 2005). For example, MacDonald et al. (Study 2; 2005) asked participants to complete a hurt proneness scale (Leary & Springer, 2000) and then ostracized or included them via a Cyberball game. After the game, participants' pain thresholds were measured using a pressure algometer. On the basis of this procedure, MacDonald et al. (2005) reported that participants high in hurt proneness were significantly less sensitive toward pain when they were ostracized compared with when they were included, and that this pattern was not present in those low in hurt proneness. We (Study 3; Chen, 2008) also asked participants to complete the hurt proneness scale (Leary & Springer, 2000) at the beginning of the experiment; however, individual differences in hurt proneness did not moderate the difference in pain sensitivity in the social pain and physical pain conditions. That is, social pain recall, compared with physical pain recall, led to decreased sensitivity to physical pressure, regardless of the individual's level of hurt proneness.

In addition, MacDonald (2008) excluded participants via Cyberball (Study 1) or describing emotions associated with a past rejection experience (Studies 2 and 3). The experimenter measured participants' pain threshold and their pain tolerance before and after this manipulation. Across three studies, participants with both high baseline pain thresholds and high anxious attachment reported high postmanipulation pain thresholds following social exclusion. In these studies (MacDonald, 2008), social exclusion manipulations influenced participants' pain thresholds but not pain tolerance. These differences could be caused by the manipulations in different studies. As MacDonald mentioned, the manipulations in his studies were less strong, whereas manipulations in DeWall and Baumeister's (2006) research and in our own research are stronger.

Together, the studies from our lab provide converging evidence that social pain can be more easily relived than physical pain as revealed through both direct and indirect measures. Individuals reported that past physical pain was hurtful, and they recalled in great detail what happened to them, yet they were unable to reexperience past physical pain. This finding is consistent with pain memory research regarding physical pain; however, social pain is different from physical pain: It can be reexperienced.

Why does social pain linger longer than does physical pain? It is possible that people use different coping strategies to deal with social pain and physical pain. In many cultures, showing social pain or hurt feelings can be embarrassing or be seen as a sign of weakness. Thus, people may be less willing to reveal their social wounds and they may even be motivated to ignore, deny, or suppress these hurtful feelings, although from a clinical perspective, a better way to cope with social suffering seems to be open acknowledgment and processing.

SOCIAL PAIN IS MORE EASILY PRELIVED THAN PHYSICAL PAIN

A psychological process related to pain reliving is mentally visualizing or preliving future experiences. Mental imagery has long been known to have an important impact on cognition, behavior, and emotion (see Taylor, Pham, Rivkin, & Armor, 1998), and social psychologists often use different mental images to manipulate moods. For example, Larsen and Ketelaar (1991) asked participants to imagine positive events (e.g., winning a lottery or taking a vacation) or negative events (e.g., being expelled from school in an embarrassing manner or having a close friend die). Participants were asked to write down their mental imageries to facilitate the mood induction. A manipulation check showed that each of the mood manipulations led to the corresponding mood.

Recent studies have suggested that preliving a future experience may involve processes common to reliving a past experience (Schacter, Addis, & Buckner, 2007). For example, Addis, Wong, and Schacter (2007), using neuroimaging techniques, found remarkable overlaps in regions comprising the autobiographical memory retrieval network when participants were asked to elaborate on past experiences and when they were instructed to elaborate on future experiences. These regions included the medial prefrontal regions, medial posterior regions, posterior regions in the medial and lateral parietal cortex (extending into the precuneus and the retrosplenial cortex), the lateral temporal cortex, and the medial temporal lobe (Addis et al., 2007; Schacter et al., 2007). These similarities suggest that preliving future experiences may induce feelings of pain in a fashion similar to how reliving past experiences induces feelings of pain. In particular, preliving a future socially painful event should lead to feelings of pain more easily and more intensely than should preliving a physically painful event.

We recently tested this hypothesis by asking participants to imagine either that they would be betrayed by their romantic partners in the future (social pain condition) or that they would suffer from a physical injury in the future (physical pain condition; Chen & Williams, 2008). Participants were instructed to write down in detail what they had imagined, including what would happen, how it would happen, and how they would feel. Before imagining these future experiences, participants were asked to rate on the Pain Slide how much pain they would feel if the event were to happen (i.e., anticipated pain). Immediately after imagining the event, participants were asked to indicate their feelings of pain (i.e., prelived pain) on the Pain Slide as well as the MPQ. Participants in the social pain and the physical pain conditions reported the same level of anticipated pain; however, participants in the social pain condition prelived more intense pain than did those in the physical pain condition, as measured by the Pain Slide as well as the MPQ. The feeling of pain that participants prelived in this study is different from negative affect triggered by the negative nature of these mental imageries. This study measured participants' mood following the measurement of prelived pain, using the Positive and Negative Affect Schedule (Watson, Clark, & Tellegen, 1988). Participants in the social pain condition and the physical pain condition did not differ in their self-reported positive affect or their negative affect. That is, although imagining being betrayed by one's romantic partner and imagining suffering a physical injury are equally negative, only the former leads to feelings of pain.

Past research has shown that people differ in the vividness of their visual images (Marks, 1973; McKelvie, 1994; McKelvie & Demers, 1979). Because the prelived pain was associated with mental imagery about future events, the feelings of pain that people prelived should be positively correlated with the vividness of their mental imageries. We measured participants' capacity for mentally visualizing future events, using the Vividness of Visual Imagery Questionnaire (VVIQ; Marks, 1973). The VVIQ asks participants to imagine various scenarios and to rate how vivid their mental images are. This study found that participants who scored higher on the VVIQ experienced higher levels of pain following the pain preliving than did those who scored lower in imagery vividness. Further analysis indicated that this effect was limited to the social pain condition. That is, the positive association between the vividness of mental imagery and the prelived pain was observed in the social pain condition but not in the physical pain condition. Participants in the physical pain condition did not experience pain, regardless of the vividness of their mental imagery.

Consistent with the difference between social pain reliving and physical pain reliving, our research suggests that people are able to prelive social pain but not physical pain. Unlike reliving a past experience, preliving a future experience deals with experiences that have not yet happened. However, because preliving a future experience relies heavily on past experiences, it is possible that pain preliving shares the same mechanisms as does pain reliving.

Can social pain preliving impair cognition in the same way that social pain reliving does? Chen (2008) recently asked participants to imagine being betrayed by their romantic partners in the future or having a physical injury in the future. Participants were asked to write down what they had imagined and how they would feel if the event was to happen. Following the pain preliving, participants were asked to work on the lexical decision task and the Stroop task. Similar to the pain reliving study, participants had equally high performance on the lexical decision task following social pain preliving and physical pain preliving; however, participants responded significantly more slowly on the Stroop task following social pain preliving than they did following physical pain preliving.

Another recent study directly asked participants to imagine being betrayed by one's romantic partner in the future or having a physical injury in the future (Study 6; Chen, 2008). Participants' pain sensitivity was measured before the pain preliving (baseline measure) as well after the pain preliving. To measure pain sensitivity, an experimenter applied a pain pressure algometer perpendicularly to the second, third, fourth, and fifth fingers of the participant's dominant hand. For the pain threshold measure, participants were asked to report when they began to feel pain from the pressure; for the pain tolerance measure, participants were asked to report when they felt the pressure was too much to bear. This study found that following social pain preliving, compared with physical pain preliving, participants became less sensitive to physical pressure, such that they had higher pain tolerance scores as well as higher pain threshold scores. In summary, imagining future socially painful experiences (i.e., social pain preliving) not only leads to feelings of pain but also impairs the function of cognitive activity; however, no such effects have been found for physical pain reliving or preliving.

IMPLICATIONS AND CONCLUSIONS

The famous statement that "no man is an island" not only emphasizes that it is part of human nature to connect with others but also implies the detrimental impact that can result when such connections are threatened. Mounting evidence suggests that the system responsible for monitoring closeness with others overlaps with the physical pain system that alerts people of dangers in the environment. We agree with other researchers, including many of the contributors to this volume, that threats to social inclusion status are likely processed at the same basic level as survival threats, and we concur that the social pain system may have been built on the preexisting physical pain system over evolutionary history. The set of studies discussed in the chapter, however, suggests some substantial differences between these two systems. Pain associated with social experiences can be reinstated through memory retrievals, but pain caused by physical injury cannot be reinstated and fades with time. Imagining a future socially painful experience can trigger pain, but imagining a physically painful experience cannot. Such differences reflect that the two pain systems might differ in their activation mechanisms but also suggest that the two pain systems may cope with pain differently. Further studies are needed to fully understand these effects.

A common practice in social psychological research involves using physical injury as a control condition when studying the effect of social pain. For example, Baumeister and colleagues (Baumeister, Twenge, & Nuss, 2002; DeWall & Baumeister, 2006; Twenge, Catanese, & Baumeister, 2003) asked participants to work on a bogus personality test (e.g., the Eysenck Personality Questionnaire; Eysenck & Eysenck, 1975) and then told them that the test indicated that they would live alone in the future (future alone condition), that they would have a future filled with several meaningful and lasting relationships (future belonging condition), or that they would have a lot of accidents in the future (accident prone condition). In addition, terror management research (Greenberg, Pyszczynski, & Solomon, 1986; Pyszczynski, Greenberg, & Solomon, 1999) argues that individuals are motivated to boost their self-esteem and worldviews to fight against the terror of death when their own mortality is salient. It is common to compare the effects of mortality salience induction (e.g., ask participants to imagine their own death) with a control condition asking participants to recall or imagine a painful dental visit. The death of oneself can be thought of as a threat to social bonds because relationships end when one dies (see Baumeister & Leary, 1995), and the primary suffering people have about their own death is the concern of being separated from friends and families (Bednarski & Leary, 1994). The studies presented in this chapter suggest that both the future alone manipulation and the mortality salience manipulation may have different impacts on pain system than do their corresponding control conditions, which may confound the results in studies using these paradigms.

The differences between social pain and physical pain reported in this chapter also lead to interesting lines of future research. Could the differences between social pain and physical pain in reliving and preliving be extended to other social pain situations? Our studies included in this chapter focused on a specific type of social pain: betrayal. How about other painful situations, such as the loss of a loved one, extreme loneliness, and so on? Would age or past experiences affect people's capacity to relive or prelive social pain? What if people had forgiven the offender? Would they still reinstate past social pain? Addressing these questions will help to delineate the overlap and boundaries of social pain and physical pain.

REFERENCES

Addis, D. R., Wong, A. T., & Schacter, D. L. (2007). Remembering the past and imagining the future: Common and distinct neural substrates during event construction and elaboration. *Neuropsychologia, 45,* 1363–1377. doi:10.1016/j.neuro psychologia.2006.10.016

Bartholomew, K., & Horowitz, L. M. (1991). Attachment styles among young adults: A test of a four-category model. *Journal of Personality and Social Psychology, 61,* 226–244. doi:10.1037/0022-3514.61.2.226

Baumeister, R. F., & Leary, M. R. (1995). The need to belong: Desire for interpersonal attachments as a fundamental human motivation. *Psychological Bulletin, 117,* 497–529. doi:10.1037/0033-2909.117.3.497

Baumeister, R. F., Twenge, J. M., & Nuss, C. K. (2002). Effects of social exclusion on cognitive processes: Anticipated aloneness reduces intelligent thought. *Journal of Personality and Social Psychology, 83,* 817–827. doi:10.1037/0022-3514.83.4.817

Bednarski, R., & Leary, M. R. (1994). *Self-esteem and fear of death.* Unpublished manuscript, Wake Forest University, Winston-Salem, NC.

Bowlby, J. (1958). The nature of the child's tie to his mother. *The International Journal of Psycho-Analysis, 39,* 350–373.

Bowlby, J. (1959). Separation anxiety. *The International Journal of Psycho-Analysis, 41,* 89–113.

Bowlby, J. (1960). Grief and mourning in infancy and early childhood. *The Psychoanalytic Study of the Child, VX,* 3–39.

Chen, Z. (2008). *Psychological impact of social pain: The pain that doesn't heal.* Unpublished doctoral dissertation, Purdue University, West Lafayette, IN.

Chen, Z., & Williams, K. D. (2008, May). *Social pain but not physical pain can be pre-lived.* Paper presented at the annual meeting of the Midwestern Psychological Association, Chicago, IL.

Chen, Z., Williams, K. D., Fitness, J., & Newton, N. C. (2008). When hurt won't heal: Exploring the capacity to relive social pain. *Psychological Science, 19,* 789–795. doi:10.1111/j.1467-9280.2008.02158.x

DeWall, C. N., & Baumeister, R. F. (2006). Alone but feeling no pain: Effects of social exclusion on physical pain tolerance and pain threshold, affective forecasting, and interpersonal empathy. *Journal of Personality and Social Psychology, 91,* 1–15. doi:10.1037/0022-3514.91.1.1

Donne, J. (1959). *Devotions upon emergent occasions: Together with death's duel.* Ann Arbor: University of Michigan Press. (Original work published 1624)

Eccleston, C., & Crombez, G. (1999). Pain demands attention: A cognitive-affective model of the interruptive function of pain. *Psychological Bulletin, 125,* 356–366. doi:10.1037/0033-2909.125.3.356

Eisenberger, N. I., & Lieberman, M. D. (2004). Why rejection hurts: The neurocognitive overlap between physical and social pain. *Trends in Cognitive Sciences, 8,* 294–300. doi:10.1016/j.tics.2004.05.010

Eisenberger, N. I., Lieberman, M. D., & Williams, K. D. (2003, October 10). Does rejection hurt? An fMRI study of social exclusion. *Science, 302,* 290–292. doi:10.1126/science.1089134

Erskine, A., Morley, S., & Pearce, S. (1990). Memory for pain: A review. *Pain, 41,* 255–265. doi:10.1016/0304-3959(90)90002-U

Eysenck, H. J., & Eysenck, S. B. G. (1975). *Manual of the Eysenck Personality Questionnaire.* San Diego, CA: EDITS.

Finch, J. F., Okun, M. A., Pool, G. J., & Ruehlman, L. S. (1999). A comparison of the influence of conflictual and supportive social interactions on psychological distress. *Journal of Personality, 67,* 581–621. doi:10.1111/1467-6494.00066

Gray, J. A., & McNaughton, N. (2000). *The neuropsychology of anxiety.* New York, NY: Oxford University Press.

Greenberg, J., Pyszczynski, T., & Solomon, S. (1986). The causes and consequences of the need for self-esteem: A terror management theory. In R. F.

Baumeister (Ed.), *Public self and private self* (pp. 189–212). New York, NY: Springer-Verlag.

Hansson, R., Jones, W., & Fletcher, W. (1990). Troubled relationships in later life: Implications for support. *Journal of Social and Personal Relationships, 7*, 451–463. doi:10.1177/0265407590074003

Hazan, C., & Shaver, P. (1987). Romantic love conceptualized as an attachment process. *Journal of Personality and Social Psychology, 52*, 511–524. doi:10.1037/0022-3514.52.3.511

Hazan, C., & Shaver, P. (1994). Attachment as an organizational framework for research on close relationships. *Psychological Inquiry, 5*, 1–22. doi:10.1207/s15327965pli0501_1

James, W. (1950). *The principles of psychology* (Vol. 1). New York, NY: Dover. (Original work published 1890)

Larsen, R. J., & Ketelaar, T. (1991). Personality and susceptibility to positive and negative emotional states. *Journal of Personality and Social Psychology, 61*, 132–140. doi:10.1037/0022-3514.61.1.132

Leary, M., & Springer, C. A. (2000). Hurt feelings: The neglected emotion. In R. Kowalski (Ed.), *Behaving badly: Aversive behaviors in interpersonal relationships* (pp. 151–176). Washington, DC: American Psychological Association.

Locksley, A., Ortiz, V., & Hepburn, C. (1980). Social categorization and discriminatory behavior: Extinguishing the minimal intergroup discrimination effect. *Journal of Personality and Social Psychology, 39*, 773–783. doi:10.1037/0022-3514.39.5.773

MacDonald, G. (2008). Use of pain threshold reports to satisfy social needs. *Pain Research & Management, 13*, 309–319.

MacDonald, G., Kingsbury, R., & Shaw, S. (2005). Adding insult to injury: Social pain theory and response to social exclusion. In K. D. Williams, J. P. Forgas, & W. von Hippel (Eds.), *The social outcast: Ostracism, social exclusion, rejection, and bullying* (pp. 77–90). New York, NY: Psychology Press.

MacDonald, G., & Leary, M. R. (2005). Why does social exclusion hurt? The relationship between social and physical pain. *Psychological Bulletin, 131*, 202–223. doi:10.1037/0033-2909.131.2.202

Marks, D. F. (1973). Visual imagery differences in the recall of pictures. *The British Journal of Psychology, 64*, 17–24.

Maslow, A. H. (1968). *Toward a psychology of being*. New York, NY: Van Nostrand.

McFarlin, D. B., & Blascovich, J. (1984). On the Remote Associates Test (RAT) as an alternative to illusory performance feedback: A methodological note. *Basic and Applied Social Psychology, 5*, 223–229. doi:10.1207/s15324834basp0503_5

McKelvie, S. J. (1994). The vividness of Visual Imagery Questionnaire as a predictor of facial recognition memory performance. *The British Journal of Psychology 85*(Pt. 1), 93–104.

McKelvie, S. J., & Demers, E. G. (1979). Individual differences in reported visual imagery and memory performance. *The British Journal of Psychology, 70*, 51–57.

Melzack, R. (1975). The McGill Pain Questionnaire: Major properties and scoring methods. *Pain, 1*, 277–299. doi:10.1016/0304-3959(75)90044-5

Melzack, R. (1983). *Pain measurement and assessment.* New York, NY: Raven Press.

Morley, S. (1993). Vivid memory for "everyday" pains. *Pain, 55*, 55–62. doi:10.1016/0304-3959(93)90184-Q

Nelson, E. E., & Panksepp, J. (1998). Brain substrates of infant–mother attachment: Contributions of opioids, oxytocin, and norepinephrine. *Neuroscience and Biobehavioral Reviews, 22*, 437–452. doi:10.1016/S0149-7634(97)00052-3

Panksepp, J. (1998). *Affective neuroscience: The foundations of human and animal emotions.* London, England: Oxford University Press.

Porter, S., & Peace, K. A. (2007). The scare of memory: A prospective, longitudinal investigation of the consistency of traumatic and positive memories in adulthood. *Psychological Science, 18*, 435–441. doi:10.1111/j.1467-9280.2007.01918.x

Price, D. D. (1988). *Psychological and neural mechanisms for pain.* New York, NY: Raven Press.

Pyszczynski, T., Greenberg, J., & Solomon, S. (1999). A dual-process model of defense against conscious and unconscious death-related thoughts: An extension of terror management theory. *Psychological Review, 106*, 835–845. doi:10.1037/0033-295X.106.4.835

Robertson, J., & Bowlby, J. (1952). Responses of young children to separation from their mothers. *Courrier of the International Children's Centre, Paris, II*, 131–140.

Robinson, J. A., & Swanson, K. L. (1990). Autobiographical memory: The next phase. *Applied Cognitive Psychology, 4*, 321–335. doi:10.1002/acp.2350040407

Safer, M. A., Bonanno, G. A., & Field, N. P. (2001). "It was never that bad": Biased recall of grief and long-term adjustment to the death of a spouse. *Memory (Hove, England), 9*, 195–203. doi:10.1080/09658210143000065

Salovey, P., Sieber, W. J., Jobe, J. B., & Willis, G. (1994). The recall of physical pain. In N. Schwarz & S. Sudman (Eds.), *Autobiographical memory and the validity of retrospective reports* (pp. 89–105). New York, NY: Springer-Verlag.

Schacter, D. L., Addis, D. R., & Buckner, R. L. (2007). Remembering the past to imagine the future: The prospective brain. *Nature Reviews. Neuroscience, 8*, 657–661. doi:10.1038/nrn2213

Sherif, M., Harvey, O. H., White, B. J., Hood, W. R., & Sherif, C. W. (1988). *The Robbers Cave Experiment: Intergroup conflict and cooperation.* Middletown, CT: Wesleyan University Press. (Original work published 1961)

Tajfel, H. (1970). Experiments in intergroup discrimination. *Scientific American, 223*, 96–102. doi:10.1038/scientificamerican1170-96

Tajfel, H., Flament, C., Billig, M. G., & Bundy, R. F. (1971). Social categorization and intergroup behaviour. *European Journal of Social Psychology, 1*, 149–178. doi:10.1002/ejsp.2420010202

Taylor, S. E., Pham, L. B., Rivkin, I., & Armor, D. A. (1998). Harnessing the imagination: Mental simulation and self-regulation of behavior. *American Psychologist, 53*, 429–439.

Twenge, J. M., Catanese, K. R., & Baumeister, R. F. (2003). Social exclusion and the deconstructed state: Time perception, meaninglessness, lethargy, lack of emotion, and self-awareness. *Journal of Personality and Social Psychology, 85*, 409–423. doi:10.1037/0022-3514.85.3.409

Watson, D., Clark, L. A., & Tellegen, A. (1988). Development and validation of brief measures of positive and negative affect: The PANAS scales. *Journal of Personality and Social Psychology, 54*, 1063–1070. doi:10.1037/0022-3514.54.6.1063

Weiss, R. S. (1979). The emotional impact of marital separation. In G. Levinger & O. C. Moles (Eds.), *Divorce and separation: Context, causes, and consequences* (pp. 201–210). New York, NY: Basic Books.

Wilder, D. A., & Thompson, J. E. (1980). Intergroup contact with independent manipulations of in-group and out-group interaction. *Journal of Personality and Social Psychology, 38*, 589–603. doi:10.1037/0022-3514.38.4.589

Williams, K. D. (2001). *Ostracism: The power of silence*. New York, NY: Guilford Press.

Williams, K. D. (2007). Ostracism. *Annual Review of Psychology, 58*, 425–452. doi:10.1146/annurev.psych.58.110405.085641

Williams, K. D., Cheung, C. K. T., & Choi, W. (2000). CyberOstracism: Effects of being ignored over the Internet. *Journal of Personality and Social Psychology, 79*, 748–762. doi:10.1037/0022-3514.79.5.748

Williams, K. D., Forgas, J. P., & von Hippel, W. (Eds.). (2005). *The social outcast: Ostracism, social exclusion, rejection, and bullying*. New York, NY: The Psychology Press.

Wittstein, I. S., Thieman, D. R., Joao, M. D., Lima, A. C., Kenneth, M. D., Baughman, M. D., . . . Champion, H. C. (2005). Neurohumoral features of myocardial stunning due to sudden emotional distress. *The New England Journal of Medicine, 352*, 539–548. doi:10.1056/NEJMoa043046

III

HEALTH CONSEQUENCES
OF SOCIAL PAIN

8

THE BIOPSYCHOSOCIAL PERSPECTIVE OF PAIN AND EMOTION

ROBERT J. GATCHEL AND NANCY D. KISHINO

In this chapter, we review the biopsychosocial perspective of pain and emotion. As other chapters in this volume have shown, social pain (e.g., fear of public speaking, public embarrassment, and even thoughts of humiliation or failure) often generates the same array of physiological and behavioral effects that actual physical pain stimuli elicit. Before we discuss this specific topic more, a brief overview of the general biopsychosocial perspective of pain is needed. Indeed, this biopsychosocial perspective is now accepted as the most heuristic approach to comprehensively understanding pain syndromes (e.g., Gatchel, 2005; Gatchel, Peng, Peters, Fuchs, & Turk, 2007; Turk & Monarch, 2002). It emphasizes the complex interaction among physiological, psychological, and social factors that perpetuate and may even worsen the clinical presentation. For a full understanding of an individual's perception and response to pain (and its emotional concomitants), the interrelationships among biological changes, psychological status, and the sociocultural context all need to be considered. Any model that focuses on only one of these dimensions will be incomplete and inadequate. In presenting the biopsychosocial model, Gatchel, Peng, Peters, Fuchs, and Turk (2007) thoroughly reviewed the basic neuroscience processes of pain (the *bio* part of biopsychosocial) as well as the psychosocial factors. This informative review spans the extensive scientific literature on how psychological and social factors can interact with brain processes to help influence emotional and physical health and illness.

In an earlier discussion of this biopsychosocial model, Gatchel (2004) presented a conceptual model of the interactive processes involved in pain or illness and health (see Figure 8.1). So, for example, pain is not a purely perceptual phenomenon. Rather, the injury that has caused the pain also disrupts the body's homeostatic regulation systems, which, in turn, produces stress and initiates complex programs to restore homeostasis. As can be seen, there are central processes (involving biological, somatic, cognitive, and affective components) that interact with peripheral processes, as well as social factors.

PAIN AND EMOTION

As historically reviewed by Gatchel (2005), pain was traditionally viewed as a symptom secondary to the presence of some tissue pathology and, therefore, as being of secondary importance. Of course, from this perspective, it fol-

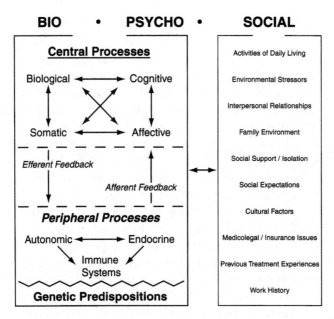

Figure 8.1. A Conceptual Model of the Biopsychosocial Interactive Processes Involved in Pain/Illness and Health. From "Comorbidity of Chronic Mental and Physical Health Disorders: The Biopsychosocial Perspective," by R. J. Gatchel, 2004, *American Psychologist, 59,* p. 798. Copyright 2004 by the American Psychological Association.

lowed that once this pathology was resolved, the pain would subside. However, research did not substantiate this perspective but rather suggested that the end-experience of pain was a composite of sensory–discriminative, cognitive–evaluative, and motivational features (Gatchel et al., 2007). Pain is ultimately a subjective, private experience, but one that is also described in terms of sensory and affective properties. Indeed, various organizations, such as the International Association for the Study of Pain, view pain as a sensation in specific parts of the body that is always unpleasant with a common concomitant negative emotional experience associated with it. Subsequent research has unequivocally supported the significant and interactive roles of sensory information and emotional states (e.g., Fernandez, 2002; Turk & Monarch, 2002). This emotional component of pain incorporates many different affective states, but they are primarily negative in nature (e.g., anxiety, anger, and depression). These emotional distress states are reviewed in the next sections.

Anxiety

Anxiety is a common emotional response to pain, especially in the case of chronic pain. In fact, individuals with chronic or persistent pain become anxious about the meaning of their pain symptoms and what those symptoms might mean for their future activities, their ability to work, the potential for more permanent disability, and so on. Such fear and anxiety, in turn, may keep them from engaging in activities that might exacerbate or worsen their symptoms. Such fear often leads to avoidance and motivates inactivity (e.g., Boersma & Linton, 2005). Moreover, such fear contributes to increased muscle tension and physiological arousal that may further exacerbate and maintain pain symptoms (Gatchel, 2005).

Many investigators have suggested that the fear of pain alone (driven by the anticipation of pain and not by the sensory experience of pain itself) produces significant negative reinforcement for the persistence of avoidance behavior and the resultant functional disability in pain patients (Gatchel et al., 2007). Such avoidance leads to even more maladaptive behavior and then to a vicious cycle of increased fear → more limited activity → decreased physical functioning → more susceptibility to flare-ups of pain → further increased fear, and so on. In fact, several studies have shown that fear of movement and fear of injury or reinjury are stronger predictors of functional limitations than are biomedical indices or even pain severity or duration measures (e.g., Turk, Robinson, & Burwinkle, 2004). Thus, pain-related fear and concerns about avoiding further harm exacerbate pain symptoms. As Gatchel (2005) noted, there is a reciprocal relationship between an emotional state (e.g., anxiety) and cognitive–interpretative processes: Thinking affects mood, and mood influences appraisals (e.g., harm avoidance) and, ulti-mately, the experience of pain.

Anger

Anger is often present in people suffering from chronic pain (Gatchel, 2005). For example, approximately 98% of patients referred to a multidiscipli-nary pain rehabilitation center reported some degree of anger at the time of their initial assessment (Okifuji, Turk, & Curran, 1999). Fernandez and Turk (1995) speculated that this negative emotional response is due to anger as a reaction to the presence of recurrent and recalcitrant pain symptoms that are unsubstantiated by purely objective medical findings and unrelieved by various medical treatments. Fernandez and Turk also noted that the presence of anger may increase autonomic nervous system arousal while also blocking motivation toward adherence to treatment programs. Moreover, besides the anger and frus-tration related to the persistence of pain symptoms, there may also be anger gen-erated by the perception of lack of sympathy by employers, family members, and the health care system in general. In fact, Okifuji, Turk, and Kalauokalani (1999) found the following targets of this anger: 60% toward health care providers, 39% toward significant others, 30% toward insurance companies, 26% toward employers, and 20% toward attorneys. Finally, the correlations between anger and pain severity have been found to be statistically significant (ranging from .17 to .35; Gatchel et al., 2007). Thus, although the precise biopsychosocial mechanisms by which anger and frustration exacerbate pain symptoms are not totally known, such affect is intricately linked to the overall pain experience.

Depression

A great deal of clinical research has consistently documented that 40% to 50% of chronic pain patients have depressive disorders (e.g., Dersh, Gatchel, Mayer, Polatin, & Temple, 2006). One question often raised is what occurred first—the chronic pain or the depression? For chronic low back pain, the answer is both; one half of the sample evaluated had depressive sympto-matology before the onset of the initial injury causing the pain, and the other half had it after the injury (Polatin, Kinney, Gatchel, Lillo, & Mayer, 1993). It is also interesting to note that there are potentially common pathogenic mechanisms involved in psychiatric disorders, such as depression, and pain (e.g., Okasha et al., 1999; Polatin 1991). Both nociceptive and affective path-ways coincide anatomically. Furthermore, norepinephrine and serotonin, the two neurotransmitters most implicated in the psychopathology of mood dis-orders, are also involved in the gate-control mechanisms of pain. Finally, certain antidepressants have been found to have a mitigating effect on chronic pain, even at doses considered to be subtherapeutic for depression. Gallagher (2002) further documented the close neurochemical connection between pain and depression.

A Final Caveat: Social and Physical Pain

Walco and Harkins (1999), in a review of life span developmental approaches to pain, appropriately pointed out the importance of psychosocial and cognitive factors in the perception of, and reaction to, different types of pain. For example, they discussed research findings that indicate older chronic pain patients report less pain-related negative affect and suffering, but not less pain intensity, relative to younger chronic pain patients. They went on to interpret such findings as possibly reflecting a generalized reduction of emotionality with increasing age, coupled with a comparable impact on sensory acuity for pain.

Walco and Harkins (1999) provided a further example of this dissociation when considering loss of teeth in children. In the United States, complete loss of teeth (i.e., edentulousness) is no longer a common occurrence because of better oral hygiene, nutrition, and education. Therefore, currently, edentulousness is not to be expected. When it does occur, it is unexpected and emotionally distressing. Indeed, as noted by Walco and Harkins (1999), it has been found that younger individuals who lost their teeth reported significantly greater emotional distress and health care concerns than did age-matched peers with natural dentition.

These findings take the biopsychosocial framework one step further in suggesting that social pain (e.g., the experience of embarrassment because of edentulousness) leads to additional psychosocial distress above and beyond any lasting sensory pain associated with tooth loss. Thus, social pain may trigger the comparable biopsychosocial reactions to purely physical pain stimuli. This phenomenon also relates to earlier research on vicarious emotional conditioning through observation of emotional reactions displayed by others. For example, Berger (1962) demonstrated that when subjects observed another individual receive a pain-producing electric shock, even though they themselves had no direct contact with the noxious shock, they demonstrated a comparable increase in their emotional responding. Such vicarious classical conditioning can also take place through high-order conditioning processes, when a conditioned stimulus modifies a formerly neutral stimulus with which it becomes contiguously associated, with the capacity to elicit elevated autonomic arousal states (Mischel, 1968). Thus, an individual who becomes publicly embarrassed may then develop a full-blown phobia for social situations that could potentially produce a recurrence of that embarrassment, with its negative heightened arousal reactivity that is painful to experience. Such social pain is an interesting area for future research.

Summary of Emotional Factors and Pain

As reviewed earlier, there is a significant amount of scientific clinical research documenting the key role of negative emotional states, such as anxiety, anger, and depression, in patients with chronic pain. Dersh, Polatin, and Gatchel (2002) also provided a more comprehensive review of the close comorbidity of chronic pain and psychopathological states such as anxiety, depression, substance abuse, and personality disorders. From a clinical treatment point of view, such a comorbidity between psychopathology and chronic pain must be considered in any pain management program. Thus, again, a biopsychosocial approach has to be taken, in which attention must be focused on not only physical pathology and somatic factors involved in persistent pain but also psychosocial factors such as mood or emotional states. If these emotional states are not appropriately treated in a comprehensive manner with other variables, then a vicious cycle of events can occur to prevent recovery. As succinctly noted by Gatchel et al. (2007),

> It is important to be aware of the significant role of negative mood in chronic pain patients, because it is likely to influence treatment motivation and compliance with treatment recommendations. For example, patients who are anxious may fear engaging in what they perceive as demanding activities, patients who are depressed and who feel helpless may have little initiative to comply, and patients who are angry with their health care system are not likely to be motivated to respond to recommendations from yet another health care professional. (p. 602)

Gatchel and colleagues (2007) went on to review the ever-growing neuroscience research that is beginning to isolate how these emotional, pain, and physiological and anatomical factors interact to produce various symptom patterns. In the next section, we review neuroscience research on brain imaging.

THE BRAIN, PAIN, AND EMOTION

Gatchel, Robinson, Peng, Benitez, and Noe (2008) recently discussed how, with the availability of functional magnetic resonance imaging (fMRI) of the brain, the underlying physiological and anatomical mechanisms of pain (and its emotional concomitants) can be more fully comprehended. This new fMRI technology has provided the ability to identify a variety of cortical and subcortical structures involved with the cerebral response to nociceptive (painful) stimuli in humans. For example, Ploghaus et al. (1999) evaluated the anticipating aspects of the pain experience using fMRI and found greater activation in the rostral anterior insular cortex and medial prefrontal cortex when a subject was anticipating pain, and greater activation in the caudal insula and anterior cingulate cortex when an individual experienced pain.

Such fMRI studies have also allowed the investigation of emotionally related phenomena that had previously been relatively poorly understood. Wager et al. (2004), for instance, evaluated the placebo effect using fMRI. They reported that the rostral anterior cingulate cortex and the brainstem were associated with increased activation in both a placebo condition and an actual analgesic condition, both of which blunted the experience of pain and its emotional concomitant.

Furthermore, in a study of empathy, Singer and colleagues (2004) evaluated subjects who personally experienced a physically painful stimulus and then compared their brain activity with when they were observing a loved one also undergoing a physically painful stimulus. Similar patterns of brain activity were revealed in both conditions: an increase in activity in the anterior insula and rostral anterior cingulate cortex as well as in areas of the brainstem and cerebellum. Moreover, the amount of activation in the anterior insula and anterior cingulate cortex was closely correlated with these subjects' scores on measures of empathy. In addition, Mackey et al. (2003) demonstrated a relationship between fMRI indices and empathy-related pain. Finally, Eisenberger and coworkers (2003) also found greater activation of the anterior cingulate cortex when someone was experiencing emotional pain (specifically, emotional distress over being excluded). The prefrontal cortex was also found to play a role in the processing of this emotional pain.

What are the clinical implications of these findings? As elucidated by Eippert et al. (2007), once these brain regions have been more clearly mapped out on the basis of this past research, then the next important scientific step will be to have subjects voluntarily regulate emotions through the use of fMRI feedback to increase or decrease activity in the brain regions associated with those emotions. As these investigators noted, because dysfunction in emotional-regulation processes have been found in both clinical and nonclinical populations, real-time fMRI protocols can be developed to help individuals gain control of and eliminate such dysfunction. Indeed, deCharms and colleagues (2004) have already made a start in this direction. They trained healthy volunteers to increase or decrease activation of the rostral anterior cingulate cortex. Subsequently, the subjects' perception of pain during an acute thermal pain stimulus changed in the expected direction (i.e., decreased pain sensation corresponding to decreased activation of the rostral anterior cingulate cortex). Moreover, these investigators also found that patients with chronic pain were able to decrease levels of ongoing pain by decreasing activation of the same region of the brain. These findings clearly demonstrate how brain–pain–emotion interactions can potentially be managed for positive health outcomes.

IMPLICATIONS FOR BIOPSYCHOSOCIAL TREATMENT

Because of the complexity of pain syndromes, especially when they become chronic in nature, traditional unimodal treatment approaches, such as pharmacotherapy, invasive methods (e.g., injections, surgery), and physical therapy, when administered alone in an uncoordinated fashion, have not been found to be therapeutically effective (Gatchel & Okifuji, 2006). However, interdisciplinary pain management programs that involve the integrated care of patients by a comprehensive treatment team (consisting of a physician, psychologist or psychiatrist, physical therapist, and occupational therapist) have been found to be the most therapeutically effective and cost-effective methods of successfully managing pain and increasing patient functioning and quality of life (Gatchel & Okifuji, 2006). That is because a host of biopsychosocial components are included: physician oversight of any physical pathology, medication management, and injections, if needed; physical therapy to address any physical deconditioning relative to such areas as strength, range of motion, and cardiovascular conditioning; behavioral medicine treatment, including stress management, biofeedback, and cognitive–behavioral therapy; and occupational therapy, including help in transitioning back to normal work status and activities of daily living. The major goals of an interdisciplinary pain management program are to

- increase physical functioning,
- decrease pain,
- manage negative mood states,
- increase sleep quality,
- return to work and normal activities of daily living,
- eliminate unnecessary medications, and
- increase one's sense of control over pain management as well as acquire appropriate adaptive coping skills.

The tremendous success of this biopsychosocial interdisciplinary treatment approach is due to the fact that all the important aspects of the pain syndrome—the experiential pain component, emotion, and physical underpinnings—are all treated and tailored to the specific needs of patients. Thus, the biopsychosocial approach to pain has revolutionized the successful treatment of this prevalent and costly medical (societal) problem.

CONCLUSIONS

The biopsychosocial perspective is now viewed as the most heuristic approach to comprehensively understanding pain syndromes and other illness states. The hallmark of this perspective is its focus on the complex interaction among physiological, psychological, and social factors that perpetuate and may even worsen the clinical presentation of symptoms. As such, these significant emotional components contribute to the ultimate experience of pain. Three of the major emotional states involved in this comorbidity were reviewed: anxiety, anger, and depression. As discussed, it is essential to be aware of the significant role of these negative emotional states in chronic pain conditions because they are likely to influence patients' treatment motivation and compliance with treatment recommendations. Interdisciplinary treatment programs based on the biopsychosocial perspective have been found to be clinically effective in reducing pain and its associated emotional concomitants.

Neuroscience research is beginning to isolate how the various emotional, physiological or anatomical, and pain factors interact to produce various symptom patterns. This research will begin to answer questions such as, Why do two individuals exposed to the same painful stimulus react to it so differently in terms of its reported severity? Why do some individuals develop depression, some anxiety, and some neither when pain becomes chronic in nature? Why do some people respond to an injury with a great deal of disability when there is no underlying pathology, whereas others do not respond even when there is some pathology present? We hope that future research will begin answering these important questions. One important new technology being used in this quest is brain imaging, especially fMRI. We reviewed various studies that have isolated brain areas involved in different pain- and emotionally related phenomena, as well as the clinical treatment implications of such findings. Even greater new insights into brain–pain–emotion mechanisms will surely also arise.

REFERENCES

Berger, S. M. (1962). Conditioning through vicarious instigation. *Psychological Review, 69*, 450–466. doi:10.1037/h0046466

Boersma, K., & Linton, S. J. (2005). Screening to identify patients at risk: Profiles of psychological risk factors for early intervention. *The Clinical Journal of Pain, 21*, 38–43. doi:10.1097/00002508-200501000-00005

deCharms, R. C., Christoff, K., Glover, G. H., Pauly, J. M., Whitfield, S., & Gabrieli, J. D. (2004). Learned regulation of spatially localized brain activation using real-time fMRI. *NeuroImage, 21*, 436–443. doi:10.1016/j.neuroimage.2003.08.041

Dersh, J., Gatchel, R. J., Mayer, T., Polatin, P., & Temple, O. R. (2006). Prevalence of psychiatric disorders in patients with chronic disabling occupational spinal disorders. *Spine, 31,* 1156–1162. doi:10.1097/01.brs.0000216441.83135.6f

Dersh, J., Polatin, P., & Gatchel, R. (2002). Chronic pain and psychopathology: Research findings and theoretical considerations. *Psychosomatic Medicine, 64,* 773–786. doi:10.1097/01.PSY.0000024232.11538.54

Eippert, F., Veit, R., Weiskopf, N., Erb, M., Birbaumer, N., & Anders, S. (2007). Regulation of emotional responses elicited by threat-related stimuli. *Human Brain Mapping, 28,* 409–423. doi:10.1002/hbm.20291

Eisenberger, N. I., Lieberman, M. D., & Williams, K. D. (2003). Does rejection hurt? An fMRI study of social exclusion. *Science, 302,* 290–292. doi:10.1126/science.1089134

Fernandez, E. (2002). *Anxiety, depression, and anger in pain: Research implications.* Dallas, TX: Advanced Psychology Resources.

Fernandez, E., & Turk, D. C. (1995). The scope and significance of anger in the experience of chronic pain. *Pain, 61,* 165–175. doi:10.1016/0304-3959(95)00192-U

Gallagher, R. M. (2002). *The pain-depression conundrum: Bridging the body and mind.* Retrieved from http://www.medscape.com/viewprogram/2030

Gatchel, R. J. (2004). Comorbidity of chronic mental and physical health disorders: The biopsychosocial perspective. *American Psychologist, 59,* 795–805. doi:10.1037/0003-066X.59.8.795

Gatchel, R. J. (2005). *Clinical essentials of pain management.* Washington, DC: American Psychological Association. doi:10.1037/10856-000

Gatchel, R. J., & Okifuji, A. (2006). Evidence-based scientific data documenting the treatment- and cost-effectiveness of comprehensive pain programs for chronic nonmalignant pain. *The Journal of Pain, 7,* 779–793. doi:10.1016/j.jpain.2006.08.005

Gatchel, R. J., Peng, Y., Peters, M. L., Fuchs, P. N., & Turk, D. C. (2007). The biopsychosocial approach to chronic pain: Scientific advances and future directions. *Psychological Bulletin, 133,* 581–624. doi:10.1037/0033-2909.133.4.581

Gatchel, R. J., Robinson, R. C., Peng, Y., Benitez, O. J., & Noe, C. E. (2008). The brain and pain: What have we learned using fMRI? *Practical Pain Management, 8*(5), 28–40.

Mackey, S., Ochsner, K., Ludlow, D., Knierim, K., Hanelin, K., & Glover, G. (2003). Do I feel what you feel? A functional imaging study of empathy of pain. *Journal of Pain, 4*(2, Suppl. 1), 54.

Mischel, W. (1968). *Personality and assessment.* New York, NY: Wiley.

Okasha, A., Ismail, M. K., Khalil, A. H., El Fiki, R., Soliman, A., & Okasha, T. (1999). A psychiatric study of nonorganic chronic headache patients. *Psychosomatic Medicine, 40,* 233–238.

Okifuji, A., Turk, D. C., & Curran, S. L. (1999). Anger in chronic pain: Investigations of anger targets and intensity. *Journal of Psychosomatic Research, 47,* 1–12.

Okifuji, A., Turk, D. C., & Kalauokalani, D. (1999). Clinical outcomes and economic evaluation of multidisciplinary pain centers. In A. R. Block, E. F. Kremer, & E. Fernandez (Eds.), *Handbook of pain syndromes* (pp. 77–97). Mahwah, NJ: Erlbaum.

Ploghaus, A., Tracey, I., Gati, J. S., Clare, S., Menon, R. S., Matthews, P. M., & Rawlins, J. N. P. (1999, June 18). Dissociating pain from its anticipation in the human brain. *Science, 284,* 1979–1981. doi:10.1126/science.284.5422.1979

Polatin, P. (1991). Predictors of low back pain. In A. White & R. Anderson (Eds.), *Conservative care of low back pain* (pp. 265–273). Baltimore, MD: Williams & Wilkins.

Polatin, P. B., Kinney, R. K., Gatchel, R. J., Lillo, E., & Mayer, T. G. (1993). Psychiatric illness and chronic low-back pain. The mind and the spine—Which goes first? *Spine, 18,* 66–71. doi:10.1097/00007632-199301000-00011

Singer, T., Seymour, B., O'Doherty, J., Kaube, H., Dolan, R. J., & Frith, C. D. (2004, February 20). Empathy for pain involves the affective but not sensory components of pain. *Science, 303,* 1157–1162. doi:10.1126/science.1093535

Turk, D. C., & Monarch, E. S. (2002). Biopsychosocial perspective on chronic pain. In D. C. Turk & R. J. Gatchel (Eds.), *Psychological approaches to pain management: A practitioner's handbook* (2nd ed., pp. 3–29). New York, NY: Guilford Press.

Turk, D. C., Robinson, J. P., & Burwinkle, T. (2004). Prevalence of fear of pain and activity in fibromyalgia syndrome patients. *The Journal of Pain, 5,* 483–490. doi:10.1016/j.jpain.2004.08.002

Wager, T. D., Rilling, J. K., Smith, E. E., Sokolik, A., Casey, K. L., Davidson, R. G., . . . Cohen, J. D. (2004, February 20). Placebo-induced changes in fMRI in the anticipation and experience of pain. *Science, 303,* 1162–1167. doi:10.1126/science.1093065

Walco, G. A., & Harkins, W. (1999). Lifespan developmental approaches to pain. In D. C. Turk & R. J. Gatchel (Eds.), *Psychosocial factors in pain: A critical perspective* (pp. 107–117). New York, NY: Guilford Press.

9

SOCIAL STRESSORS, SOCIAL PAIN, AND HEALTH

ANDREW BAUM, CARROLL MICHELLE LEE,
AND ANGELA LIEGEY DOUGALL

Quietly but steadily, depictions of health and illness have changed. Major scientific breakthroughs, changes in disease prevalence and mortality patterns, and more subtle changes in approach to treatment have resulted in a marked modification of the medical model among health care practitioners and laypeople alike. Where theory once focused exclusively on injury or on pathogens and host resistance, prevailing opinion now includes genetic, environmental, and lifestyle variables, and it is no longer unusual for behaviors, attitudes, emotions, and social processes to be incorporated into models of disease etiology, progression, and treatment.

The recognition that social processes affect health and well-being is not new but has been particularly important over the past 30 years in emerging, holistic perspectives in health. Social phenomena such as support, integration, loneliness, and victimization have been discussed as causes or facilitators of illness or as supporting good health (e.g., Cohen, 2004; Uchino et al., 1996). With the development of social psychophysiology and social neuroscience (e.g., Cacioppo, Berntson, Sheridan, & McClintock, 2000) and the introduction of constructs such as social pain, it has become possible to begin to model the processes by which these social phenomena affect maintenance of health and coping with illness. Considerable attention has been directed at benefits of social support and social integration and ways in which social phenomena facilitate adaptation and well-being. Less attention has been paid to consequences of social stressors or sources of social pain. In this chapter, we consider the possibility that social pain and social stressors affect health and illness.

SOCIAL PAIN

Social pain refers to the experience of social loss, situations in which valued social relationships and intimacy are threatened, harmed, or lost. Being ignored, ostracized, or left out of a group; loss of close social contacts because of death, relocation, or other means; loneliness; and other conditions that produce social pain appear to evoke some of the same responses and appear to be mediated by some of the same neural pathways as physical pain (Eisenberger & Lieberman, 2004; Panksepp, 2003). The similarities across social and physical pain are striking, and a rapidly growing literature has established at least circumstantial evidence that the two share important characteristics. One of these overlapping properties is stress, also driven by similar neuroendocrine pathways and commonly associated with social and physical injury. The commonalities across physical and social pain are likely to include the facts that both are stressful and that many of the pathways by which pain is generated and perceived are shared with stress processes. This commonality provides a basis for predicting health consequences of social pain and adds parsimony to an emerging area of inquiry.

As we have suggested, stress provides a pathway by which the extent of health effects associated with social loss or pain can be explained and predicted. There is something special and uniquely influential about interpersonal stressors; theory has focused on the critical qualities of social stressors, suggesting that they often pose considerable threat. Research tends to support this distinction. It appears that social stressors have larger or more persistent effects than do nonsocial stressors on some of the systems that mediate effects of these stressors on health (Dickerson & Kemeny, 2004). As far as we know, there is less evidence of qualitatively different responses to social and nonsocial stressors, although it seems that interpersonal aspects of nonsocial stressors add significantly to the burden carried.

This chapter was developed to consider potential health effects of social pain, and casting the chapter in a stress model is useful in this regard. Pain is typically a symptom of real or potential dysfunction, be it tissue damage, pressure, neuropathies, or other problems. It is adaptive as a signal that something is "wrong," that damage is likely, and that something needs to be done, as a means of motivating an organism to rest, avoid, or cope with whatever is amiss. As a stressor, it is much the same: a source of information or alarm and a motivator of remedial action. Although one can readily conceptualize pain as a stressor or as a cause or promoter of some health problem, relatively little research takes this perspective. For social pain, the same is generally the case; some research has confirmed that interactions with other people can be a source of stress, but much of what is known is tentative. It is fairly clear, as we briefly consider later in this chapter, that social stressors and social pain can have predictable effects on health and well-being.

We have suggested and available evidence supports the notion that social or interpersonal stressors are "worse" than nonsocial stressors and the effects of social stressors are more persistent or intense and more likely to affect health outcomes (e.g., Cohen, 2004; Edwards, Hershberger, Russell, & Markert, 2001). It is worth considering why social stressors might be more persistent, more intense, and more harmful. The most common explanation has to do with the basic human needs for social connectedness and the fact that disruption to such basic needs is more salient and hence has more of an impact. Such explanations derive from decades of etiology research and studies of *social species*, animals that thrive in groups. They also rest on the many forms of mutual support and assistance that derive from these groups. In the context of this view, one can begin to describe the specific benefits that humans harvest from social relationships and how threats to these benefits may produce or exacerbate stress. A partial list of the kinds of assistance and benefits of social relationships would include existential and self-directed concerns about feeling valued by and part of a group, instrumental assistance with tasks or problems, opinion validation, and evaluation of coping strategies. Loss of social resources that reinforce self-esteem, including a sense of being valued, or that provide instrumental assistance or opinion validation should be particularly stressful. Threats to these basic needs may be appraised as more threatening overall than are those many nonsocial events, and threats to these social resources may have direct effects like any other stressors. In other words, nonspecific responses to threat result in specific responses and, for example, may intensify the threat in a setting. At the same time, social assets that help people cope may also be affected. We consider this again in the next section.

SOCIAL PAIN AND STRESS

The complex relationship between pain and stress is difficult to disentangle and produces similar kinds of effects. The perception of pain, for example, is carried out in many of the same branches of the nervous system as is stress or arousal of the sympathetic nervous system and the hypothalamic–pituitary–adrenal–cortical axis. Stress appears to modulate the experience of pain, and pain appears to affect the experience of stress. Similar phenomena mediate or moderate pain and stress as well. To some extent this may be due to the likelihood that pain is stressful or that conditions that produce pain (e.g., tissue damage, muscle tension, pressure, blood flow) also cause stress independently of pain. It is clear that the processes involved in nociception are distinct and there are many differences between pain and stress or emotional arousal. However, the similarities between and the cooccurrence of pain and stress raise questions about the best ways to describe the impact of painful events.

Examination of the literature on social pain also reinforces the notion that stress and pain are linked and that social loss or harm can cause a syndrome that looks like these two phenomena. Several studies refer to the fact that people spontaneously use "pain" words to describe social loss or rejection, including terms such as *broken heart* or *hurt feelings* (e.g., Eisenberger, Jarcho, Lieberman, & Naliboff, 2006). Social pain is defined as a result of social injury (involving harm, loss, or threat) and as "distressing experience arising from the perception of actual or potential psychological distance from close others or a social group" (Eisenberger & Lieberman, 2004, p. 294). This definition is parallel to definitions of social or interpersonal stressors as in harm, threat, or loss associated with interpersonal phenomena.

Evidence also suggests that some of the same areas in the brain that are involved in physical pain are also involved in social pain. A major source of many different functions, the anterior cingulate cortex (ACC) participates in a range of performance and affective responses and the emotional distress associated with physical and social pain is mediated by this pathway. There is considerable overlap of functions at this site and sympathetic and hypothalamic–pituitary–adrenal axis activity is associated with ACC activation as well. In fact, the dorsal ACC involved in pain experience is also related to sympathetic modulation of heart rate (Critchley et al., 2003). This association suggests that the ACC supports effortful activity across a range of functions (e.g., Bush, Luu, & Posner, 2000; Gianaros et al., 2005), reflecting considerable overlap of function by neural and endocrine systems across physical pain, social pain, and stress pathways.

Our premise, then, is that stress may be a common pathway linking painful stimuli, either physical or social, with the emotional experience of these stimuli and with potential health consequences of social pain. In addition to the specific aspects of a stressor that warrant coping attention, thresholds and sensitivity to further stimulation may be altered by pain, and stress reactivity to acute events may be affected as well. More important, the persistence and magnitude of social stressors in general and social loss in particular may initiate a cascade of stress responses that may cause changes in most bodily functions and predispose illness and disability.

Stress has been defined in many ways, and its complexity is matched only by the extent and nature of its effects on the mind and body. The term refers to a largely nonspecific, readying response that accompanies environmental change, anticipated change, or other stimuli. In other words, organisms that encounter threats or danger are "provided" with a readied state by biobehavioral aspect of the stress response. These general responses, which are similar across stressors, occur as a means of supporting more specific coping directed at the source or experience of stress and appear to have chronic ramifications if they are extremely intense or frequent. Many of the nonspecific responses do not appear to be well-suited to chronic or episodic stressors. Also, stress is typically accompanied by discomfort, which serves as a motivator to impel the organism to act in some way. What this means is that most stressors evoke both a generic, nonspecific readying response that mobilizes an organism's resources and a specific set of responses aimed at eliminating the source of stress or reducing its aversiveness (see Figure 9.1). The generic readying response increases strength and alertness and facilitates access to stored energy for use if needed. Blood flow is diverted from vulnerable areas and organs that are not central to coping and is directed toward supporting increases in the supply of nutrients and the speed by which they can be taken to the brain and musculature. This increase also increases attention and vigilance, performance of well-learned tasks is enhanced, and these changes generally support coping. Stress produces a state of arousal and readiness to deal with any stressor with a broad, general response and with resources and motivation to cope with it. Its cognitive components are related to its phenomenologic impact: Stress makes people feel different, with anxiety, sadness, tension, aggressiveness, and discomfort accompanying many bodily changes. It is likely that this aversive experience serves to motivate people to do something about the situation or their relationship to it.

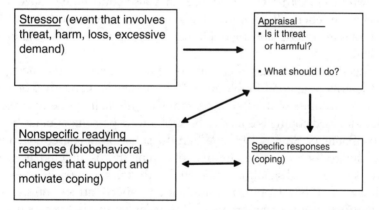

Figure 9.1. The stress process includes the environmental conditions or events that threaten, harm, or otherwise tax individuals, a nonspecific readying response, and a specific coping directed at the situation or the person's relationship with the situation.

Stress provides an energized "platform" for launching specific coping targeted specifically at the causes of discomfort. Lazarus (1966) and Lazarus and Folkman (1984) have also argued that psychological appraisal is important in this process, and evidence supporting this contention is extensive. The nature and strength of the stressor, reflected in the magnitude of threat, harm, loss, or demand and the relevant assets, resources, and experiences an individual may have had, are evaluated and interpreted (Lazarus & Folkman, 1984). This appraisal yields a specific conclusion about how strong or immediate a response should be and what coping mechanisms are more or less likely to be useful. The product of this appraisal includes the generic arousal described earlier and judgments about the specific set of conditions and sources of demand or threat. These judgments guide decisions about coping and are specific to environmental conditions and the interpretation of them. In this way, experience and appraisal of stressors can produce both nonspecific stress and specific, targeted coping.

The notion of coping essentially describes what people do to eliminate or tolerate (i.e., accommodate) a stressor or the way it makes them feel. Several taxonomies of coping have been presented, and volumes discuss the study and modification of coping, but the bottom line is that coping reflects organized activity in the service of stress reduction. People may act in different ways to eliminate its impact on how they feel. First, people are motivated to eliminate the discomfort associated with appraisal of environmental conditions or nonspecific arousal. People often rely on perceptions of their hearts beating to infer anxiety or distress. When people can feel a strong or rapid heartbeat, they may believe it is because of anxiety and the like; because stress increases heart rate in a way that many people can detect, it may lead to the perception of one's own mood. Other bodily changes may also contribute to specific concerns or more general discomfort. Changes in gastrointestinal (GI) motility as a result of sympathetic slowing of GI may be interpreted as a serious problem or malaise.

Together, these kinds of conditions reflect sensations that most people would describe as uncomfortable and possibly of specific concern. Coping that removes or inhibits sources of stress removes the main cause of stress; this problem-focused coping is effective but not always possible or plausible (e.g., Collins, Baum, & Singer, 1983). When the situation or sources of stress are not modifiable or cannot be eliminated, coping that is directed at reducing the aversiveness or discomfort associated with stress may prove more useful (Collins et al., 1983). Coping may include a balanced "attack" on situational and emotional fronts or a more focused singular approach. Successful coping reduces the aversiveness of the situation and reduces motivation to change it (see Figure 9.2). The likelihood of success appears to depend, in part, on the additional resources and support provided by stress.

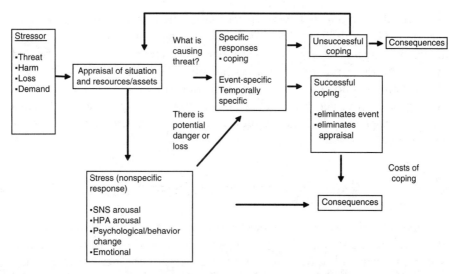

Figure 9.2. A model of stress and coping. Stressors—events that convey threat, harm, loss, or extensive demand—are appraised, and specific ways of coping with these stressors are selected. At the same time, generic stress responses motivate some action against the stressors and support specific targeted coping. HPA = hypothalamic–pituitary–adrenal; SNS = sympathetic nervous system.

STRESS, COPING, AND HEALTH

We have described stress in the context of several models of stress that evolved over the past century and reflect most modern thought about stress. Stress is, in most cases, an adaptive process by which the organism prepares to respond to a threat and then responds to it. The biological and psychological changes that occur during stress are useful in the short term and recede once adaptation is achieved. However, the changes involved in this readying response are generated by neural and endocrine stimulation and two-way communication between the central and peripheral nervous system, and as a result their effects are not limited to adaptive targets; epinephrine, a primary neuroendocrine component of stress, can have effects on circulation and respiration that help the organism cope but also can have inhibitory effects on immune cells or other tissues that express adrenergic receptors. In other words, many of the changes during stress that are helpful for coping may have other effects that could be negative. In particular, when stress is unusually prolonged, persistent, repetitive, or intense, these effects may have "unintended" effects that may affect health and well-being, reflecting both "costs of coping" and "collateral damage" of stress and coping.

In addition, stress affects a range of emotions, decision making, problem-solving performance, and behavioral phenomena that also have positive and negative effects. Some behaviors, particularly when they are directed toward accommodating discomfort or "self-medicating" anxiety, involve withdrawal or increased drug use, including alcohol and tobacco use. Stress-related increases in these and other behaviors can affect health and illness as surely as physical changes do, and when these behaviors directly involve health, this impact can be stronger. Stress-related disruption of positive health behaviors (e.g., exercise) and adherence to prevention and early detection recommendations can have health effects as well.

SOCIAL STRESSORS AND HEALTH

As we noted, stressors include those events that can cause harm or the loss of something or someone who is highly valued, or otherwise introduce threat or excessive demand. When stressors involve interpersonal activity (e.g., being ignored, being bullied, loneliness, loss of friendship), they are considered to be social stressors. Compared with events that do not have clear interpersonal components (e.g., loss of property in a disaster, urban noise), they appear to cause stronger effects and they also seem to have more extensive implications for future responding. Independent of cause, most stressors are capable of having indirect effects on social processes. Effects on one's social order, one's roles, other people's behavior, and the usefulness and availability of important social outcomes may all be influenced by stress. This complexity suggests that social processes that are related to social pain or stress caused by social events or conditions have a number of primary and secondary effects that can affect health and illness.

There are a number of sources of social pain. Many appear to be acute events, such as being ignored or bullied at school, but most have the capacity to become more persistent and chronic. This issue is critical and will go a long way toward determining whether the nature and extent of health effects warrant separate attention. Stressors that cause health problems are generally thought to be chronic. Although some acute stressors facilitate events that may contribute to pathogenesis or expression of underlying disease, most pathways linking stress and health appear to presume chronic experience of stress, which causes long-term disruption of bodily systems and communication among them. For example, many investigators believe that stress can cause disruption of immune system activity, which may open windows of heightened vulnerability for infection, tumor growth, or viral replication (e.g., Cohen et al., 2003; Kiecolt-Glaser & Newton, 2001; Uchino, Cacioppo, & Kiecolt-Glaser, 1996). In most cases, the chronicity of the stressors is a key component of this heightened vulnerability. Recent evidence is consistent with this for infectious illness, and many or most of the stressors studied in related research are not acute (Cohen et al., 1998).

This complexity may not map well onto some of the social stressors that define social pain, particularly acute events such as interpersonal aggression or being ignored. However, events can become chronic in many ways, related to the duration of perceived threat or harm, the duration of the event (stressor), or the duration of response (e.g., Baum, O'Keeffe, & Davidson, 1990). It is not necessary for stressor events to be chronic for stressors to persist. For example, episodic events—acute events strung together in a series—may occur frequently enough to resemble chronic stress. Episodic stressors are common and may characterize much of people's daily experiences. These stressors are typically easy to adjust to and people are often adaptable concerning discrete events, but they pose a cumulative burden that may create difficulties. People who commute to work may find the trip stressful, perhaps only for the period in which commuting occurs. However, the commute and associated distress are repeated twice a day, 5 days a week and anticipation of the stressful commute may help to link this repetitive stressor across time.

These episodic stressors may contribute to the overall burden carried by an individual and may actually become chronic by virtue of their repetitive, periodic nature. It is possible that people may habituate to stressors such as commuting and may develop methods of minimizing chronic stress, but for particularly salient situations, this may be rarer. For example, a single instance of social victimization is likely a stressful experience, may ordinarily be considered acute, and by itself may not have an impact on someone's development or well-being. However, when this victimization is repeated on a regular basis (e.g., daily), it may cause a more chronic perception of threat; perturbation of bodily systems may not fully recover between events (i.e., the frequency or intervals between events may be short enough to cause interference with recovery and extension of stressful responding over time). In addition, stigmatization, painful anticipation of additional victimization, and other aspects of episodic victimization can extend stress in time and potentially contribute to chronic dysfunction and pathophysiology.

By this reasoning, it is possible that a range of acute and chronic social stressors can contribute to poor health or illness by initiating stress and limiting typical responses when social stressors are compromised. It suggests the possibility of health consequences by virtue of acutely painful social stressors when they become chronic because of periodic repetitive experience. In addition, some social losses cause distress that goes well beyond immediate or acute effects. Loss of loved ones, close friends, valued social relationships, and other social resources may pose more chronic effects that extend as long as or longer than the healing process. Outcomes are complicated by the fact that the social conditions are not just stressors; they also affect appraisal, the extent to which an event or change is perceived as stressful, and what kinds of coping are used (e.g., Cohen & Wills, 1985; Uchino et al., 1996).

Social support, though often defined or measured differently, has been shown in study after study to buffer stress, reduce stressful experiences, and minimize negative consequences of stress. Many of the attributes or benefits of social support are relevant; having trusted, supportive others around allows one to obtain information, validate opinions and reactions, and experience greater perceived control and efficacy. It can enhance one's ability to cope, provide instrumental or tangible aid, and otherwise influence one's responses to stressors (Cohen, 1988). Rarely have psychosocial variables such as social support been this consistently linked with stress and stress outcomes, and the evidence seems irrefutable. It is generally better (healthier and less stressful) to have social support, particularly when encountering stressors.

So what happens when the source of one's social support becomes the source of stress? Married couples are often a self-contained support unit; each member of the couple is a primary source of social support. Though not exclusively drawn from this unit, social support from the union should be useful to each when dealing with stressors. If the couple splits up, each will likely experience social loss, which can be a notable stressor. In addition, each might experience reduction of one's support, leading to a ripple effect where the loss of social support affects coping with a vast array of stressors. Interpersonal stressors are stressors that occur among people's personal relationships. Studies investigating the link between life stress and susceptibility to the common cold report that of various chronic stressors (i.e., stressors lasting more than 1 month) interpersonal conflict was among the most potent, and those experiencing this kind of stress were more susceptible to the development of a viral infection when exposed than were those who did not have these conflicts (Cohen, 1988). Social loss can thus be identified as an interpersonal stressor, whether it stems from simply being ignored or left out or from the death of a spouse. In addition, it may reduce the buffering of stress experienced with an intact, unaffected support system and affect experience in a range of situations.

Negative Social Exchanges and Loss

Calhoun (1962) and others have defined stress in terms of a balance between gratifying and nongratifying social encounters. If animals or people are to live in groups, they must arrive at a comfortable, functional balance between positive and negative interactions. Optimal social conditions promote a satisfying balance and maintain healthy living. Negative social exchanges refer to unpleasant or generally aversive interactions or social experiences that result from conflict, rejection, or neglect and criticism (Newsom, Mahan, Rook, &

Krause, 2008). Several kinds of interaction or failure by group members can contribute, and these situations can produce emotional distress (e.g., August et al., 2007; Rook, 1998). One might expect some of these problems to be more common among older people, and in fact, they are reported relatively frequently in this population. A 2-year longitudinal study of older (65 years and older) adults found that higher levels of negative social exchange were related to poorer self-reported health and more health complaints (Newsom et al., 2008). Investigation of younger participants has yielded similar findings and also supports the relevance of negative social exchanges for health (Edwards, Hershberger, Russell, & Markert, 2001). College students who reported the greatest negative social interactions were more likely to report greater numbers of physical symptoms (Edwards et al., 2001).

A number of studies have suggested that negative social interactions are important factors in mental health, changes in immune and neuroendocrine activity, and chronic disease and disability (e.g., August et al., 2007; Krause & Shaw, 2002). These types of studies typically are not directed at identifying mechanisms or pathways that may mediate effects of negative social exchanges on health-impairing processes. An exception to this is a study by Kiecolt-Glaser and colleagues (2005) in which married couples participated by having a "suction blister" raised on their arm and performing two tasks (one eliciting social support and the other eliciting conflict). Through observation the individual husbands and wives were grouped into high- and low-hostile groups according to their interactions. The blisters healed more slowly after the conflict task than after the social support task, and interestingly, the high-hostile groups healed considerably (60%) more slowly than did the low-hostile groups, regardless of the task (Kiecolt-Glaser et al., 2005). This study suggests that negative social interactions can adversely impact health, particularly when the immune responses involved in healing are undermined by negative interactions. Negative social interactions could have a much greater impact on people with chronic conditions. For example, pain and long-term functional disability are strongly related to problematic social support and low social support in patients with rheumatoid arthritis (Evers et al., 2003; Riemsma et al., 1998). Studies like these are correlational and retrospective and are limited by these and other problems. Regardless, the composite notion of negative social exchange is consistent with the extension of acute events in time and may be important in shaping health behaviors and outcomes.

This notion supports the continued use of acute models of negative exchanges by suggesting that accumulations of acute events may add up to constitute a more major chronic one. As we have noted, some of the events are brief; being ignored or being treated as stigmatized or otherwise being denied a "rightful" place in a group may take place in one or a few settings, may be isolated occurrences, and may not last long enough or be important enough to cause major problems or upset. However, these events can blend together, particularly if they are regular, predictable, or uncontrollable, and may form the basis for extension of the duration or prominence of the negative social exchange. These more chronic, more influential stressors may ultimately be responsible for syndromes that can characterize social experience and open "windows" for illness-related events and pathogenic processes that can significantly affect an organism's health and well-being. We focus on the sources of stress in this section.

Ostracism and Social Rejection

Ostracism and social rejection are extreme forms of negative social contact that occur when a person is overtly excluded and ignored. Frequently, no explanations are given for this, and people are left to interpret the situation with varying information (Williams, 2007b). Ostracism and social rejection are typically brief events and may cause short-lived distress including acute increases in blood pressure and cortisol levels (Stroud, Tanofsky-Kraff, Wilfley, & Salovey, 2000). Men who are sensitive to rejection and tend to expect rejection appear to be more prone to respond with hostility (Downey, Feldman, & Ayduk, 2000). At the same time, men who are high in rejection sensitivity may avoid social situations in general (similar to a flight response) when faced with a stressor (Downey & Feldman, 1996). Hostility may result when this avoidance breaks down. Further, complicating matters is the observation that under some conditions, social rejection or ignoring people may be normative and part of routine coping with social overload (e.g., Cohen, 1978). In such cases, these instances may be viewed as benign or neutral. Riders of New York City subways may ignore and avoid contact with others around them, but this conduct is likely to be viewed as normative and benign. Although research linking chronic ostracism and social rejection to physical health is not conclusive, there appear to be clearer links to psychological health. Depression, learned helplessness, alienation, and low self-worth are among the consequences associated with long-term social rejection and ostracism (Cacioppo & Hawkley, 2005; Williams, 2007b).

Loss of Social Relationships

There are many ways in which people can lose an important relationship; death, relocation, disability, and conflict can all contribute to the end of a specific relationship or to a class of relationships (divorce, having friends or family move away, imprisonment, illness, and loss of a loved one are all instances of these stressors), and many of the depictions of social stressors as painful rely on situations in which relationships are lost. Losses may be due to stigmatizing circumstances, as is reported by patients with HIV and hepatitis who lose relationships and support because of their illness (e.g., Blasiole, Shinkunas, LaBrecque, Arnold, & Zickman, 2006). A unique form of loss can occur when a patient develops Alzheimer's disease. Such cases usually require caregivers, many of whom are family members, and even though the patient is not physically gone, many of the qualities and characteristics that made that person special and loved are no longer intact. Caregivers often experience grief while the person is still living, with studies reporting that between 47% and 59% of caregivers exhibit grief symptoms while the patient is still alive (Adams & Sanders, 2004; Collins, Liken, King, & Kokinakis, 1993).

Caregivers for patients still in the early stages of the disease expressed loss regarding activities shared with the person, including future goals, plans, and dreams (Adams & Sanders, 2004). As the disease progressed, losses experienced were more internalized, such as loss of personal time, freedom, and social interactions. Finally, in the latter stages of the disease, grief seemed to come to a peak and the loss of the interpersonal relationship was grieved (Adams & Sanders, 2004). Functional impairment appears to be positively associated with grief (Sanders, Ott, Kelber, & Noonan, 2008). One of the most commonly endorsed themes observed among caregivers was yearning for the past and aspects such as personality traits that had been lost because of the encroaching dementia. Spouses and adult children of the patients endured different types of grief. Grief experienced by adult children was more likely to include guilt and regret, whereas spouses were more likely to emphasize loss of their main means of social support (Sanders et al., 2008). These differences may magnify the impact of the loss and add to the burden carried by an already taxed system. Under these conditions, people may become vulnerable to loneliness.

Social Integration and Loneliness

Research in psychology and other social and behavioral sciences has drawn sharp distinctions between people who are well-integrated into social networks and those who are not. It is desirable to be well-embedded in one or more social networks, typically deriving social support and other supports and benefits from group membership. Loss of integration, or loss of a sense of being an active part of a social network, represents a major social loss and can lead to loneliness. Socially integrated adults have lower mortality and better health than do adults who are more isolated (Cohen, 2004; Uchino et al., 1996). Loneliness represents an extreme level of social loss that appears to be stressful and develops out of people's feeling estranged from, rejected, or misunderstood by others or a lack of social partners (Rook, 1984). To some extent, loneliness represents an extension of many instances that by themselves have considerably less impact.

Bereavement

Perhaps the most profound form of social loss is bereavement and loss of a loved one. Different from other losses in its irrevocable permanent nature, bereavement is also an excellent example of social pain. Experience shows that losses hurt, and grieving and other means of coping with it can affect one's health. Here bereavement is meant to represent the experience of loss of a close confidante, friend, or family member that follows the death of a loved one. Death is uncontrollable and to some extent unknowable, and these factors may intensify distress experienced in its wake. There are variables that increase or decrease the stressfulness of bereavement, including circumstances surrounding the death, social impact of the loss, previous experience, and the relationship with the deceased. Bereavement ultimately affects everyone and anyone, regardless of age, gender, and "station in life," and may produce intense acute distress, numbing, and persistent social pain.

This kind of distress can affect sleep, quality of social interaction, and a range of behavioral and biological functions that are often associated with health. Several studies have found effects of social loss on sleep; a study on adjustment after the loss of a spouse reported that more than half of the bereaved felt tired and experienced disturbed sleep or lack of sleep (Carlsson & Nilsson, 2007). Along with the sleep disturbances, participants reported muscular and skeletal physical symptoms that did not change throughout the year. Many of the participants attributed these ailments to the loss of their spouse (Carlsson & Nilsson, 2007). These kinds of findings are consistent with general findings in the literature indicating that bereaved people are at considerably elevated risk of morbidity and mortality compared with nonbereaved people of similar age and background (e.g., Mellström, Nilsson, Odēn, Rundgren, & Svanborg, 1982; Murrell et al., 1988; Van Eijk et al., 1988).

Prospective studies have considered widows and widowers after various intervals of grieving. One study of bereaved men and women in the eastern United States followed participants for 12 years and matched those who were widowed to a comparable, married participant (Helsing, Szklo, & Comstock, 1981). Men had a higher mortality risk than did women, and widows had a greater risk than did men with living spouses. There was also a substantial difference between widowed men who remarried and those who did not; men who did not remarry were at greater risk even when poor health was taken into account. For both men and women, mortality rates were significantly greater when the widowed person lived alone (1981). These findings suggest that "replacing" a lost social role (e.g., a spouse) may provide potent stress relief and that health effects associated with loss may be buffered by having a close social network or by negating social losses as quickly as possible.

A similar study was conducted in Finland by Martikainen and Valkonen (1996). Earlier studies did not control for cause of death variation, and all accidental deaths were excluded. This study accounted for these variables. Bereaved men were again at greater risk of mortality than were bereaved women. Distinct from the earlier study were findings related to accidental or violent causes of death, where the risk for mortality ranged from 94% among bereaved men to 51% among bereaved women, with suicide accounting for the largest amount of excess mortality among violent deaths. Specific diseases, such as cancer, circulatory diabetes, or respiratory disease, also showed significant excess mortality, and alcohol- and tobacco-related diseases were significantly higher as well. These findings suggest that the loss of a spouse is especially stressful when the death was violent or unexpected, and for some it is shortly followed by death.

Bereavement can last for variable amounts of time, and may be cross-cut by other aging- or loss-related changes that may exacerbate effects of social losses already incurred. One of the most common of these is relocation, when a bereaved spouse is relocated to a retirement or nursing home. As people age, they may lose the ability to take care of a home and require assisted living. However, they may not recognize this need or may resent or otherwise oppose the move. Relocation itself is a threat to one's sense of control and independence and may affect social support. All of these factors contribute to stress. People who moved were more likely to die during bereavement (Martikainen & Valkonen, 1996).

Data also support the assumption that bereaved people are more likely to be relocated or institutionalized (Nihtilä et al., 2008). Widowers were 71% and widows were 49% more likely to enter an institution than were their married counterparts. The highest rates appeared during the first month after the death of a spouse.

Bereavement after the loss of a spouse, parent, child, or close associate appears to cause distress on the part of many of those people left behind. The extent to which this represents the loss of a particular person or a social role or major source of support is unclear, but one would expect each type of loss to have independent and interactive effects. For example, caregiving could mitigate some of the distress by permitting anticipatory grieving and by modifying attributions about and interpretations of the loss. Evidence suggests that pre-existing relationships are strong determinants of stress and strain during caregiving (e.g., Schulz et al., 2001).

There have been some attempts to reduce distress associated with bereavement. A sample of 50 widowers (men and women) were invited to participate in a program of medical and psychological support over a 1-year period (Grimby & Johansson, 2008). The intervention included three psychological support sessions (at 1, 3, and 12 months after enrollment) and three medical support sessions. Comparisons with comparable, married, non-bereaved participants indicated that at the start, bereaved participants reported poorer quality of life than did married controls, but that over a 10-year period, there were no differences between bereaved and nonbereaved participants in health care utilization (Grimby & Johansson, 2008). These results suggest either a healing effect of the intervention, an indicator that those who will experience long-term distress are more likely to die or become ill soon after loss (making it less likely that more affected people did not participate), or that the normal pattern of response to loss is largely restricted to intense acute effects. Consistent with this, the nature of a specific loss and the chronicity or stressful impact of caregiving appear to shape subsequent consequences (e.g., Burton, Haley, & Small, 2006).

CONCLUSIONS

It is clear that bereavement is stressful and appears to be exacerbated by specific events or characteristics that make the loss more painful. Men appear to be more likely to experience health problems and death in the wake of loss, and age, where they live, and extent of social networks available may affect how much distress is experienced. In part, this greater impact on men may be due to social support investment strategies in which men invest heavily in their spouse (so when the spouse is lost, men suffer a larger hit to their overall support).

A number of studies have examined various aspects of immune, endocrine, and cardiovascular function as a function of bereavement. The picture that emerges is that bereavement is stressful and affects health-related biobehavioral processes, but that stress lessens over time and resolves readily. Effects are largely limited to the period during which stress is expressed. Martin and Dean (1993) found commonly observed psychological changes such as depression, traumatic stress, sedative use, or suicidal ideation. Biological stress responses have been linked to loneliness and in many contexts, these responses can predispose illness, death, and disability (e.g., Steptoe, Owen, Kunz-Ebrecht, & Brydon, 2004). Loneliness has been linked to shorter survival after coronary artery bypass graft (CABG) surgery (Herlitz et al., 1998) and has been associated with diseases such as emphysema and heart disease in older people (Tomaka, Thompson, & Palacios, 2006). In CABG patients, loneliness was the only aspect of quality of life that predicted survival (Herlitz et al., 1998). A broader investigation of loneliness involved longitudinal study of healthy middle-aged men and women in the United Kingdom. Among women, loneliness was associated with increased diastolic blood pressure reactivity to challenge, fibrinogen, and cardiovascular disease risk factors (Steptoe et al., 2004).

Natural killer cells are key antiviral and antitumor cells, and during stress were inversely related to loneliness, suggesting the possibility that loneliness could impair immune system function.

Healthy behaviors are also affected by loneliness and represent another pathway by which loneliness may affect health. A comparison study of health behaviors (smoking, sedentary behavior, and overweight or obesity) in lonely and nonlonely populations found significant differences in smoking and weight-related behaviors: Lonely people were most likely to smoke cigarettes and have a higher body mass index than were nonlonely people (Lauder, Mummery, Jones, & Caperchione, 2006).

We have considered several examples of social conditions that can be cast as examples of social pain and interpersonal stress, and we have described a pathway by which social stressors can have effects on health and illness. Some of these sources of social pain are clearly related to health because they are sufficiently intense and prolonged to affect key systems that maintain host defense and thereby increase the potential for pathophysiological development. Other instances of social pain are more time limited and may not be strong enough to perturb basic activity and communication among key bodily systems. However, frequent experience of relatively minor, acute events may sustain more chronic stress and may contribute to behavioral syndromes that are associated with more extreme and persistent stress. One brief act of incivility, for example, may not be much by itself but may contribute to larger patterns of harassment, discrimination, or victimization that can generate stress-related effects on health and well-being.

Many of these aspects of social pain are not well-studied, and doing so would be best served by collaboration among those interested in social phenomena and those who study pathways by which social stressors exert health effects. Theories and model building can focus on ways in which social pain contributes to stress and how critical windows of vulnerability to illness may open and close. Several themes have emerged in the development of psychology as a life science, including how external events such as social loss or victimization are translated into biobehavioral phenomena that can cause health problems. How these social and environmental events can "get under the skin" (Cohen, 2004) and how their progression toward dysfunction can be halted or redirected are important research topics and may uncover relationships among real-world variables that are not widely known.

REFERENCES

Adams, K. B., & Sanders, S. (2004). Alzheimer's caregiver differences in experience of loss, grief reactions and depressive symptoms across stage of disease: A mixed-method analysis. *Dementia: The International Journal of Social Research and Practice, 3,* 195–210.

Baum, A., O'Keeffe, M., & Davidson, L. (1990). Acute stressors and chronic response: The case of traumatic stress. *Journal of Applied Social Psychology, 20,* 1643–1654.

Blasiole, J., Shinkunas, L., LaBrecque, D., Arnold, R., & Zickmund, S. (2006). Mental and physical symptoms associated with lower social support for patients with hepatitis C. *World Journal of Gastroenterology, 12,* 4665–4672.

Burton, A. M., Haley, W. E., & Small, B. J. (2006). Bereavement after caregiving or unexpected death: Effects on elderly spouses. *Aging & Mental Health, 10,* 319–326. doi:10.1080/13607860500410045

Bush, G., Luu, P., & Posner, M. I. (2000). Cognitive and emotional influences in anterior cingulate cortex. *Trends in Cognitive Sciences, 4,* 215–222. doi:10.1016/S1364-6613(00)01483-2

Cacioppo, J. T., Berntson, G. G., Sheridan, J. F., & McClintock, M. K. (2000). Multi-level integrative analyses of human behavior: The complementing nature of social and biological approaches. *Psychological Bulletin, 126,* 829–843.

Cacioppo, J. T., & Hawkley, L. C. (2005). People thinking about people: The vicious cycle of being a social outcast in one's own mind. In K. D. Williams, J. P. Forgas, & W. von Hippel (Eds.), *The social outcast: Ostracism, social exclusion, rejection, and bullying* (pp. 91–108). New York, NY: Psychology Press.

Calhoun, J. B. (1962). Population density and social pathology. *Scientific American, 206,* 139–150.

Carlsson, M. E., & Nilsson, I. M. (2007). Bereaved spouses' adjustment after the patients' death in palliative care. *Palliative & Supportive Care, 5,* 397–404. doi: 10.1017/S1478951507000594

Cohen, S. (1978). Environmental load and the allocation of attention. In A. Baum, J. E. Singer, & S. Valins (Eds.), *Advances in environmental psychology: Vol. I. The urban environment.* Hillsdale, NJ: Erlbaum.

Cohen, S. (1988). Psychosocial models of the role of social support in the etiology of physical disease. *Health Psychology, 7,* 269–297. doi:10.1037/0278-6133.7.3.269

Cohen, S. (2004). Social relationships and health. *American Psychologist, 59,* 676–684. doi:10.1037/0003-066X.59.8.676

Cohen, S., Frank, E., Doyle, W. J., Skoner, D. P., Rabin, B. S., & Gwaltney, J. M., Jr. (1998). Types of stressors that increase susceptibility to the common cold in healthy adults. *Health Psychology, 17,* 214–223. doi:10.1037/0278-6133. 17.3.214

Cohen, S., Turner, R., Alper, C. A., & Skoner, D. P. (2003). Sociability and susceptibility to the common cold. *Psychological Science, 14,* 389–395. doi:10.1111/1467-9280.01452

Cohen, S., & Wills, T. A. (1985). Stress, social support and the buffering hypothesis. *Psychological Bulletin, 98,* 310–357.

Collins, C., Liken, M., King, S., & Kokinakis, C. (1993). Loss and grief among family caregivers of relatives with dementia. *Qualitative Health Research, 3*, 236–253. doi:10.1177/104973239300300206

Collins, D. L., Baum, A., & Singer, J. E. (1983). Coping with chronic stress at Three Mile Island: Psychological and biochemical evidence. *Health Psychology, 2*, 149–166. doi:10.1037/0278-6133.2.2.149

Critchley, H. D., Mathias, C. J., Josephs, O., O'Doherty, J., Zanini, S., Dewar, B.-K., . . . Dolan, R. J. (2003). Human cingulate cortex and autonomic control: Converging neuroimaging and clinical evidence. *Brain. Journal of Neurology, 126*, 2139 2152.

Dickerson, S. S., & Kemeny, M. E. (2004). Acute stressors and cortisol responses: A theoretical integration and synthesis of laboratory research. *Psychological Bulletin, 130*, 355–391. doi:10.1037/0033-2909.130.3.355

Downey, G., & Feldman, S. I. (1996). Implications of rejection sensitivity for intimate relationships. *Journal of Personality and Social Psychology, 70*, 1327–1343. doi:10.1037/0022-3514.70.6.1327

Downey, G., Feldman, S., & Ayduk, O. (2000). Rejection sensitivity and male violence in romantic relationships. *Personal Relationships, 7*(1), 45–61. doi:10.1111/j.1475-6811.2000.tb00003.x

Edwards, K. J., Hershberger, P. J., Russell, R. K., & Markert, R. J. (2001). Stress, negative social exchange, and health symptoms in university students. *Journal of American College Health, 50*(2), 75–79. doi:10.1080/07448480109596010

Eisenberger, N. I., Jarcho, J. M., Lieberman, M. D., & Naliboff, B. D. (2006). An experimental study of shared sensitivity to physical pain and social rejection. *Pain, 126*(1–3), 132–138. doi:10.1016/j.pain.2006.06.024

Eisenberger, N. I., & Lieberman, M. D. (2004). Why rejection hurts: A common neural alarm system for physical and social pain. *Trends in Cognitive Sciences, 8*, 294–300. doi:10.1016/j.tics.2004.05.010

Evers, A. W. M., Kraaimaat, F. W., Geene, R., Jacobs, J. W. G., & Bijlsma, J. W. J. (2003). Pain coping and social support as predictors of long-term functional disability and pain in early rheumatoid arthritis. *Behaviour Research and Therapy, 41*, 1295–1310. doi:10.1016/S0005-7967(03)00036-6

Gianaros, P. J., Dearbyshire, S. W. G., May, J. C., Siegle, G. J., Gamalo, M. A., & Jennings, J. R. (2005). Anterior cingulate activity correlates with blood pressure during stress. *Psychophysiology, 42*, 627–635. doi:10.1111/j.1469-8986.2005.00366.x

Grimby, A., & Johansson, A. K. (2008). Does early bereavement counseling prevent ill health and untimely death? *American Journal of Hospice & Palliative Medicine, 24*, 475–478. doi:10.1177/1049909107305651

Helsing, K. J., Szklo, M., & Comstock, G. W. (1981). Factors associated with mortality after widowhood. *American Journal of Public Health, 71*, 802–809. doi:10.2105/AJPH.71.8.802

Herlitz, J., Brandrup-Wognsen, G., Karlsson, T., Haglid, M., & Sjöland, H. (1998). Predictors of death and other cardiac events within 2 years after coronary artery bypass grafting. *Cardiology, 90,* 110–114. doi:10.1159/000006828

Kiecolt-Glaser, J. K., Loving, T. J., Stowell, J. R., Malarkey, W. B., Lemeshow, S., Dickinson, S. L., & Glaser, R. (2005). Hostile marital interactions, pro-inflammatory cytokine production, and wound healing. *Archives of General Psychiatry, 62,* 1377–1384. doi:10.1001/archpsyc.62.12.1377

Kiecolt-Glaser, J. K., & Newton, T. L. (2001). Marriage and health: His and hers. *Psychological Bulletin, 127,* 472–503.

Krause, N., & Shaw, B. A. (2002). Negative interaction and changes in functional disability during late life. *Journal of Social and Personal Relationships, 19,* 339–359.

Lauder, W., Mummery, K., Jones, M., & Caperchione, C. (2006). A comparison of health behaviours in lonely and non-lonely populations. *Psychology, Health and Medicine, 11,* 233–245. doi:10.1080/13548500500266607

Lazarus, R. S. (1966). *Psychological stress and the coping process.* New York, NY: McGraw-Hill.

Lazarus, R. S., & Folkman, S. (1984). *Stress, appraisal, and coping.* New York, NY: Springer.

Martikainen, P., & Valkonen, T. (1996). Mortality after the death of a spouse: Rates and causes of death in a large Finnish cohort. *American Journal of Public Health, 86*(8, Pt. 1), 1087–1093. doi:10.2105/AJPH.86.8_Pt_1.1087

Martin, J. L., & Dean, L. (1993). Effects of AIDS-related bereavement and HIV-related illness on psychological distress among gay men: A 7-year longitudinal study, 1985-1991. *Journal of Consulting and Clinical Psychology, 61,* 94–103. doi:10.1037/0022-006X.61.1.94

Mellström, D., Nilsson, A., Oden, A., Rundgren, Å., & Svanborg, A. (1982). Mortality among the widowed in Sweden. *Scandinavian Journal of Social Medicine, 10,* 33–41.

Murrell, S. A., Himmelfarb, S., & Phifer, S. F. (1988). Effects of bereavement/loss and pre-event states on subsequent physical health in older adults. *International Journal of Aging & Human Development, 27,* 89–107.

Newsom, J. T., Mahan, T. L., Rook, K. S., & Krause, N. (2008). Stable negative social exchanges and health. *Health Psychology, 27,* 78–86. doi:10.1037/0278-6133.27.1.78

Nihtilä, E. K., Martikainen, P. T., Koskinen, S. V. P., Reunanen, A. R., Noro, A. M., & Häkkinen, U. T. (2008). Chronic conditions and the risk of long-term institutionalization among older people. *European Journal of Public Health, 18,* 77–84. doi:10.1093/eurpub/ckm025

Panksepp, J. (2003, October 10). Neuroscience. Feeling the pain of social loss. *Science, 302,* 237–239. doi:10.1126/science.1091062

Riemsma, R. P., Rasker, J. J., Taal, E., Griep, E. N., Wouters, J. W., & Wiegman, O. (1998). Fatigue in rheumatoid arthritis: The role of self-efficacy and problematic social support. *British Journal of Rheumatology, 37,* 1042–1046. doi:10.1093/rheumatology/37.10.1042

Rook, K. S. (1984). The negative side of social interaction: Impact on psychological well-being. *Journal of Personality and Social Psychology, 46,* 1097–1108. doi:10.1037/0022-3514.46.5.1097

Rook, K. S. (1998). Investigating the positive and negative sides of personal relationships: Through a lens darkly? In B. H. Spitzberg & W. R. Cupach (Eds.), *The dark side of close relationships* (pp. 369–393). Mahwah, NJ: Erlbaum.

Sanders, S., Ott, C. H., Kelber, S. T., & Noonan, P. (2008). The experience of high levels of grief in caregivers of persons with Alzheimer's disease and related dementia. *Death Studies, 32,* 495–523. doi:10.1080/07481180802138845

Schulz, R., Beach, S. R., Lind, B., Martire, L., Zdaniuk, B., Hirsch, M. D., . . . Burton, L. (2001). Involvement in caregiving and adjustment to death of a spouse. *JAMA, 285,* 3123–3129. doi:10.1001/jama.285.24.3123

Steptoe, A., Owen, N., Kunz-Ebrecht, S. R., & Brydon, L. (2004). Loneliness and neuroendocrine, cardiovascular, and inflammatory stress responses in middle-aged men and women. *Psychoneuroendocrinology, 29,* 593–611. doi:10.1016/S0306-4530(03)00086-6

Stroud, L. R., Tanofsky-Kraff, M., Wilfley, D. E., & Salovey, P. (2000). The Yale Interpersonal Stressor (YIPS): Affective, physiological, and behavioral responses to a novel interpersonal rejection paradigm. *Annals of Behavioral Medicine, 22,* 204–213. doi:10.1007/BF02895115

Tomaka, J., Thompson, S., & Palacios, R. (2006). The relation of social isolation, loneliness, and social support to disease outcomes among the elderly. *Journal of Aging and Health, 18,* 359–384. doi:10.1177/0898264305280993

Uchino, B. N., Cacioppo, J. T., & Kiecolt-Glaser, J. K. (1996). The relationship between social support and physiological processes: A review with emphasis on underlying mechanisms and implications for health. *Psychological Bulletin, 119,* 488–531. doi:10.1037/0033-2909.119.3.488

Van Eijk, J., Smits, A., Huygen, F., & van der Hoogen, H. (1988). Effects of bereavement on the health of remaining family members. *Family Practice, 5,* 278–282. doi:10.1093/fampra/5.4.278

Williams, K. D. (2007a). Ostracism. *Annual Review of Psychology, 58,* 425–452. doi:10.1146/annurev.psych.58.110405.085641

Williams, K. D. (2007b). Ostracism: The kiss of social death. *Social and Personality Psychology Compass, 1*(1), 236–247. doi:10.1111/j.1751-9004.2007.00004.x

10

BULLYING AND ITS LONG-TERM HEALTH IMPLICATIONS

JENNIFER M. KNACK, HAYLIE L. GOMEZ,
AND LAURI A. JENSEN-CAMPBELL

Researchers have long argued that humans have a fundamental need to belong and to have ongoing positive significant relational bonds (Baumeister & Leary, 1995; Bowlby, 1973; Maslow, 1968; Taylor, 2007). Research has begun to examine the outcomes of injury or damage to interpersonal relationships (e.g., death, the end of a romantic relationship, bullying, rumors), collectively known as *social pain* (e.g., Eisenberger & Lieberman, 2004, 2005; MacDonald & Leary, 2005). Current models of social pain suggest biological systems play an important role in the emotional experience of pain caused when relationships are disrupted or ended. In other words, having a "broken heart" is not simply in one's mind; rather, there is a biological basis for the emotional pain associated with social pain experiences.

Evidence suggests that the neural correlates associated with the emotional experience of social pain overlap those of physical pain (e.g., anterior cingulate cortex or ACC; Eisenberger, Lieberman, & Williams, 2003; MacDonald & Leary, 2005). This overlap is observed in animals such that the neurochemicals linked to social loss also regulate the emotional experience of physical pain (Panksepp, 2003). Similarly, increased sensitivity to physical pain in humans is associated with increased sensitivity to social pain (Eisenberger, Jarcho, Lieberman, & Naliboff, 2006). People who experienced personal failure report higher pain ratings on a subsequent cold pressor task (van den Hout, Vlaeyen, Peters, Englehard, & van den Hout, 2000). DeWall and colleagues (see Chapter 5, this volume) even found that individuals who took acetaminophen (vs. a placebo) for 2 weeks reported fewer instances of hurt feelings during that time period. This evidence suggests that acute exposure to one pain type (e.g., social) influences subsequent sensitivity to the other pain type (e.g., physical).

Very little attention, however, has been paid to how chronic social pain influences pain sensitivity and physical health. In this chapter, we examine the effects of chronic social pain on pain sensitivity by focusing specifically on being the victim of bullying by peers. For the purpose of this discussion, victims are individuals who are persistently the recipient of negative, aggressive acts from one or more individuals for extended periods (e.g., 6 months; Aalsma, 2008).

THEORETICAL MODEL AND CHAPTER OVERVIEW

We posit that chronic peer victimization leads to increased sensitivity to future experiences of victimization (see Figure 10.1). First, we expect that being a frequent target of peer victimization leads to abnormal levels of basal cortisol and altered brain functioning in the ACC, the right ventral prefrontal cortex (RVPFC), and the insula. We expect that these neural and neuroendocrine alterations will lead to poorer physical health (e.g., more frequent and severe stomachaches) and mental health (e.g., loneliness, depression) outcomes. Peer victimization that is harsher in nature or longer in duration should lead to greater alterations in these biological systems. Furthermore, some individuals

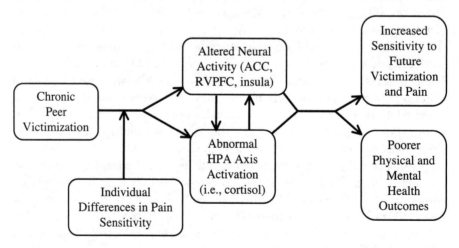

Figure 10.1. Theoretical model: How chronic victimization leads to increased sensitivity to future experiences of victimization. ACC = anterior cingulate cortex; HPA = hypothalamic–pituitary–adrenal; RVPFC = right ventral prefrontal cortex.

may be more vulnerable to pain sensitivity than other individuals. We postulate that physical health complaints of victimized children are not simply "in their head" but instead are meaningful biological alterations that may reflect changes in sensitivity to pain responses.

We first address the immediate and short-term effects associated with peer victimization. We also examine the idea that chronic peer victimization has lasting effects on neural activity, neuroendocrine functioning, and physical and psychological health. We then consider how chronic social pain may influence pain sensitivity by examining the posttraumatic stress disorder (PTSD) literature. We conclude with a discussion of the alternative hypothesis that chronic pain experiences may numb people to future experiences of social pain rather than increase their sensitivity.

PEER VICTIMIZATION

A certain degree of exposure to negative behaviors from others is normal, but some individuals are consistently targets of aggression. Estimates of American children who report being repeatedly bullied by their peers have ranged from 10% to 30% (e.g., Grills & Ollendick, 2002). These aggressive acts can include attempts to harm an individual's relationships (i.e., relational victimization; Crick & Grotpeter, 1995) and can include social isolation, discrediting, being the target of rumors, and being called names. Peer victimization can start as young as preschool, usually peaks in early adolescence, and often remains fairly stable throughout high school (e.g., K. R. Williams & Guerra, 2007). Bullying by peers has recently moved from the school yard to electronic media, such as cell phones and the Internet, making it even harder for the victim to escape bullying (David-Ferdon & Hertz, 2007).

Research consistently demonstrates that children who have poor peer relations suffer from mental health problems (e.g., Kupersmidt, Coie, & Dodge, 1990). These effects are often persistent; adults who were victimized as adolescents report higher depression and lower self-esteem than do their nonvictimized peers (Olweus, 1978). In addition, low peer acceptance and lack of friends in childhood predict overall life status adjustment problems, psychopathological symptoms, and general low self-worth in early adulthood (Bagwell, Newcomb, & Bukowski, 1998).

Peer victimization may be especially influential on health outcomes during periods of rapid developmental change. Early adolescence is one such period when children undergo a number of major physiological changes, including puberty, changes in hypothalamic–pituitary–adrenal (HPA) axis activation, maturation of the immune system, and rapid brain maturation (Spear, 2000; Walker, 2002; Walker, Walder, & Reynolds, 2001). The magnitude of developmental changes in adolescence is on par with those seen in infancy and early childhood; many of these changes influence stress responses and emotional reactivity (Spear, 2000). Adolescence in particular is seen as a sensitive period for reorganization of regulatory systems that are implicated in pain (Steinberg, 2005).

In addition to physiological changes, adolescents undergo a number of changes in their social environment (Larson & Richards, 1994). Peers and friends begin to play an increasingly important socialization role (Hartup, 1996). As the influence of peers increases, adolescents also experience a peak in victimization, as evidenced by both longitudinal and cross-sectional studies (Nansel et al., 2001; Nylund, Bellmore, Nishina, & Sandra, 2007). When adolescents are the most vulnerable to environmental stressors, they are also most likely to become victims of peer abuse. Because early adolescence is a time of increased vulnerability to stressful events, the consequence is ultimately greater pain sensitivity and poorer health outcomes for victims (Walker et al., 2001).

VICTIMIZATION AND PHYSICAL PAIN

Research has begun to focus on how harmful relationships can affect physical health. Findings indicate victimized individuals experience more physical health problems than do their nonvictimized peers (Greco, Freeman, & Dufton, 2007; Rigby, 2003). Even after controlling for initial health differences, victimized children continue to have poorer physical health outcomes 3 years later (Rigby & Slee, 1999). In a prospective longitudinal study, victims of bullying were more likely to develop new somatic problems; children with somatic problems, however, were not more likely to become victims (Fekkes, Pijpers, Fredricks, Vogels, & Verloove-Vanhorick, 2006). Most somatic complaints associated with victimization involve physical pain symptoms such as abdominal pain, headaches, chest pain, back pain, and pain in arms, legs, and joints (Garber, Walker, & Zeman, 1991).

We wanted to further examine whether victimization was related to reports of physical pain. College students completed measures of victimization, pain disability, and health as part of a larger online study on interpersonal relationships. They also completed a brief cardiac measure as part of a larger prescreening. Being victimized was positively associated with the frequency and severity of negative health outcomes; specifically, victims reported more physical pain symptoms such as stomachaches, muscle aches and pains, headaches, sore throats, and fever and chills. Being bullied was also positively associated with pain disability (Gatchel, Mayer, & Theodore, 2006). Victimized individuals reported more physical pain, took more pain medication, and saw doctors more often for their pain than did their nonvictimized counterparts. College

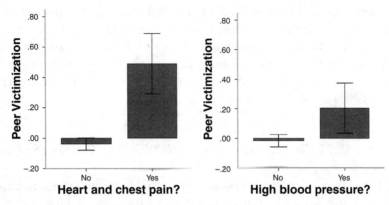

Figure 10.2. Victimization levels by heart or blood pressure problems.

students who reported frequent chest and heart pains in the initial cardiac prescreening were more victimized than were individuals who did not report these pains. Bullied students were also more likely to be told by their doctor that they had higher blood pressure than were their nonbullied counterparts (see Figure 10.2).

In other preliminary data that are part of a larger project, we found that victimized adolescents report more frequent and more severe physical health problems than do nonvictimized adolescents. Victimization significantly predicted abdominal pain (see Figure 10.3), which is in line with previous research examining the characteristics of children with high abdominal pain.

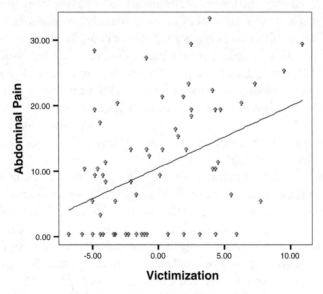

Figure 10.3. Victimization predicts abdominal pain.

Greco, Freeman, and Dufton (2007) found children who experienced greater abdominal pain tended to experience more victimization than did children who experienced less abdominal pain. Perhaps more interesting is the finding that adolescent victims are also more likely to use medication for physical pain than are nonvictimized adolescents (Due, Hansen, Merlo, Andersen, & Holstein, 2007).

OVERLAP BETWEEN PHYSICAL AND SOCIAL PAIN SYSTEMS

The overlap of biological systems associated with the emotional experience of physical and social pain is important for two reasons. First, it provides evidence of a complex interplay between social interactions and biological and psychological functioning. Second, it suggests that examining research on chronic physical pain and chronic stress may elucidate how prolonged social pain, namely, chronic peer victimization, may influence pain sensitivity and health outcomes.

Most researchers would agree that the plasticity of the nervous system predisposes individuals to alterations in the pattern of neural connections based on environmental inputs (e.g., Cicchetti & Walker, 2003). Chronic physical pain is believed to change physiological and psychological processes associated with pain unpleasantness (Baliki et al., 2006; Price, 2000). For example, pain affect includes *secondary pain affect,* which is the set of emotions associated with the long-term implications of having pain (Price, 2000). Chronic pain sufferers may become more sensitive to potential harm and attempt to avoid (or even overreact to) these situations despite the fact that they may be easily tolerable. Chronic pain sufferers do indeed avoid activities that they believe might increase pain (Sharp & Harvey, 2001). Anxiety and fear are also strongly associated with painful experiences, and chronic pain sufferers are more likely to experience anxiety and panic disorders (McWilliams, Cox, & Enns, 2003). Individuals who are more anxious and neurotic also have lower thresholds for pain unpleasantness (Harkins, Price, & Braith, 1989; Phillips & Gatchel, 2000).

Current models of psychopathology also posit that environmental factors can alter the normal course of development, making individuals more sensitive to future painful experiences (Cicchetti & Walker, 2003; Dersh, Polatin, & Gatchel, 2002). Early psychological trauma is thought to increase neurophysiological reactivity and emotional sensitization (Cicchetti, 2003). Foy et al. (1987) illustrated how residual stress from prior painful events can lead to the development of PTSD. PTSD, in turn, is associated with alterations in HPA axis activation (Inslicht et al., 2006; Yehuda, 2002).

It is interesting to note that victims of workplace bullying have been found to exhibit symptoms of PTSD (Matthiesen & Einarsen, 2004; Mikkelsen & Einarsen, 2002). In Mikkelsen and Einarsen's (2002) sample, 76% of workplace victims evidenced symptoms of PTSD; 29% of the victims met all *Diagnostic and Statistical Manual of Mental Disorders* (4th ed., text revision) criteria for PTSD. The remainder failed to report threats to their physical well-being (i.e., the A1 criterion). More severe experiences of victimization were more strongly associated with symptoms of PTSD. Bullied workers also report more somatization, which includes physical pain symptoms, than do their nonbullied counterparts (Hansen et al., 2006).

NEURAL CORRELATES OF PAIN

The emotional experience of pain is associated with the medial nociceptive system, which includes the ACC, insula, and medial thalamic nuclei; controlling the emotional experiences of pain has been associated with the prefrontal cortex (PFC; Treede, Kenshalo, Gracely, & Jones, 1999). If there is an overlap between the emotional experiences of social and physical pain, social pain should activate the same neural systems as does physical pain. Eisenberger, Lieberman, and Williams (2003) were among the first to examine how being excluded from a group compared with being included in a group affected neural processing. They found that people excluded from a group via an online ball-tossing game evidenced greater ACC and RVPFC activity. These findings are noteworthy because the ACC is part of the pain system and is active when experiencing or controlling negative affect associated with physical pain (e.g., Posner, Rothbart, Sheese, & Tang, 2007). MacDonald, Kingsbury, and Shaw (2005) reviewed a series of studies on corresponding pain sensitivity between social and physical pain demonstrating that when people are highly sensitive to one pain type, they are also sensitive to the other pain type. Eisenberger et al. (2006) found that sensitivity to physical pain predicted sensitivity to social pain (i.e., being excluded in a ball-tossing game) and that increased reports of social distress were associated with increased reports of pain unpleasantness.

In light of the plasticity of humans' neural systems (e.g., Cicchetti & Walker, 2003) and the differential neural activity evidenced during periods of social exclusion compared with social inclusion (Eisenberger et al., 2003), the direct role that chronic victimization plays with respect to sensitivity to pain should be via repeated activation of the neural pathways associated with pain. The reorganization of pain systems and the regulatory systems associated with pain management should be most malleable during a period of rapid developmental change, such as adolescence. During adolescence, unused connections between neurons are eliminated via synaptic pruning, and neural pathways repeatedly activated are strengthened (Steinberg, 2005). As an adolescent is exposed to chronic social pain, these pain pathways should strengthen, leading to nontrivial changes in pain sensitivity.

Recent research has replicated Eisenberger et al.'s (2003) findings that both the ACC and PFC are more active during presentation of rejection versus acceptance (Kross, Egner, Ochsner, Hirsch, & Downey, 2007). More important, people high in rejection sensitivity showed lower activity in left inferior and right dorsal frontal regions of the brain than did those with low rejection sensitivity. This activation was negatively correlated with self-reported distress such that individuals high on rejection sensitivity reported higher levels of distress but lower frontal activation.

We further examined whether individual differences in being victimized differentially affected a person's neural activity during exclusion. Twenty women who were in late adolescence (18–21 years) completed a modified version of the Children's Social Experiences Questionnaire as a measure of their current experiences of victimization as part of a larger prescreening session. Several months later participants played Cyberball, a simulated online ball-tossing game, in which participants were excluded from the game (i.e., they did not receive the ball) following the procedures of Eisenberger et al. (2003). Our results suggest there are individual differences in the neural experience of exclusion. First, women who were victimized evidenced greater ACC and insula activation. The insula is involved in pain processing (Augustine, 1985, 1996). We also found a relationship between victimization and RVPFC activity such that more victimized persons evidenced higher RVPFC activation. Finally, victimized women reported more distress than did their nonvictimized counterparts. Victimized people may therefore be unable to effectively self-regulate affective pain during instances of social exclusion.

The research discussed thus far suggests an important relationship between social interactions and psychological and biological functioning such that victimization may actually alter the neurological experience of later instances of victimization. In the next section, we consider how chronic stress, especially chronic social stress, affects the neuroendocrine system to influence future pain sensitivity.

CHRONIC STRESS AND THE NEUROENDOCRINE SYSTEM

Both chronic physical and social pain are associated with chronic stress and relatively permanent changes in neuroendocrine functioning. Cortisol, a hormone that is an end product of HPA activation, is associated with many regulatory roles (e.g., metabolism) and stress reactions (Lovallo & Thomas, 2000). Cortisol inhibits immune functioning and, together with other systems (e.g., the sympathetic nervous system), regulates bodily responses, helping the body to perform more effectively during times of stress. The responses of the neuroendocrine system are often beneficial in the short term, but the extended response associated with chronic exposure to stressors can place individuals at risk of adverse psychological and physical outcomes (e.g., immune suppression, increased pain). The negative outcomes associated with exposure to cortisol have been seen as early as 2 months of age (Glynn et al., 2007). Glynn et al. (2007) found that higher maternal plasma cortisol levels in mothers who breast-feed their infants (i.e., pass along breast milk higher in cortisol) predicted more fearful infant behavior (e.g., startling to loud noises). In other words, early increases in exposure to cortisol can lead to changes in temperament and thus alter how a person responds to the environment. It is likely that such exposure can influence biological development and therefore lead to long-term changes in temperament and pain responses. It is likely that chronic social pain increases allostatic load (McEwen, 1998) and wear and tear on physiological stress pathways, which leads to greater physical illnesses and pain symptomatology (Friedman & McEwen, 2004).

Social stressors have been found to influence neuroendocrine functioning (Cicchetti & Rogosch, 2001; De Bellis et al., 1999; Gillespie & Nemeroff, 2007) and have been associated with poorer psychological, immunological, and health outcomes (Dickerson, Gruenewald, & Kemeny, 2004; Dougall & Baum, 2001; House, Landis, & Umberson, 1988; Taylor, 2007). For example, maltreated children evidence hypercortisolism, demonstrated through elevated average daily cortisol levels and higher cortisol levels in the morning and afternoon (Cicchetti & Rogosch, 2001). Peer-rejected preschoolers similarly exhibit higher cortisol levels in the classroom than do their more popular peers (Gunnar & Quevedo, 2007). Adolescents who are neglected by their peers also show higher cortisol levels (Adam, 2006). Gunnar and Quevedo (2007) further suggested that social pain (e.g., social threats, aversive interactions) is most likely involved in these stress reactions.

Recent work has examined the influence of chronic peer victimization on neuroendocrine functioning. Vaillancourt and colleagues (2008) examined the link between self-reported experiences of bullying for 12-year-olds over a 3-month period and cortisol levels (assessed in the morning and evening). They found that both occasional and frequent verbal abuse by peers were associated with changes in HPA activity, namely, hypersecretion of cortisol for boys and hyposecretion of cortisol for girls (Vaillancourt et al., 2008). For adults, experiencing bullying in the workplace was also associated with lower awakening cortisol (Hansen et al., 2006). Lower awakening cortisol has also been linked with PTSD and chronic fatigue (Hansen et al., 2006).

Our own work also offers evidence that peer victimization during adolescence alters biological functioning (Knack, Jensen-Campbell, & Baum, in press). Young adolescents completed daily cortisol assessments over school days. They then returned to the laboratory to participate in the Trier Social Stress Test (TSST), which consisted of preparing and delivering a 5-min speech about why they would be the ideal class president. When examining the diurnal cortisol pattern associated with victimized and nonvictimized adolescents, we found that victimized adolescents had lower daily cortisol levels. More interesting, perhaps, is that bullied children also had a flattened cortisol awakening response, which was associated with poorer health outcomes. These findings are consistent with Vaillancourt et al.'s (2008) results, suggesting that peer victimization influences neuroendocrine functioning.

During the TSST, victimized adolescents reported feeling less accepted during the task and reported feeling that the task was more stressful. Victims also showed a different cortisol reactivity pattern than did their nonvictimized adolescents; bullied children showed higher cortisol immediately after the stress task and lower cortisol 30 min after the stressor than did the non-bullied children. These findings suggest victimized adolescents are showing greater sensitivity to social pain during a social stressor than are their non-victimized peers.

In the preceding sections, we have outlined the adverse consequences of peer victimization in adolescence. Our preliminary findings have demonstrated that peer victimization not only negatively impacts adolescents' mental health but also impacts physical pain sensitivity, the neural processing of future experiences of victimization, and overall neuroendocrine functioning. In the next section, we examine the clinical literature on how social traumas may have a long-term influence on pain responses to provide more evidence that chronic social pain should lead to greater physical pain sensitivity.

Posttraumatic Stress Disorder

PTSD involves experiencing or witnessing a traumatic or extremely stressful event and involves a symptom set following that trauma that includes feelings of helplessness, fear, and horror (McCann, Sakheim, & Abrahamson, 1988). Psychophysiological disturbances can include (a) reexperiencing the trauma through intrusive thoughts, images, dreams and (b) numbness or avoidant responses. Some researchers have even suggested that PTSD symptoms can develop after less clear-cut traumatic events that involve social pain, such as divorce (Mol et al., 2005). The number of traumatic events is also related to the severity of symptoms (Sledjeski, Speisman, & Dierker, 2008).

As stated in previous sections, we believe chronic social pain will influence biological systems and pain pathways in the brain, creating relatively permanent changes that make individuals more sensitive to pain, especially for individuals who may be more vulnerable to pain. We come back to individual differences in pain vulnerability later in this chapter.

PTSD has been repeatedly associated with greater sensitivity to pain, specifically with respect to chronic widespread pain, fibromyalgia, and persistent pain (Arguelles et al., 2006; Asmundson, Stein, & McCreary, 2002; Cohen et al., 2002). It is interesting to note that the original trauma does not need to involve physical injury for the association with physical pain to develop but can involve a social injury or life event (e.g., divorce, childhood neglect, sudden death of a loved one; Mol et al., 2005; Stam, 2007). There is a higher rate of both opiate and nonopiate analgesic medication use among those who have PTSD (Schwartz et al., 2006). Treatment that is successful in caring for the psychiatric symptoms associated with PTSD also seems to ease physical pain symptoms (Muse, 1986). Taken together, these findings provide further support that social and physical symptoms overlap and chronic or traumatic social pain can lead to greater physical pain sensitivity.

Alternative Hypothesis: Baumeister's Numbing Hypothesis

This chapter has, to this point, focused solely on how repeated episodes of social pain result in increased sensitivity to future rejection and pain sensitivity. However, it is important to note that an alternative hypothesis does exist, namely Baumeister's (1990) numbing hypothesis. This hypothesis posits that individuals become numb and detached in the face of social exclusion and enter into a state of cognitive deconstruction characterized by flat affect, altered time perception, aversion to self-awareness, and feelings of meaninglessness. Subsets of PTSD patients do in fact experience not only numbness or avoidant responses but also reduced pain sensitivity (Stam, 2007).

DeWall and Baumeister (2006) examined the effects of social exclusion on pain tolerance, affective forecasting, and empathy in a series of five experiments. They proposed that because the social and physical pain systems share the same neural mechanisms (Eisenberger et al., 2003), interpersonal events that tax the system would influence physical pain tolerance. On the basis of the hypothesis that physical pain is linked to emotions and that as physical analgesia set in so might emotional analgesia, they proposed excluded participants should become numb to physical pain after being ostracized and that physical numbness should be correlated with emotional numbness. Participants took a personality test and received bogus feedback about the implications of their test results on the quality of their future relationships (i.e., future alone, meaningful relationship, no feedback); pain threshold, pain tolerance, empathy for the pain of others, emotionality, mood, and affective forecasting of future reactions to positive or negative events were all evaluated after participants received the feedback. In Experiments 1 through 5, participants in the "future alone" condition exhibited greater pain threshold and pain tolerance, less empathy for the pain of others, and more neutral affective forecasting than did participants who were told they would have meaningful relationships or those given no feedback. These results provide support for DeWall and Baumeister's hypothesis that physical analgesia and emotional analgesia are linked, possibly by the same physiological mechanisms, and serve to temporarily numb the pain of current or forecasted exclusion.

Sensitization Versus Habituation

Habituation, or numbing, and sensitization are thought to be independent processes that influence stress responses (Groves & Thompson, 1970; Gump & Matthews, 1999). Although some support has been found for Baumeister's numbness hypothesis, a large number of studies suggest that chronic pain leads to increasing sensitivity to pain experiences (Cicchetti & Walker, 2003; Dersh et al., 2002; Eisenberger et al., 2006; Eisenberger et al., 2003; K. D. Williams & Sommer, 1997; K. D. Williams, Cheung, & Choi, 2000). None of the work to date by Baumeister and his colleagues examined how chronic pain influences these systems. Instead, Baumeister and his colleagues examined the immediate influence of a social stressor on pain responses. Although these research findings are important to advance knowledge of how pain systems overlap, they do not provide information on how chronic social pain influences pain sensitivity over time.

An important question involves when habituation versus sensitization may occur in socially painful situations. There is wide variability in how biological pathways are altered after trauma (Lanius, Bluhm, Lanius, & Pain, 2006). For example, there are differences in neural activation in PTSD patients who relive their traumatic events and those who become numb or dissociative (Lanius et al., 2006). These findings suggest that there are boundary conditions that may produce sensitization under certain situations and habituation under other situations.

First, the intensity of the painful event should be associated with greater sensitization. For example, animal research has found that sensitization is more likely to occur when the stressor involves a high-intensity stimulus (regardless of the frequency of exposure), whereas habituation is more likely to occur with exposure to low-to-medium intensity stimuli (Groves, Lee, & Thompson, 1969; Gump & Matthews, 1999). It is therefore possible that both acute, intense social pain (e.g., loss of a loved one, traumatic event) and chronic (and intense) social pain (e.g., peer victimization) should lead to sensitization. Conversely, increased exposure to low-to-medium intensity social pain episodes should lead to numbing or habituation.

Second, the duration of the painful event has been associated with greater sensitization (Gump & Matthews, 1999). Lepore, Miles, and Levy (1997) found a strong relationship between a chronic stressor and acute reactivity but a weaker (and nonsignificant) relationship between a short-term stressor and reactivity. Dealing with an ongoing stressor has been found to lead to diminished coping resources and slower recovery following exposure to an acute stressor (i.e., greater sensitization; Gump & Matthews, 1999). Matthews and her colleagues (1997) also found that acute stressor reactivity was influenced by the frequency of the stressors; children with higher frequency stressors showed the greatest cardiovascular reactivity.

Third, the number of painful events can influence sensitivity. The number of traumas or painful events experienced influences the relationship between pain sensitivity and chronic pain (Sledjeski, Speisman, & Dierker, 2008). Indeed, sequential traumatization lowers threshold sensitivity to future stressors (Keilson, 1992; van der Hal-Van Raalte, Van IJzendoorn, & Bakermans-Kranenburg, 2007; Van IJzendoorn, Bakermans-Kranenburg, & Sagi-Schwartz, 2003). Poor-quality child care after the war for young Holocaust survivors was associated with more PTSD symptoms, more physical illnesses, and lower well-being 60 years later (van der Hal-Van Raalte et al., 2007). These negative associations were not found for Holocaust survivors who did not experience the secondary trauma of poor child care after the war.

Finally, the characteristics of the person may influence whether there is sensitization versus habituation to pain. Some children may be constitutionally more at risk than others of developing pain sensitization when exposed to peer victimization. The notion that the developmental outcomes of a particular individual involve the interaction between hereditary and environmental factors is widely accepted (e.g., Caspi & Moffitt, 2006). For example, Way and Taylor (see Chapter 4, this volume) found that the G allele (relative to the A allele) of the polymorphism A118G is associated with greater rejection sensitivity; greater cortisol responses during the TSST, which suggests responses to social threats; and greater ACC activity when excluded.

Genomic studies of the 5-HTT polymorphism have found that people who carry the short (s) allele have higher baseline cortisol levels (Jabbi et al., 2007), are more neurotic (Munafo, Clark, Roberts, & Johnstone, 2006), show greater levels of anxiety and harm avoidance (Lesch et al., 1996), and show stronger amygdala activation in response to aversive images (Heinz et al., 2004). In addition to biases toward neuroticism, individuals who carry the short allele are also less capable of coping with life stressors and are more vulnerable in developing internalizing problems when exposed to traumatic life events

(Caspi et al., 2003; Eley et al., 2004; Gibb, McGeary, Beevers, & Miller, 2006; Grabe et al., 2005; Kaufman et al., 2004; Kendler, Kuhn, Vittum, Prescott, & Riley, 2005). These results suggest there may be genetic risks for developing sensitivity to pain especially when the individual is exposed to environmental stressors. Future research should seek to further identify the various boundary conditions to determine when social pain events lead to numbness and when they lead to sensitization.

CONCLUSIONS

Throughout this chapter, we have considered whether chronic social pain leads to increased sensitivity to future instances of physical pain. We have presented a wide range of research suggesting chronic social pain does indeed lead to increased sensitivity to future experiences of social pain as well as a plethora of physical and mental health problems. We have also suggested the importance of considering individual differences (e.g., different genetic polymorphisms) and how such differences may alter pain sensitivity. These findings highlight the need to adequately assess the long-term influence of peer victimization (and well as other chronic social pains) on biological systems, health, and physical pain outcomes. Understanding the mechanisms underlying the connections between peer victimization and poorer health outcomes is essential to better understand where the chain of events leading to these negative consequences can be interrupted.

REFERENCES

Aalsma, M. C. (2008). Editorial: What is bullying? *The Journal of Adolescent Health, 43*, 101–102. doi:10.1016/j.jadohealth.2008.06.001

Adam, E. K. (2006). Transactions among adolescent trait and state emotion and diurnal and momentary cortisol activity in naturalistic settings. *Psychoneuroendocrinology, 31*, 664–679. doi:10.1016/j.psyneuen.2006.01.010

Arguelles, L. M., Afari, N., Buchwald, D. S., Clauw, D. J., Furner, S., & Goldberg, J. (2006). A twin study of posttraumatic stress disorder symptoms and chronic widespread pain. *Pain, 124*, 150–157. doi:10.1016/j.pain.2006.04.008

Asmundson, G. J. G., Stein, M. B., & McCreary, D. R. (2002). Posttraumatic stress disorder symptoms influence health status of deployed peacekeepers and nondeployed military personnel. *Journal of Nervous and Mental Disease, 190*, 807–815. doi:10.1097/00005053-200212000-00002

Augustine, J. R. (1985). The insular lobe in primates including humans. *Neurological Research, 7*, 2–10.

Augustine, J. R. (1996). Circuitry and functional aspects of the insular lobe in primates including humans. *Brain Research, 22,* 229–244. doi:10.1016/S0165-0173 (96)00011-2

Bagwell, C. L., Newcomb, A. F., & Bukowski, W. M. (1998). Preadolescent friendship and peer rejection as predictors of adult adjustment. *Child Development, 69,* 140–153.

Baliki, M. N., Chialva, D. R., Geha, P. Y., Levy, R. M., Harden, N., Parrish, T. B., & Appkarian, A. V. (2006). Chronic pain and the emotional brain: Specific brain activity associated with spontaneous fluctuations of intensity of chronic back pain. *The Journal of Neuroscience, 26,* 12165–12173. doi:10.1523/JNEUROSCI.3576-06.2006

Baumeister, R. F. (1990). Suicide as escape from self. *Psychological Review, 97,* 90–113. doi:10.1037/0033-295X.97.1.90

Baumeister, R. F., & Leary, M. R. (1995). The need to belong: Desire for interpersonal attachments as a fundamental human motivation. *Psychological Bulletin, 117,* 497–529. doi:10.1037/0033-2909.117.3.497

Bowlby, J. (1973). *Attachment and loss: Vol. 2. Separation: Anxiety and anger.* New York, NY: Basic Books.

Caspi, A., & Moffitt, T. E. (2006). Gene-environment interactions in psychiatry: Joining forces with neuroscience. *Nature Reviews. Neuroscience, 7,* 583–590. doi:10. 1038/nrn1925

Caspi, A., Sugden, K., Moffitt, T. E., Taylor, A., Craig, I. W., Harrington, H. L., ... Poulton, R. (2003, July 18). Influence of life stress on depression: Moderation by a polymorphism in the 5-HTT gene. *Science, 301,* 386–389. doi: 10.1126/science.1083968

Cicchetti, D. (2003). Experiments of nature: Contributions to developmental theory. *Development and Psychopathology, 15,* 833–835. doi:10.1017/S0954579403000397

Cicchetti, D., & Rogosch, F. A. (2001). Diverse patterns of neuroendocrine activity in maltreated children. *Development and Psychopathology, 13,* 677–693. doi:10. 1017/S0954579401003145

Cicchetti, D., & Walker, E. F. (Eds.). (2003). *Neurodevelopmental mechanisms in psychopathology.* New York, NY: Cambridge University Press. doi:10.1017/ CBO9780511546365

Cohen, J. A., Perel, J. M., De Bellis, M. D., Friedman, M. J., & Putnam, F. W. (2002). Treating traumatized children: Clinical implications of the psychobiology of posttraumatic stress disorder. *Trauma, Violence & Abuse, 3,* 91–108. doi:10.1177/ 15248380020032001

Crick, N. R., & Grotpeter, J. K. (1995). Relational aggression, gender, and social-psychological adjustment. *Child Development, 66,* 710–722. doi:10.2307/1131945

David-Ferdon, C., & Hertz, M. (2007). Electronic media, violence, and adolescents: An emerging public health problem. *The Journal of Adolescent Health, 41,* S1–S5. doi:10.1016/j.jadohealth.2007.08.020

De Bellis, M. D., Baum, A. S., Birmaher, B., Keshavan, M. S., Eccard, C. H., Boring, A. M., . . . & Ryan, N. D. (1999). Developmental traumatology, Part I: Biological stress systems. *Biological Psychiatry, 45,* 1259–1270. doi:10.1016/S0006-3223(99)00044-X

Dersh, J., Polatin, P. B., & Gatchel, R. J. (2002). Chronic pain and psychopathology: Research findings and theoretical considerations. *Psychosomatic Medicine, 64,* 773–786. doi:10.1097/01.PSY.0000024232.11538.54

DeWall, C. N., & Baumeister, R. F. (2006). Alone but feeling no pain: Effects of social exclusion on physical pain tolerance and pain threshold, affective forecasting, and interpersonal empathy. *Journal of Personality and Social Psychology, 91,* 1–15. doi:10.1037/0022-3514.91.1.1

Dickerson, S. S., Gruenewald, T. L., & Kemeny, M. E. (2004). When the social self is threatened: Shame, physiology, and health. *Journal of Personality, 72,* 1191–1216.

Dougall, A. L., & Baum, A. (2001). Stress, health, and illness. In A. Baum, T. A. Revenson, & J. E. Singer (Eds.), *Handbook of health psychology* (pp. 321–337). Mahwah, NJ: Erlbaum.

Due, P., Hansen, E. H., Merlo, J., Andersen, A., & Holstein, B. E. (2007). Is victimization from bullying associated with medicine use among adolescents? A nationally representative cross-sectional survey in Denmark. *Pediatrics, 120,* 110–117. doi:10.1542/peds.2006-1481

Eisenberger, N. I., Jarcho, J. M., Lieberman, M. D., & Naliboff, B. D. (2006). An experimental study of shared sensitivity to physical pain and social rejection. *Pain, 126,* 132–138. doi:10.1016/j.pain.2006.06.024

Eisenberger, N. I., & Lieberman, M. D. (2004). Why rejection hurts: A common neural alarm system for physical and social pain. *Trends in Cognitive Sciences, 8,* 294–300. doi:10.1016/j.tics.2004.05.010

Eisenberger, N. I., & Lieberman, M. D. (2005). Why it hurts to be left out: The neurocognitive overlap between physical and social pain. In K. D. Williams, J. P. Forgas, & W. V. Hippel (Eds.), *The social outcast: Ostracism, social exclusion, rejection, and bullying* (pp. 109–123). New York, NY: Psychology Press.

Eisenberger, N. I., Lieberman, M. D., & Williams, K. D. (2003, October 10). Does rejection hurt? An fMRI study of social exclusion. *Science, 302,* 290–292. doi:10.1126/science.1089134

Eley, T. C., Sugden, K., Corsico, A., Gregory, A. M., Sham, P., McGuffin, P., . . . Craig, I. W. (2004). Gene-environment interaction analysis of serotonin system markers with adolescent depression. *Molecular Psychiatry, 9,* 908–915. doi:10.1038/sj.mp.4001546

Fekkes, M., Pijpers, F. R. M., Fredricks, A. M., Vogels, T., & Verloove-Vanhorick, S. P. (2006). Do bullied children get ill, or do ill children get bullied? A prospective cohort study on the relationship between bullying and health-related symptoms. *Pediatrics, 117,* 1568–1574. doi:10.1542/peds.2005-0187

Foy, M. R., Stanton, M. E., Levine, S., & Thompson, R. F. (1987). Behavioral stress impairs long-term potentiation in rodent hippocampus. *Behavioral and Neural Biology, 48*, 138–149. doi:10.1016/S0163-1047(87)90664-9

Friedman, M. J., & McEwen, B. S. (2004). Posttraumatic stress disorder, allostatic load, and medical illness. In P. P. Schnurr & B. L. Green (Eds.), *Trauma and health: Physical health consequences of exposure to extreme stress* (pp. 157–188). Washington, DC: American Psychological Association. doi:10.1037/10723-007

Garber, J., Walker, L. S., & Zeman, J. (1991). Somatization symptoms in a community sample of children and adolescents: Further validation of the Children's Somatization Inventory. *Psychological Assessment. Journal of Consulting and Clinical Psychology, 3*, 588–595.

Gatchel, R. J., Mayer, T. G., & Theodore, B. R. (2006). The pain disability questionnaire: Relationships to one-year functional and psychosocial rehabilitation outcomes. *Journal of Occupational Rehabilitation, 16*, 72–91. doi:10.1007/s10926-005-9005-0

Gibb, B. E., McGeary, J. E., Beevers, C. G., & Miller, I. W. (2006). Serotonin transporter (5-HTTLPR) genotype, childhood abuse, and suicide attempts in adult psychiatric inpatients. *Suicide & Life-Threatening Behavior, 36*, 687–693. doi:10.1521/suli.2006.36.6.687

Gillespie, C. F., & Nemeroff, C. B. (2007). Corticotropin-releasing factor and the psychobiology of early-life stress. *Current Directions in Psychological Science, 16*, 85–89. doi:10.1111/j.1467-8721.2007.00481.x

Glynn, L. M., Davis, E. P., Schetter, C. D., Chicz-DeMet, A., Hobel, C. J., & Sandman, C. A. (2007). Postnatal maternal cortisol levels predict temperament in healthy breastfed infants. *Early Human Development, 83*, 675–681. doi:10.1016/j.earlhumdev.2007.01.003

Grabe, H. J., Lange, M., Wolff, B., Völzke, H., Lucht, M., Freyberger, H. J., . . . Cascorbi, I. (2005). Mental and physical distress is modulated by a polymorphism in the 5-HT transporter gene interacting with social stressors and chronic disease burden. *Molecular Psychiatry, 10*, 220–224. doi:10.1038/sj.mp.4001555

Greco, L. A., Freeman, K. E., & Dufton, L. (2007). Overt and relational victimization among children with frequent abdominal pain: Links to social skills, academic functioning, and health service use. *Journal of Pediatric Psychology, 32*, 319–329. doi:10.1093/jpepsy/jsl016

Grills, A. E., & Ollendick, T. H. (2002). Peer victimization, global self-worth, and anxiety in middle school children. *Journal of Clinical Child and Adolescent Psychology, 31*, 59–68.

Groves, P. M., Lee, D., & Thompson, R. F. (1969). Effects of stimulus frequency and intensity on habituation and sensitization in acute spinal cat. *Physiology & Behavior, 4*, 383–388. doi:10.1016/0031-9384(69)90194-2

Groves, P. M., & Thompson, R. F. (1970). Habituation: A dual-process theory. *Psychological Review, 77*, 419–450. doi:10.1037/h0029810

Gump, B. B., & Matthews, K. A. (1999). Do background stressors influence reactivity to and recovery from acute stressors? *Journal of Applied Social Psychology, 29,* 469–494. doi:10.1111/j.1559-1816.1999.tb01397.x

Gunnar, M., & Quevedo, K. (2007). The neurobiology of stress and development. *Annual Review of Psychology, 58,* 145–173. doi:10.1146/annurev.psych.58.110405.085605

Hansen, A. M., Hogh, A., Persson, R., Karlson, B., Garde, A. H., & Orbaek, P. (2006). Bullying at work, health outcomes, and physiological stress response. *Journal of Psychosomatic Research, 60,* 63–72. doi:10.1016/j.jpsychores.2005.06.078

Harkins, S. W., Price, D. D., & Braith, J. (1989). Effects of extraversion and neuroticism on experimental pain, clinical pain, and illness behavior. *Pain, 36,* 209–218. doi:10.1016/0304-3959(89)90025-0

Hartup, W. W. (1996). The company they keep: Friendships and their developmental significance. *Child Development, 67,* 1–13. doi:10.2307/1131681

Heinz, A., Braus, D. F., Smolka, M. N., Wrase, J., Puls, I., Hermann, D., . . . Büchel, C. (2004). Amygdala-prefrontal coupling depends on a genetic variation of the serotonin transporter. *Nature Neuroscience, 8,* 20–21. doi:10.1038/nn1366

House, J. S., Landis, K. R., & Umberson, D. (1988, July 29). Social relationships and health. *Science, 241,* 540–545. doi:10.1126/science.3399889

Inslicht, S. S., Marmar, C., Meylan, T., Metzler, T., Hart, S., Otte, C., . . . Baum, A. (2006). Increased cortisol in women with intimate partner violence-related posttraumatic stress disorder. *Annals of the New York Academy of Sciences, 1071,* 428–429. doi:10.1196/annals.1364.035

Jabbi, M., Korf, J., Kema, I. P., Hartman, C., van der Pompe, G., Minderaa, R. B., . . . den Boer, J. A. (2007). Convergent genetic modulation of the endocrine stress response involves polymorphic variations of 5-HTT, COMT and MAOA. *Molecular Psychiatry, 12,* 483–490.

Kaufman, J., Yang, B. Z., Douglas-Palumberi, H., Houshyar, S., Lipschitz, D., Krystal, J. H., & Gelernter, J. (2004). Social supports and serotonin transporter gene moderate depression in maltreated children. *Proceedings of the National Academy of Sciences of the United States of America, 101,* 17316–17321. doi:10.1073/pnas.0404376101

Keilson, H. (1992). *Sequential traumatization in children.* Jerusalem, Israel: Magnes Press.

Kendler, K. S., Kuhn, J. W., Vittum, J., Prescott, C. A., & Riley, B. (2005). The interaction of stressful life events and a serotonin transporter polymorphism in the prediction of episodes of major depression. *Archives of General Psychiatry, 62,* 529–535. doi:10.1001/archpsyc.62.5.529

Knack, J. M., Jensen-Campbell, L. A., & Baum, A. (in press). Worse than sticks and stones: Bullying is related to altered HPA axis functioning and poorer health. *New Directions in the Neuroscience of Aggression and Victimization: Brain and Cognition.*

Kross, E., Egner, T., Ochsner, K., Hirsch, J., & Downey, G. (2007). Neural dynamics of rejection sensitivity. *Journal of Cognitive Neuroscience, 19*, 945–956. doi: 10.1162/jocn.2007.19.6.945

Kupersmidt, J. B., Coie, J. D., & Dodge, K. A. (1990). Predicting disorder from peer social problems. In S. R. Asher & J. D. Coie (Eds.), *Peer rejection in childhood* (pp. 274–305). New York, NY: Cambridge University Press.

Lanius, R. A., Bluhm, R., Lanius, U., & Pain, C. (2006). A review of neuroimaging studies in PTSD: Heterogeneity of response to symptom provocation. *Journal of Psychiatric Research, 40*, 709–729. doi:10.1016/j.jpsychires. 2005.07.007

Larson, R., & Richards, M. H. (1994). *Divergent realities: The emotional lives of mothers, fathers, and adolescents*. New York, NY: Basic Books.

Lepore, S. J., Miles, H. J., & Levy, J. S. (1997). Relation of chronic and episodic stressors to psychological distress, reactivity, and health problems. *International Journal of Behavioral Medicine, 4*, 39–59. doi:10.1207/s15327558 ijbm0401_3

Lesch, K. P., Bengel, D., Heils, A., Sabol, S. Z., Greenberg, B. D., Petri, S., . . . Murphy, D. L. (1996, November 29). Association of anxiety-related traits with a polymorphism in the serotonin transporter gene regulatory region. *Science, 274*, 1527–1531. doi:10.1126/science.274.5292.1527

Lovallo, W. R., & Thomas, T. L. (2000). Stress hormones in psychophysiological research: Emotional, behavioral, and cognitive implications. In J. T. Cacioppo, L. G. Tassinary, & G. Berntson (Eds.), *Handbook of psychophysiology* (pp. 342–367). New York, NY: Cambridge University Press.

MacDonald, G., Kingsbury, R., & Shaw, S. (2005). Adding insult to injury: Social pain theory and response to social exclusion. In K. Williams, J. Forgas, & W. van Hippel (Eds.), *The social outcast: Ostracism, social exclusion, rejection, and bullying* (pp. 77–90). New York, NY: Psychology Press.

MacDonald, G., & Leary, M. R. (2005). Why does social exclusion hurt? The relationship between social and physical pain. *Psychological Bulletin, 131*, 202–223. doi:10.1037/0033-2909.131.2.202

Maslow, A. H. (1968). *Toward a psychology of being* (2nd ed.). New York, NY: Van Nostrand Reinhold.

Matthews, K. A., Gump, B. B., Block, D. R., & Allen, M. T. (1997). Does background stress heighten or dampen children's cardiovascular responses to acute stress? *Psychosomatic Medicine, 59*, 488–496.

Matthiesen, S. B., & Einarsen, S. (2004). Psychiatric distress and symptoms of PTSD among victims of bullying at work. *British Journal of Guidance & Counselling, 32*, 335–356. doi:10.1080/03069880410001723558

McCann, I. L., Sakheim, D. K., & Abrahamson, D. J. (1988). Trauma and victimization: A model of psychological adaptation. *The Counseling Psychologist, 16*, 531–594. doi:10.1177/0011000088164002

McEwen, B. S. (1998). Stress, adaptation, and disease: Allostasis and allostatic load. *Annals of the New York Academy of Sciences, 840*, 33–44. doi:10.1111/j.1749-6632.1998.tb09546.x

McWilliams, L. A., Cox, B. J., & Enns, M. W. (2003). Mood and anxiety disorders associated with chronic pain: An examination in a nationally representative sample. *Pain, 106*, 127–133. doi:10.1016/S0304-3959(03)00301-4

Mikkelsen, E. G., & Einarsen, S. (2002). Basic assumptions and symptoms of post-traumatic stress among victims of bullying at work. *European Journal of Work and Organizational Psychology, 11*, 87–111. doi:10.1080/13594320143000861

Mol, S. S. L., Arntz, A., Metsemakers, J. F. M., Dinant, G. J., Vilters-Van, M., Pauline, A. P., & Knottnerus, J. A. (2005). Symptoms of post-traumatic stress disorder after non-traumatic eventus: Evidence from an open population study. *British Journal of Psychiatry, 186*, 494–499.

Munafo, M. R., Clark, T. G., Roberts, K. H., & Johnstone, E. C. (2006). Neuroticism mediates the association of the serotonin transporter gene with lifetime major depression. *Neuropsychobiology, 53*, 1–8.

Muse, M. (1986). Stress-related, posttraumatic chronic pain syndrome: Behavioral treatment approach. *Pain, 25*, 389–394.

Nansel, T. R., Overpeck, M., Pilla, R. S., Ruan, W. J., Simmons-Morton, B., & Schmidt, P. (2001). Bullying behaviors among US youth. *JAMA, 285*, 2094–2100. doi:10.1001/jama.285.16.2094

Nylund, K., Bellmore, A., Nishina, A., & Sandra, G. (2007). Subtypes, severity, and structural stability of peer victimization: What does latent class analysis say? *Child Development, 78*, 1706–1722. doi:10.1111/j.1467-8624.2007.01097.x

Olweus, D. (1978). *Aggression in the schools: Bullies and whipping boys*. Washington, DC: Hemisphere Publication Services.

Panksepp, J. (2003). Can anthropomorphic analyses of separation cries in other animals inform us about the emotional nature of social loss in humans? Comment on Blumberg and Sokoloff (2001). *Psychological Review, 110*, 376–388. doi:10.1037/0033-295X.110.2.376

Phillips, J. M., & Gatchel, R. J. (2000). Extraversion-introversion and chronic pain. In R. J. Gatchel & J. N. Weisberg (Eds.), *Personality characteristics of patients with pain* (pp. 181–202). Washington, DC: American Psychological Association. doi:10.1037/10376-008

Posner, M. I., Rothbart, M. K., Sheese, B. E., & Tang, Y. (2007). The anterior cingulate gyrus and the mechanism of self-regulation. *Cognitive, Affective & Behavioral Neuroscience, 7*, 391–395. doi:10.3758/CABN.7.4.391

Price, D. D. (2000, June 9). Psychological and neural mechanisms of the affective dimension of pain. *Science, 288*, 1769–1772. doi:10.1126/science.288.5472.1769

Rigby, K. (2003). Consequences of bullying in schools. *Canadian Journal of Psychiatry, 48*, 583–590.

Rigby, K., & Slee, P. (1999). Suicidal ideation among adolescent school children, involvement in bully-victim problems, and perceived social support. *Suicide & Life-Threatening Behavior, 29*, 119–130.

Schwartz, A. C., Bradley, R., Penza, K. M., Sexton, M., Jay, D., Haggard, P. J., . . . Ressler, K. J. (2006). Pain medication use among patients with posttraumatic stress disorder. *Psychosomatics: The Journal of Consultation and Liaison Psychiatry, 47*, 136–142.

Sharp, T. J., & Harvey, A. G. (2001). Chronic pain and posttraumatic stress disorder: Mutual maintenance? *Clinical Psychology Review, 21*, 857–877. doi:10.1016/S0272-7358(00)00071-4

Sledjeski, E. M., Speisman, B., & Dierker, L. C. (2008). Does number of lifetime traumas explain the relationship between PTSD and chronic medical conditions? Answers from the National Comorbidity Survey-Replication (NCS-R). *Journal of Behavioral Medicine, 31*, 341–349. doi:10.1007/s10865-008-9158-3

Spear, L. P. (2000). Neurobehavioral changes in adolescence. *Current Directions in Psychological Science, 9*, 111–114. doi:10.1111/1467-8721.00072

Stam, R. (2007). PTSD and stress sensitization: A tale of brain and body: Part 1: Human Studies. *Neuroscience and Biobehavioral Reviews, 31*, 530–557. doi:10.1016/j.neubiorev.2006.11.010

Steinberg, L. (2005). Cognitive and affective development in adolescence. *Trends in Cognitive Sciences, 9*, 69–74. doi:10.1016/j.tics.2004.12.005

Taylor, S. E. (2007). Social support. In H. S. Friendman & R. C. Silver (Eds.), *Foundations of health psychology* (pp. 145–171). New York, NY: Oxford University Press.

Treede, R.-D., Kenshalo, D. R., Gracely, R. H., & Jones, A. K. P. (1999). The cortical representation of pain. *Pain, 79*, 105–111. doi:10.1016/S0304-3959(98)00184-5

Vaillancourt, T., Duku, E., Decatanzaro, D., Macmillan, H., Muir, C., & Schmidt, L. A. (2008). Variation in hypothalamic-pituitary-adrenal axis activity among bullied and non-bullied children. *Aggressive Behavior, 34*, 294–305. doi:10.1002/ab.20240

van den Hout, J. H., Vlaeyen, J. W., Peters, M. L., Englehard, I. M., & van den Hout, M. A. (2000). Does failure hurt? The effects of failure on pain report, pain tolerance, and pain avoidance. *European Journal of Pain, 4*, 335–346. doi:10.1053/eujp.2000.0195

van der Hal-Van Raalte, E., Van IJzendoorn, M. H., & Bakermans-Kranenburg, M. J. (2007). Quality of care after early childhood trauma and well-being in later life: Child Holocaust survivors reaching old age. *American Journal of Orthopsychiatry, 77*, 514–522. doi:10.1037/0002-9432.77.4.514

Van IJzendoorn, M. H., Bakermans-Kranenburg, M. J., & Sagi-Schwartz, A. (2003). Are children of Holocaust survivors less well-adapted? A meta-analytic investigation of secondary traumatization. *Journal of Traumatic Stress, 16*, 459–469. doi:10.1023/A:1025706427300

Walker, E. F. (2002). Adolescent neurodevelopment and psychopathology. *Current Directions in Psychological Science, 11*, 24–28. doi:10.1111/1467-8721.00161

Walker, E. F., Walder, D. J., & Reynolds, F. (2001). Developmental changes in cortisol secretion in normal and at-risk youth. *Development and Psychopathology, 13*, 721–732. doi:10.1017/S0954579401003169

Williams, K. D., Cheung, C. K. T., & Choi, W. (2000). Cyberostracism: Effects of being ignored over the Internet. *Journal of Personality and Social Psychology, 79*, 748–762. doi:10.1037/0022-3514.79.5.748

Williams, K. D., & Sommer, K. L. (1997). Social ostracism by one's coworkers: Does rejection lead to loafing or compensation? *Personality and Social Psychology Bulletin, 23*, 693–706. doi:10.1177/0146167297237003

Williams, K. R., & Guerra, N. G. (2007). Prevalence and predictors of internet bullying. *The Journal of Adolescent Health, 41*, S14–S21. doi:10.1016/j.jadohealth.2007.08.018

Yehuda, R. (2002). Current status of cortisol findings in post-traumatic stress disorder. *The Psychiatric Clinics of North America, 25*, 341–368. doi:10.1016/S0193-953X(02)00002-3

CONCLUSION: SOCIAL PAIN RESEARCH—ACCOMPLISHMENTS AND CHALLENGES

GEOFF MacDONALD AND LAURI A. JENSEN-CAMPBELL

Although the research described in this volume provides compelling support for the notion of overlap between physical and social pain mechanisms, assembling the relevant evidence into one body of work brings starkly into view a number of questions that remain unanswered. Social pain research is clearly in its infancy, with a series of fundamental issues yet to be resolved. The fact that social pain research is in its early stages limits the claims one can make about the phenomenon but also provides opportunities for researchers to make meaningful contributions at the foundational level of a topic of potentially great importance. In this closing chapter, we give an overview of the evidence provided in this volume for the social pain hypothesis. We also highlight issues and challenges that emerge from this work in an attempt to identify central questions that may be useful in guiding researchers interested in advancing understanding of social pain.

Perhaps the most convincing aspect of the growing empirical evidence for overlap between physical and social pain mechanisms is the use of varied methodologies that point to multiple points of intersection. Naomi Eisenberger's program of research (Chapter 2) centers on functional magnetic resonance imaging analyses of activation in the dorsal anterior cingulate cortex (dACC), a brain area previously identified as related to physical pain affect, in response to social exclusion. Her chapter discusses work showing such dACC activation to be related to greater self-reported distress during exclusion in the lab and higher levels of social distress in daily life. She also shows dACC activation to be related to theoretically relevant individual differences such as trait rejection sensitivity and a genetic polymorphism related to heightened aggression. Jennifer Knack, Haylie Gomez, and Lauri Jensen-Campbell (Chapter 10) also relate heightened anterior cingulate cortex (ACC) activation during exclusion to a history of relational victimization.

Sally Dickerson's contribution (Chapter 3) highlights elevated levels of cortisol and increased proinflammatory cytokine production as two more potential markers of social pain experience. Her work shows that release of cortisol and tumor necrosis factor-alpha may not just represent generic stress responses but may also be a particular reaction to current social evaluative threats and feelings of shame and guilt (although Dickerson describes the evidence for immune system responses as preliminary). Indeed, Andrew Baum, Carroll Michelle Lee, and Angela Liegey Dougall (Chapter 9) suggest that over long periods of time such stress responses may lead to serious health problems and increased morbidity. In an impressive review of genetic bases of social pain, Baldwin Way and Shelley Taylor (Chapter 4) note other potential social pain mechanisms, such as heightened opioid release, which has been shown in response to recalling relational breakups, and elevated plasma oxytocin levels, which have been shown to be associated with impoverished social conditions. Social injuries also appear to lead to physical analgesia (DeWall, Pond, & Deckman, Chapter 5), even in response to relatively mundane experiences such as reliving old social wounds (Chen & Williams, Chapter 7) and meeting an unfriendly stranger (MacDonald, Borsook, & Spielmann, Chapter 6).

Thus, a number of markers of social pain experience appear to triangulate on the conclusion that social and physical injuries are mediated by at least some of the same physiological systems. Identifying these markers of social pain experience is clearly important and will help guide health researchers in isolating social factors underlying disease processes. However, an important research direction for growth in the field will be moving beyond this descriptive stage and beginning to pinpoint what, if any, functional significance these physiological markers hold for responses to socially painful situations (Dickerson, Gruenewald, & Kemeny, 2009). At least at the theoretical level, one marker of social pain with a clearly identified function is the ACC, which has been argued to serve as a neural alarm system (Eisenberger & Lieberman, 2004). However, the functional value of cortisol, immune system, and analgesic responses to social pain is highly unclear.

In that regard, one important idea is Baum et al.'s (Chapter 9) distinction between readying responses that are not specific to the source of stress and more specific responses that facilitate attempts to eliminate or reduce a particular source of stress. A potentially useful strategy for isolating whether a physiological marker of social pain represents a generic readying response or a targeted social response comes from Dickerson's approach of contrasting social and nonsocial stressors. This work has provided evidence that cortisol is especially elevated in response to social stressors, possibly suggesting a particular role for cortisol in managing the social situation. Further work examining relations between cortisol levels and seemingly adaptive aspects of response to socially painful situations (e.g., emotion regulation, accuracy of social perceptions, direction of attention) may help identify the specific role of the cortisol response.

Another distinction that may be useful in associating particular functions with physiological responses to socially painful situations is that between warning and coping responses. Although social pain may well serve to alert individuals to the potential for social danger (e.g., through ACC activation; Eisenberger & Lieberman, 2004), some physiological responses to social exclusion may be more involved in managing responses to social injuries. For example, it appears difficult to explain physical numbness as a means of warning an individual of social threat. DeWall and Baumeister (2006) noted that such numbness may represent a coping response that relieves suffering and facilitates adaptive responding. However, if a particular physiological marker of a socially painful experience is part of a broad stress reaction rather than a focused coping response, that marker may have no functional value or even work counter to adaptive coping. Indeed, DeWall and Baumeister (2006) also noted that analgesic responses may disrupt emotional functioning, thus hampering adaptive responding to social exclusion.

Drawing distinctions between warning and coping mechanisms may be particularly important for approaches to managing social pain. Although social pain is aversive, Jaak Panksepp's (Chapter 1) characterization of emotions as a gift of nature that aids in the healthy regulation of behavior offers a reminder that aversive feelings are not necessarily undesirable. Painful situations can open individuals to opportunities for growth; for example, MacDonald et al. (Chapter 6) found evidence that social pain triggers the approach of rewarding social partners. The chapters in this volume offer many interesting suggestions for managing social pain, including acetaminophen (DeWall et al., Chapter 5), oxytocin, and buprenorphine (Panksepp, Chapter 1). These approaches would seem to hold enormous value for quelling hyperactive social exclusion warning mechanisms that lead individuals to perceive pathologically elevated degrees of rejection. However, we would caution that physiological responses related to healthy coping that are masked or sedated may impair the process of recovery from social injury. We also find ourselves sympathetic with the holistic view advocated by the biopsychosocial model (Gatchel & Kishino, Chapter 8), which points to the value of interventions to quell chronic social pain such as social contact, music, touch, and physical exercise.

The distinction between warning and coping mechanisms is one of several categorizations that need to be clarified for research on social pain to progress. Researchers should be aware that there are multiple forms of rejection experience but that basic work on social exclusion has not yet yielded agreement as to the best ways of distinguishing and categorizing types of exclusion (Leary, 2005). For example, feeling ignored appears to promote dejection and social engagement, whereas feeling actively rejected promotes agitation and social withdrawal (Molden, Lucas, Gardner, Dean, & Knowles, 2009). The distinction between acute and chronic rejection also appears highly relevant (Baum et al., Chapter 9). As one example, cortisol release may prove to be a functional response to social exclusion in the short term, but chronic activation of stress systems can lead to debilitating conditions such as hypercortisolism or hypocortisolism, as in the case of maltreated children (Knack et al., Chapter 10). Thus, researchers should carefully consider their choices of manipulations and measures to ensure they are targeting the aspects of social exclusion most relevant to their research questions. In turn, these careful choices should help build a body of literature that can inform an understanding of the basic features of social exclusion.

In general, the work presented in this book serves as a strong reminder of the deeply social nature of human beings. When Baumeister and Leary (1995) identified belongingness as a human need, evidence for this claim at the physiological level was not abundant. The growing body of work described in this volume makes clear that the physiological systems that regulate this need are tied to some of human beings' most ancient and basic safety mechanisms. Although the work presented here strongly points to pain systems as important mechanisms for responses to social exclusion, other systems also hold promise for providing insight into the physiological basis of response to social exclusion. For example, research suggests that feelings of warmth and cold may also inform social judgments (Zhong & Leonardelli, 2008). Indeed, perhaps the most natural metaphors for the regulation of social behavior involve *closeness* and *distance*, suggesting a role for spatial mechanisms as well. Thus, although the social pain hypothesis appears to be promising and generative, pain is likely one of several points of overlap between physical and social behavior regulation.

Nevertheless, Zhansheng Chen and Kipling Williams (Chapter 7) sound an important note of caution by offering a reminder that understanding social pain requires an investigation not just of points of overlap but also of points of distinction. Their findings that relived and prelived social injuries are experienced as currently painful, whereas relived and prelived physical injuries are not, highlight the potential for social pain to linger. Indeed, these results force careful consideration of what is meant by chronic social pain given that even single episodes of rejection have the potential to be relived repeatedly.

Overall, then, understanding reactions to social exclusion in terms of pain appears to be a promising and empirically sound route for providing insight into the effects of social connection and disconnection. It is clear, however, that there are a number of fundamental questions the field has yet to answer, only some of which we touch on here. Answers to these questions appear to require the sharing of knowledge and expertise across research specialties. We hope that this volume provides readers with a starting point for that multidisciplinary conversation.

REFERENCES

Baumeister, R. F., & Leary, M. R. (1995). The need to belong: Desire for interpersonal attachments as a fundamental human motivation. *Psychological Bulletin, 117,* 497–529. doi:10.1037/0033-2909.117.3.497

DeWall, C. N., & Baumeister, R. F. (2006). Alone but feeling no pain: Effects of social exclusion on physical pain tolerance and pain threshold, affective forecasting, and interpersonal empathy. *Journal of Personality and Social Psychology, 91,* 1–15. doi:10.1037/0022-3514.91.1.1

Dickerson, S. S., Gruenewald, T. L., & Kemeny, M. E. (2009). Psychobiological responses to social self threat: Functional or detrimental? *Self and Identity, 8,* 270–285. doi:10.1080/15298860802505186

Eisenberger, N. I., & Lieberman, M. D. (2004). Why rejection hurts: A common neural alarm system for physical and social pain. *Trends in Cognitive Sciences, 8,* 294–300. doi:10.1016/j.tics.2004.05.010

Leary, M. R. (2005). Varieties of interpersonal rejection. In K. D. Williams, J. P. Forgas, & B. von Hippel (Eds.), *The social outcast: Ostracism, social exclusion, rejection, and bullying* (pp. 35–51). New York, NY: Cambridge University Press.

Molden, D. C., Lucas, G. M., Gardner, W. L., Dean, K., & Knowles, M. L. (2009). Motivations for prevention or promotion following social exclusion: Being rejected versus being ignored. *Journal of Personality and Social Psychology, 96,* 415–431. doi:10.1037/a0012958

Zhong, C. B., & Leonardelli, G. J. (2008). Cold and lonely: Does social exclusion literally feel cold? *Psychological Science, 19,* 838–842. doi:10.1111/j.1467-9280.2008.02165.x

INDEX

and psychic pain, 33
within-brain emotional effects, 13
Brain imaging. *See also* Functional
magnetic resonance imaging
and cognitive judgments, 39–40
monitoring nervous system with,
20–21
of neurochemical systems, 36
and pain responses, 41
and separation distress, 34, 42
viewing affective aspects of pain
with, 19
Brief Mood Introspection Scale (BMIS),
133
Broca's area, 56
Broken heart syndrome, 163
Bullying. *See also* Peer victimization
electronic, 217
workplace, 221, 223–224
Buprenorphine, 36–38

CABG. *See* Coronary artery bypass
surgery
Calhoun, J. B., 202
Cancer, 22, 64
Cannabinoid (CB$_1$ receptors), 131
Cardiac output, 124
Cardiac pain, 22, 218–219
Cardiovascular disease, 208
Cardiovascular responses, 85–87, 90
Caregiving, 54, 150, 163, 204, 207. *See
also* Nurturant behavior
CARE system (nurturance), 12
Carfentanil, 34
Catechol-O-methyltransferase
(COMT), 100–102
Causal analyses, 41
CB$_1$ receptors (cannabinoid), 131
Central nervous system, 128, 131
Chen, E., 83, 89
Chen, Z., 6, 61, 167–168, 171
Chickens, 25, 26
Childbirth, 22, 64
Children
adolescents, 217–218, 222–224
physical pain of, 65
toddlers, 106
Chronic pain, 89–90, 240
and activation of brain regions, 188
and allostatic load, 223

antidepressants for treatment of, 64
anxiety associated with, 133, 183
and attachment, 65
and belonging deficits, 134–136
cingulotomy for treatment of, 56
comorbidity of psychopathological
states and, 186
and depression, 99
and secondary pain affect, 220
and sensitization, 226
Chronic stress and stressors, 89, 200,
201, 222–228
Cingulate cortex damage, 18
Cingulotomy, 56
Circulation, 199
Clonidine, 27
Cognition
effects of physical pain on, 18, 166
effects of social exclusion on, 124,
221
impact of mental imagery on, 169
impairment of, 171
Cognitive deconstruction, 124
Cognitive–interpretive processes,
183–184
COMT (catechol-O-methyltransferase),
100–102
Conditioning, 18, 185
C177G polymorphism, 98
Confidence, 31
Conflict resolution, 143
Consciousness
emotional-affective aspects of, 11
evolution of, 32–33
Contact comfort, 22
Coping, 134–136, 197–200, 202, 239–240
Coronary artery bypass surgery
(CABG), 64, 208
Corr, P. J., 143
Corticotropin-release factor (CRF),
25–26, 81
Cortisol responses, 81–85, 89–90, 238,
240
and 5-HTT polymorphism, 227
future research directions, 84–85
to interpersonal conflict and
rejection, 83–84
to ostracism and rejection, 203
to peer victimization, 216, 224
to social evaluative threat, 102

Harm avoidance, 227
"Healing touch," 22
Health (physical). *See also* Mental
      health
   and chronicity of stressors, 200–201
   and coping with stress, 199–200
   effects of bereavement on, 206–208
   effects of loneliness on, 205,
         208–209
   effects of loss on, 194, 202–205
   effects of negative social exchanges
         on, 202–204
   effects of social integration on, 205
   effects of social rejection on,
         204–205
   holistic perspectives in, 193
Heart rate, 41, 85–87, 196, 198, 219
Heatherton, T. F., 145
Hepatitis, 204
HIV, 90, 204
Holistic perspectives (health), 193
Holmes, J. G., 146
Holocaust survivors, 227
Homeostatic affects, 13, 19, 32
Homeostatic regulation systems, 182
Hormones, 81, 89, 90, 100–101. *See also*
      specific hormones
Hostile affect scale, 133
HPA activity. *See* Hypothalamic–
      pituitary–adrenocortical activity
HTR2A G-1438A gene, 103
Hurt feelings, 131–132, 144, 148, 163
Hurt Feelings Scale, 133
Hurt proneness, 168–169
Hypercortisolism, 85, 223, 240
Hypnosis, 21, 56
Hypothalamic–pituitary–adrenocortical
      (HPA) activity, 81, 84, 89, 90, 195
Hypothalamus, 19, 81

Idiopathic pain, 11, 33
Illnesses, 201, 205, 208, 223, 227. *See*
      also specific illnesses
Immune responses, 21, 87–88, 90, 203,
      238
Inclusion. *See* Social inclusion
Individual differences
   in hurt proneness, 168–169
   in sensitivity, 62–63
Infection(s), 87, 200,202

Infectious illnesses, 201
Inflammation, 87, 88, 131
Injuries
   and periaqueductal gray, 127
   physical, 148
   and posttraumatic stress disorder, 225
   social, 3, 145, 238
Insensitivity, 66, 104, 106, 129–130.
      See also Sensitivity
Instinctual responses, 29
Insula, 7, 57, 216, 222
Intellectual performance, 124
Interactive processes (biopsychosocial
      perspective), 182
Interdisciplinary pain management
      programs, 188
International Association for the Study
      of Pain, 183
Interpersonal bonds, 3
Interpersonal conflict, 83–84, 202
Interpersonal rejection. *See* Rejection
Interpersonal stressors, 194–196, 202
Interpersonal transgressions, 66
Interventions, 69, 207–208, 239
Intimacy, 142, 146, 147, 149, 153–154
Isolation, social. *See* Social isolation
Isolation calls. *See* Separation-distress
      vocalizations

James, William, 161
Jelen, P., 30
Jensen-Campbell, 7, 224

Kalauokalani, D., 184
Kappa-receptors, 37
Kemeny, M. E., 80
Ketamine, 38, 39
Ketelaar, T., 170
Kiecolt-Glaser, J. K., 203
Kingsbury, R., 221
Kirschbaum, C., 83
Kishino, N., 6
Kleinman, B. M., 142
Knack, J.M., 7, 224
Knowles, M. L., 155

Laboratory rats, 25, 27–28
Language, 55, 123, 164, 196
Larsen, R. J., 170
Laureneau, J. P., 142

and pregnancy, 107–108
and psychic-pain disorders, 35

PAG. *See* Periaqueductal gray
Pain
    abdominal, 219–220
    acute, 79, 226
    cardiac. *See* Cardiac pain
    chronic. *See* Chronic pain
    defined, 18
    idiopathic, 11, 33
    neurogenic. *See* neurogenic pain.
    perception of, 195
    physical. *See* Physical pain
    postoperative, 22
    preliving, 169–172
    psychic, 20, 21, 30, 33–36
    psychological, 4, 33–34
    regulation of, 21, 63–64
    reliving, 147, 165–169
    social. *See* Social pain
    as stressor, 194–195
Pain affect, 3, 4, 131, 220
Pain control systems, 21–22
Pain events, 165
Pain experience, 165
Pain management programs, 188
Pain memory research, 165
Pain-potentiation effects, 64–66
Pain-regulation effects, 63–64
Pain sensation, 131
Pain sensitivity. *See* Sensitivity
Pain Slide, 166, 170
Pain threshold, 62, 129–130, 133, 168,
    220
Pain tolerance, 129, 168
Pain vocalizations, 16–17. *See also*
    Separation-distress vocalizations
Panadol, 130. *See also* Acetaminophen
PANIC/GRIEF system, 15–17. *See also*
    Separation distress
    evolutionary design of, 11–14
    in periaqueductal gray regions, 20
    and social learning, 40
Panksepp, J., 4, 97, 126, 163
Paracetamol. *See* Acetaminophen
Parasympathetic nervous system (PNS),
    87
Parenting, 106
Peace, K. A., 165

Peer rejection, 84
Peer victimization, 216–224, 227
    and adolescent developmental
        changes, 217–218
    chronicity of, 200, 201
    frequency of, 217
    neural effects of, 221–222
    and neuroendocrine system, 222–224
    physical pain in, 218–220
    and physical–social pain overlap,
        220–221
Peng, Y., 181, 186
Periaqueductal gray (PAG)
    and controlling physical pain, 41
    and depression, 34
    pain vocalizations in, 16
    PANIC/GRIEF system in, 20
    and physical–social pain overlap, 127
    psychic-pain system in, 21, 33
    and social distress, 60
Personality traits, 96, 144, *See also*
    specific personality traits
Peters, M. L., 181
PET studies. *See* Positron emission
    tomography studies
PFC. *See* Prefrontal cortex
Pharmacology
    manipulation of psychic pain with,
        34–35
    for pain regulation, 63–64
    and serotonin, 103
    treatment of depression and suicidal
        ideation with, 35–39
Phenotypes, 109
Phobias, social. *See* Social phobias
Physical health. *See* Health (physical)
Physical pain, 3. *See also* Physiological
    responses
    brain mechanisms of, 18–19
    control of, 41
    and dACC, 55–59
    genetic factors of, 101
    opiates for reduction of, 30
    overlap of social and. *See*
        Physical–social pain overlap
    and pain control systems, 21–22
    in peer victimization, 218–220
    with posttraumatic stress disorder, 225
    preliving, 169–172
    as protective mechanism, 13

of pain, 21, 63–64
self-, 125
Reinforcement, 31, 183
Rejection, 3
  and aggression, 100
  cardiovascular responses to, 86
  as cause of emotional pain, 147–149
  cortisol responses to, 83–84
  and dACC activity, 57, 59–60
  effects of, 240
  peer, 84
  as result of racial discrimination,
        69–71
  sensitivity to, 60–61, 90, 144, 203, 222
  and social threat, 149–151
  as stressor, 204
  and survival, 53, 54
Relationships
  damage to, 215
  importance of, 4
  interpersonal stressors from, 202
  loss of, 201, 204–205
  maintenance of, 162
  and physical–social pain overlap, 54
  rewards from, 141, 142, 148
  romantic, 135, 155. See also Couples
  social evaluative threat in, 85
  threats to, 194, 195
  withdrawal from, 151
Reliving pain, 147, 165–169
Relocation, 207
Remote association test (RAT), 167
Residual stress, 220
Respiration, 199
Reward, social. See Social reward
Rhesus monkeys, 56, 63, 98, 102–103
Right ventral prefrontal cortex (RVPFC),
        57, 58, 71, 127, 216, 222
Robinson, R. C., 186
Rohleder, N., 83
Rostral anterior insular cortex, 187
Ruehlman, L. S., 164
RVPFC. See Right ventral prefrontal
        cortex

Sadness, 17, 24, 34. See also Depression;
        Melancholia
Safer, M. A., 165
Safety needs, 162
SBP (systolic blood pressure), 85

Schacter, D. L., 170
Schaller, M., 146
Sebanc, A. M., 84
Secondary pain affect, 220
Sedation, 20
Seinfeld, Jerry, 53
Self-awareness, 42, 124, 225
Self-conscious emotions, 80–82, 85
Self-defeating behavior, 124
Self-disclosure, 142
Self-esteem, 133, 134, 144, 152, 173
Self-preservation, 5, 80
Self-regulation, 125
Sensitivity. See also Insensitivity
  and aggression, 67–69, 100
  and dACC responses, 56
  genetic factors in, 62–63, 227–228
  and hurt proneness, 169
  individual differences in, 62–63
  to physical pain, 65–66, 135,
        148–149, 171–172
  to physical pressure, 167–168
  and physical-social pain overlap,
        215–216, 220
  and posttraumatic stress disorder, 225
  to rejection, 60–61, 90, 144,
        203, 222
  to social threat, 132–133, 144, 145
Sensitization, 226–228
Sensory-affective systems, 11, 13, 16, 19
Sensory component of pain, 55, 56
Separation anxiety, 163
Separation distress. See also
        PANIC/GRIEF system
  in animals, 15–17, 23–28, 42, 56–57
  and dACC, 56–57
  and depression, 33–34
  evolutionary emergence of, 19–21
  generation of, 12
  and social–emotional systems, 39
Separation-distress vocalizations (DVs)
  by birds, 25–26
  genetic factors in, 98
  neuropharmacological analysis of,
        23–25
  and opioids, 20, 63
  and PANIC/GRIEF system, 15–17
  and psychic pain, 33
  by rats, 25, 27–28, 127
  role of dACC in, 56

responding to, 126
scales of, 142, 144–147
sensitivity to, 132–133, 144, 145
and social avoidance, 143–144,
149–154
Social victimization. *See* Peer
victimization
Soltysik, S., 30
Somatization, 218, 221
Somatosensory neocortex, 18
Speech production, 56
Spielmann, S. S., 6, 155
Squirrel monkeys, 56
STAI (State-Trait Anxiety Inventory),
133
State Self-Esteem Scale (SSES), 133
State-Trait Anxiety Inventory (STAI),
133
Strachman, A., 154
Stress
coping with, 197–200, 202
defined, 196–197
from disruption of homeostasis, 182
and perception of pain, 195–196
residual, 220
Stressor(s), 194–196
acute, 85, 200, 201, 227
bereavement as, 206–208
chronic, 89, 200–201, 222–228
coping with, 198, 199
cortisol responses to, 81–83
episodic, 201
interpersonal, 194, 202
loneliness as, 205, 208–209
loss as, 202–204
loss of social relationships as, 204–205
negative social exchanges as, 202–204
ostracism and social rejection as, 204
social integration as, 205
social support for buffering, 202
social vs. nonsocial, 194, 195
Stress process, 197
Stress tests, 98
Stroop task, 167, 171
Subcortical region, 19, 39, 40
Subjectivity, 14
Suicidal ideation, 38–39
Suicidal intent, 13
Suicide, 207
Survival, 32, 53, 54, 80, 95, 126

Sympathetic nervous system (SNS), 85,
87, 90
Sympathy, 184
Systolic blood pressure (SBP), 85

Tajfel, H., 162
Tambor, E. S., 132
Taylor, S. E., 5, 227
T-cytotoxic lymphocytes, 87
Teeth loss, 185
Temporal cortex, 19
Terdal, S. K., 132
Terror management research, 172–173
Thalamus, 17, 18, 21, 55
Threat, social. *See* Social threat
Tice, D. M., 83–84
Tissue damage, 163, 182
TNFα (tumor necrosis factor-alpha), 88
Toddlers, 106
Tolerance (addiction), 23–24, 36
Tolerance (pain). *See* Pain tolerance
Total peripheral resistance, 124
Tout, K., 84
Trait aggression, 100
Trait anxiety, 133, 134
Trauma, 220, 226, 227. *See also*
Posttraumatic stress disorder
Treatment
in biopsychosocial perspective, 188
of chronic pain, 64
with cingulotomy, 56
of depression, 22, 35–38
of physical pain, 220
of suicidal ideation, 38–39
unimodal approaches to, 188
Trier Social Stress Test, 98, 100, 224
Tumor growth, 200
Tumor necrosis factor-alpha (TNFα), 88
Turk, D. C., 181, 184
Twin studies, 96–97
Tylenol, 130. *See also* Acetaminophen

Ultrasonic vocalizations (USVs), 27
Unimodal treatment approaches, 188
Urocortin, 27
USVs (ultrasonic vocalizations), 27

Vaillancourt, T., 223
Van Dulmen, M. M. H., 84
Variants. *See* Alleles

ABOUT THE EDITORS

Geoff MacDonald, PhD, is an associate professor in the Department of Psychology at the University of Toronto. He received his PhD in social psychology at the University of Waterloo and won Social Sciences and Humanities Research Council funding to complete a postdoctoral fellowship at Wake Forest University. Prior to joining the University of Toronto, Dr. MacDonald held the position of senior lecturer at the University of Queensland School of Psychology. In addition to his work on social pain, he has examined diverse topics including social threats and rewards, romantic relationships, self-esteem, culture, social influence, and alcohol.

Lauri A. Jensen-Campbell, PhD, is a core faculty member in the doctoral programs in experimental and health psychology at the University of Texas (UT) at Arlington. She is also a distinguished teaching professor, with courses on developmental psychology and research design and statistics. She received her PhD in psychology from Texas A&M University in 1995. Before coming to UT Arlington, she was an associate professor at Florida Atlantic University in Davie, Florida. Her research is located at the intersection of personality, social, developmental, and health psychology. She is currently interested in how bullying influences health outcomes across the life span. In addition, she is interested in how individual differences in personality and genetic polymorphisms buffer or exacerbate these associations between poor peer relationships and health outcomes. Since coming to UT Arlington, Dr. Jensen-Campbell has received funding from the National Science Foundation, Timberlawn Psychiatric Research Foundation, and the Anthony Marchionne Foundation.